JESUS AND THE METAPHORS OF GOD

Studies in
Judaism and Christianity

Exploration of Issues in the
Contemporary Dialogue Between
Christians and Jews

Editor in Chief for
Stimulus Books
Helga Croner

Editors
Lawrence Boadt, C.S.P.
Helga Croner
David Dalin
Leon Klenicki
John Koenig
Kevin A. Lynch, C.S.P.
Richard C. Sparks, C.S.P.

 A STIMULUS BOOK

CONVERSATION ON THE ROAD NOT TAKEN
Volume Two

JESUS AND THE METAPHORS OF GOD

The Christs of the New Testament

Bernard J. Lee, S.M.

A STIMULUS BOOK
PAULIST PRESS ◆ NEW YORK ◆ MAHWAH

Copyright ©1993 by
Stimulus Foundation

Library of Congress Cataloging-in-Publication Data

Lee, Bernard J., 1932–
    Jesus and the metaphors of God : the Christs of the New Testament / Bernard J. Lee.
        p.   cm.—(Conversation on the road not taken : v. 2) (A Stimulus book)
    Includes bibliographical references and index.
    ISBN 0-8091-3429-2
    1. Jesus Christ—Person and offices—History of doctrines—Early church, ca. 30-600. 2. Jesus Christ—Person and offices. 3. Ruah (The Hebrew word) 4. Word of God (Theology) 5. Logos. 6. Wisdom (Biblical character) 7. God—History of doctrines—Early church, ca. 30-600. 8. God—Knowableness. I. Title. II. Series: Lee, Bernard J., 1932– Conversation on the road not taken : v. 2.
    BT198.L427 1993
        232—dc20   93-14256
                                                                                          CIP

Published by Paulist Press
997 Macarthur Boulevard
Mahwah, N.J. 07430

Printed and bound in the
United States of America

Contents

FOREWORD

The book, where everything seems possible through language that one thinks one can master and that finally turns out but to be the very *place* of its bankruptcy. All the metaphors the word can inspire lie between these two extremes. None of them really gets to the heart of it, but, between this all and this nothing, the unfathomable opening takes place.[1]

Perhaps I owe my patient but prodding publisher, my friends, and readers of *The Galilean Jewishness of Jesus* who braved a request for more, a word of explanation. For in fact, when the first volume was published, I had already in hand a nearly complete manuscript for Volume 2.

As was the case at the start of Volume 1, I experience embarrassment at beginning with autobiographical reflections. A book stands rather much on its own without that. However, I believe that finally every theological work is also autobiography anyway, so this is my way of being up front about it.

There is a new acquaintance (by writings only) who gives me the impetus to move again with the text. His name is Edmond Jabes, a Jewish academic who spent much of his adult professional life in Paris. He questions what a book is anyway, and knows that every book at best only resembles the real book toward which it nods. I know only some of his books. The Jabes you hear may not be the real one, but someone who resembles the one I think I met.

Two considerations have delayed this book. The first is easier to describe. It is the mood in the Catholic Church (the institutional side) that tends to equate theology with catechetics (which is but one of its roles) and has narrowing tolerance for constructive, speculative and/or empirical theology. The tensions between ecclesia and academia are severe. I question whether ecclesia's collective sensibilities have seriously come to terms with historical consciousness, i.e. with how our concepts and articulations are all relationalized and partialized. No interpretation can claim utter allegiance beyond the world view and the social location of its emergence. The only way to canonize a concept or articulation is to freeze the world view that is its setting. That means death to thinking.

The fall-out from historical consciousness radically questions a tradi-

1

tion that has banked so much on the perennial durability of its articulations. We are only beginning to fence with the new question, which is
how norming functions in a post-modern church. There is no identity
without norming, so how shall it happen anew?

Perhaps Rome's fierceness forces a care that the Body's well-being
requires, since the metamorphosis is so deep. I'll grant that. But many
theologians find themselves reckoning with a mood that is less than
encouraging, exactly when theological creativity ought to be notoriously
dear. The current situation, then, may also just be downright unhealthy.
I grant that possibility too, even the likelihood.

The second reason for this text's delay has to do with other things.
Deconstruction is perhaps the far end of historical consciousness, a radical awareness that "fact" is always interpreted and partly constructed.
Our constructions have some yield, of course. But every construction
always also obstructs. Interpretation never purely yields. So why write
anything at all? That's enough to make one (me, anyway) sit on a
manuscript, and sit and sit and sit. Whatever is said is tenuous and
partial and cannot avoid the systemic distortion that is even built into
grammar itself. "It is our words," Jabes writes, "that require the most
erasing."[2]

But that is all we have. Therefore, the erasible is everything for us,
so one dares a book. "Only the fallible word can be heard."[3] After
pondering Jabes' fretful grappling with the nature of writing (which he
does in writing!), I can better name my own hesitancies and resistances,
and the sense of audacity I feel about publishing anything at all ever. It
was so long ago that I was enthralled by my youthful sense of T.S. Eliot's
warning that "one has only learnt to get the better of words / For the
thing one no longer has to say, or the way in which / One is no longer
disposed to say it"; and, that given the "undisciplined squads of emotion" that haunt our cognitions, the best we can do is "make a raid on
the inarticulate."[4] Attracted by the option of silence, making the raid
remains risky.

I suspect that many writers, after many a revision, still know that
this is not yet the book one is destined to write. The destiny book hangs
around in the shadows. Forever is the time of waiting for it. Who has not
read a book and known from the beginning that the real book is inside
the entrails of the text in hand, never to be let loose. Any actual book
only more or less resembles the real book. Jabes has helped me to be
satisfied with resemblances:

Every book includes a zone of darkness, a shadow-layer which one cannot evaluate and which the reader discovers only gradually. It irritates him, but he does not sense that this is where the real book lies, the site around which the pages he is reading organize themselves. This unwritten book, both enigmatic and revealing, always slips away. And yet, only the reader's intuitive grasp of it enables him to approach the book's true dimension; this intuition enables him to judge if the writer has indeed come close to, or, to the contrary, has wandered far from the book he had the ambition to write.[5]

In the final chapters of this volume I have felt especially vulnerable on these grounds. Let me give an example.

Since preparing most of this text I have read Bernard Cooke's extraordinary book, *The Distancing of God*.[6] While his thesis is of course specific to his abiding concerns, the book brought to my conscious awareness one of my own concerns about the metaphors of God. God metaphors tell some important tales about how close God is (exactly right here this very moment), or how far (so far that mediators must bridge the chasm). Metaphors that mediate knowing do more than tell, they *make*. I think I can say now that all of these issues seem so important because metaphors of God will always underpin any Christological interpretation of Jesus. The nearness of God in Christological understanding of Jesus matters greatly. I know that at best this text hints in that direction, perhaps resembles the intent somewhat, but remains riddled with the incurable fallibility of words.

In theology there is a lot of fall-out that has to do with power and politics, for the recovery of the Jewishness of Jesus, as much as Christians can accurately interpret and absorb it, calls many later interpretations into question (especially the uninterrupted history of supercessionist Christology).

The distance between Judaism and Christianity, as I have hinted elsewhere, is not simply between Athens and Jerusalem, but between Alexandria and Usha.[7] With the destruction of the temple in 70 C.E., something ends for all Jews, including those who count themselves among the followers of Jesus. Before that the relation between Christian Jews and other Jews is frequently tense, but not ruptured. After the bitter destruction in the first war, Jewish religious leaders gathered at Jabneh in Judea, not far distant from the present city of Tel Aviv. Christian Jews do not enter into this Jewish event. It is not long now before the Christian community becomes completely separate from Judaism, and even defines itself as non-Judaism.

Both of these traditions are entering simultaneously into a productive new formative stage. After the greater destruction of the Second War, 135 C.E., Jewish religious leadership relocates in Usha in Galilee, to codify prayer life and to redact their interpretative materials on the oral tradition (the Mishnah). Between 400–500 the Jerusalem Talmud is redacted. Between 500–600 the much longer Babylonian Talmud is completed. In this period, one could not find a more deliberate back-turning on Hellenized culture. With Greek language, thought and culture all around, Usha, Jerusalem and Babylon opt radically for Hebrew and Aramaic, even though Greek press from all sides.

At the same time, the Christian interpretation of a Jewish fact named Jesus is richly concentrated in Alexandria. While the Mishnah takes shape in Usha, a great catechetical school, founded by Patenus, flourishes in Alexandria. While the Jerusalem Talmud is coming together, the great Councils of Nicea and Constantinople are shaping in Greek the faith of Christianity. By the time the Babylonian Talmud is ready, Ephesus and Chalcedon have given Christian faith a distinctive Greek shape.

Christians undertook an experiment in interpretation which had an earlier Jewish experimenter in Philo of Alexandria, an older contemporary of the younger Jesus and Paul. He gave a thoroughly Greek rendering of Jewish religiousness. Judaism flirted with it, but it was never a serious courtship. Christian interpretation, however, appropriated Stoic thought deeply, sometimes with Philo consciously as an exemplar.

Culture is not simply a *form* in which any content can be recast. Culture is always content as well when it casts experience. Experience cannot ever be entirely translated across a culture. That is why the rabbis say that every translator is a traitor. The best that one cultural understanding can do about another is "sort of" resemble it. The distance between Usha and Alexandria is not "merely" cultural, it is profoundly other yet not entirely other.

During one and the same period, the first five centuries, Judaism and Christianity are immersed in radical self-interpretation and there is no effective dialogue between them. By the end of that period the Midrashic tradition is a very rich one. The Mishnah and Talmuds are authoritative. The Tosefta supplements the Talmuds also with great power. From the same period comes the New Testament (antedated only by Paul's writings). The Apologists and the Fathers have fashioned a magnificent body of Christian literature. The Great Councils have had their say.

Now, as the beginnings of the Christian fact are nudged to speak again with Jewish voices, two things are happening. First, the classical interpretation of the Jesus event is relationalized and partialized, and on many grounds called into question. The Christian fact as we have come to know it is one of the many possible historical options that might have been realized. If it hadn't been this one, it would have been another. Christian faith can only be lived in historical options. But we become aware that it was and is one among many possible realizations. It is supple!

Secondly, this is the kind of dialogue with a tradition that discloses what in the tradition "is most hazardous and most original."[8] The emotions are correspondingly mixed between consternation and fear, pride and promise.

Within the quite Greek option, there was and is a plentiful storehouse of magnificent and compelling expressions of faith. The Stoic/Platonic/Aristotelian interpretative schemata make possible a Theophilus of Antioch, Origen, Augustine, Boethius, Aquinas, Rahner, Lonergan, to name but a few. This faith bears true resemblances to the Jewish fact of Jesus, but does not exhaust it, and that is a mighty point. Resemblance never means "interchangeable with." Resemblance has the same roots as metaphor; there is always an "is like" and an "is not like." The "is like" guides, clarifies and satisfies at the same time that the "is not like" whispers an interrogation. In times of stress the "is not like" screams instead of whispers, exploding the secrecy. "There is no rest in the kingdom of resemblances. For any question, resemblance is a treacherous dissatisfied question at the heart of felicitous phrasing."[9]

In Greek culture, the metaphysical tradition feels it can uncover first principles that are for all time non-negotiable. That cultural presupposition contrasts vigorously with the Pharisaic instinct that an oral tradition keeps Jewish faith radically open to reinterpretation. One of the fundamental Jewish values, says Jabes, "is the freedom to interrogate Judaism without ceasing to be Jewish."[10] Perhaps that is a plausible context for the freedom of the crucified Jesus to interrogate God without ceasing to be God's Son. At the core of being Jewish is a "question which does not stop questioning itself in the reply it calls forth."[11] Perhaps the question has always been more important (certainly more interesting) than the answer. Yet question was once the tentative position between answer and answer. Now I find my answers tentative positions between my questions. I know I am not alone in this.

The Hebrew religious instinct forbids images of God and insists that God's real name not be written or spoken exactly. While they may not have Paul Ricoeur's philosophical vocabulary, I think they know the danger of hopping with uncritical excitement on the resemblances, just because of the true disclosures therein. If the fix is too firm, then the correcting and/or adjusting questions slither away. Idolatry is left, the major Hebrew sin (perhaps for us all).

My first encounter with Edmond Jabes was a chance meeting. I was in Brooklyn with a colleague/friend for a symposium with the Industrial Areas Foundation. We took a free day in Manhattan. My friend bought several of Jabes' books. On the subway ride back to Brooklyn I began to page through the books. That brief exposure was titillating. I soon purchased a batch on my own. Jacques Derrida, who has been part of my grappling with the meaning of deconstruction and historical consciousness, said of Jabes in 1972 that in the previous ten years nothing of interest was written in France that did not have its precedents somewhere in the texts of Edmond Jabes. That was no minor recommendation.

Jabes writes limited writing about the limitations of writing, and produces non-books about the books he *would* write but, like every writer, will never write, because *that* book stays only and always in the shadows of the non-book. And it is somewhat in those reservations that this present non-book of mine has hidden for a while. This non-book including the book it harbors deals with metaphors for God, i.e. with resemblances that have caught our fancy and perhaps God's fancy. The metaphors are a grand religious treasure. Two and three thousand years later we need to be measured in claims about how well we have caught their first revelations. But, Jabes writes,

> We shall never unwind time without the sure help of images. . . . Images have a past and a future difficult to determine. They make us think of them both in their past and in their future. Thus they are the image of thought, of which we never know if it will plunge us into the night of our past or project us into the time to come. . . . An Image is always an image of an image which thought veils or unveils. So that there is no past or future except for thinking that has kept us alert.[12]

In these ruminations there is a lot of thinking about images and metaphors. I am curious about possible Christological futures of Jesus if metaphors indigenous to his Galilean Jewish soul lead the way, as they have not. I shall be pushing for the importance of *Ruach*/Spirit and *Dabhar*/Word. I shall say here at the beginning and again at the end that whatever privilege I claim for *Ruach* and *Dabhar* has to do with hearing an event speak nearly with its original voice. These are not the only metaphors that authentically resemble and dissemble. I hope, especially in the third and last volume, to hang in systematically with those metaphors, in conversation with Jesus the Jew, with Christians, and with any Jews interested since they, as Vatican II affirms, remain God's chosen people with whom God has never abrogated his covenant.[13] Our Christian covenant is not thereby diminished by God's continuing covenant with the Jews. I find little, however, in our imposing Christological inheritance that helps us simultaneously affirm both that continuing covenant and the mystery and splendor of our own. That is a burning issue.

So, in regard to all of this, perhaps some kind of non-book of questions is in order, and why not? Maybe even that is not the reason for the book. "Perhaps we write," writes Jabes, "only to save a few words from the fire smoldering inside us."[14] That is plausible.

Notes

1. Edmond Jabes with Marcel Cohen, *From the Desert to the Book,* tr. Pierre Joris (Barrytown: Station Hill, 1990), p. 15. [DB]
2. Edmond Jabes, *The Book of Resemblances,* tr. Rosmarie Waldrop (Hanover: Univ. Press of New England, 1990, p. 66. [BR]
3. Jabes, BR 1990, p. 66.
4. T.S. Eliot, "East Coker," *The Four Quartets* (New York: Harcourt, Brace and World, 1971), pp. 30, 31.
5. Jabes, BR 1990, p. 66.
6. Bernard J. Cooke, *The Distancing of God,* (Minneapolis: Fortress, 1990).
7. Bernard J. Lee, *Journal of Ecumenical Studies,* Winter 1991.
8. Edmond Jabes, *The Book of Dialogue,* tr. Rosemarie Waldrop (Middletown: Wesleyan Press, 1987), p. 59. [BD]
9. Jabes, BR 1990, p. 56.
10. Jabes, BD 1987, p. 58.
11. Jabes, BD 1990, p. 58.
12. Jabes, BR 1990, pp. 60, 61.
13. *Nostra Aetate,* sect. 4.
14. Jabes, BD 1987, p. 15.

1
Meta-Phors and Mega-Physics

Introduction

That Christian faith is founded in Jesus a Jew was the theme of the first volume, *The Galilean Jewishness of Jesus*. How that Jewishness might be retrieved by Christians and welcomed in the constitution of Christian selfhood today is the concern of all three volumes together, but is especially the constructive theology of volume three. We are about the work now of locating the major constructive elements for such Christological reflection by examining the metaphoric possibilities at our disposal, and indicating which of them would have been most at home in the religious world of Jesus.

The followers of Jesus in Jerusalem, under the leadership of James, the Lord's brother, were attempting to frame their faith in Jesus Christ within the Jewish faith of Pharisaic Judaism, the Jewish faith of Jesus. They were trying to walk Christian faith on this Jewish road of both the written and the oral Torah. The so-called Council of Jerusalem, however, rerouted the journey. Instead of the more detailed Halakah, community leaders settled for the fundamental essentials of the Noahide Covenant, and of Leviticus 17 and 18. Gentile Christians were to abstain from food sacrificed to idols, from blood, from the meat of strangled animals, and from illicit marriages.

In contrast with these pared down expectations, Matthew's Jesus insists that the oral tradition of the Pharisees is binding: "You must do what they tell you" (Mt 23:3). Don't follow their bad example, Jesus warns, but even the tithes on mint and cumin are legitimate and should be done (Mt 23:23). The same Jewish road that Jesus and his first followers walked was not taken. If many of the details of Pharisaic law were socializations in Jewish identity, and they were, their abandonment in the Jerusalem decision had far-reaching effects. And that local decision became, in fact, a universal pattern. Unlike Jesus who was within Judaism, Christians have passed through their history without Judaism since the late first century.

To be sure, no one knows exactly where the road not taken might have led. There are hints, perhaps, from early Jewish Christians—but not a decisive map. Nor are we secure about where that road might lead if we attempt to reconstruct it today. But there is a kind of conversation that might give kilometer to kilometer guidance. A piece of that conversation is all I am claiming. This is Volume Two of a conversation on the road not taken.

Retrieving our Jewishness is a formidable Christian task. Seeking to explore that retrieval in the first volume, *The Galilean Jewishness of Jesus,* I tried to locate Jesus within the Judaism of his day. I began with a long chapter on method which reached for some synthesis between empirical process thought, pragmatism, praxis, hermeneutics, the philosophy and epistemology of metaphor, and some elements of deconstructionist thought. I want to be the first to say that it is not (yet, perhaps) a fully wrought synthesis, but these seem like important elements of postmodern theological reflection.

In the second chapter of Volume 1, I addressed the cultural and religious texture of Palestinian Judaism. While no part of the Mediterranean world could escape Hellenistic influence, its impact upon Judaism varies from place to place. Philo of Alexandria, Jesus' contemporary, brings Greek meanings into the very heart of his Jewish self-understanding. I suggested that while Hellenism does impact in many ways upon Jewish life in Palestine, it does not make its way substantially into the interior of the Jewish soul.

The Jewish will expressed in the Maccabean revolt, in the two Jewish Wars and in the work of Palestinian rabbis in Jabneh (Judea) and Usha (Galilee) testifies, I believe, to a quite Hebraic determination of soul in the place and time of Jesus. This was the case within the larger context of considerable Greek influence from Alexander on, including some pressure from Jews themselves to assimilate Hellenism more deeply during the events that led to the Maccabean revolt.

My interest in this issue comes from the need to understand better the assumptive world in which the soul of Jesus came to consciousness. We cannot, of course, assess that world either certainly or fully. But that should not discourage us from our best efforts at hearing the life and words of Jesus upon their own horizon—a Jewish horizon.

In the final chapter of Volume 1, I explored the "kinds of Jews" that help elucidate the kind of Jew Jesus was. I indicated what I think are some clear affinities between Jesus and the Pharisees, Jesus and the figure of the teacher, Jesus and the wandering charismatics, and Jesus and the eschatological prophet. I think we should not choose one alone as *the* clue to Jesus' horizon, but should keep all of the typologies active in interpreting him. Yet he, like anyone, is always more than any or all the typologies we might invoke to illuminate his existence. And that applies as well to all of the Christologies which our faith has ever devised.

Three and a Half Metaphors

When we call Jesus "the Christ" we are already speaking metaphorically. "Christ" and its Hebrew counterpart "Messiah" literally mean "anointed with oil." Oil was poured on the heads of kings. Later in history priests were also anointed. In Jewish hope there would come an "anointed" of Yahweh who would save Yahweh's people and usher in the final reign of God. When Jesus' followers begin to call Jesus "the Christ" to interpret his meaning for them and us, they have in mind especially the last of the meanings indicated above: Jesus ushers in the reign of God. Presumably they do not experience Jesus as being literally anointed with oil. They take one of the "anointed" meanings and leave another. No other metaphor is so widely used to interpret Jesus. It is commonplace to say Jesus Christ almost as though Christ were part of his given name.

Historical biblical Christology has often gone the route of examining the other titles of Jesus in the Christian scriptures to explore the fuller scope of that earliest Christological faith in Jesus, e.g. Son of God, Son of Man, Son of David, Lord, etc. These also are metaphors.

No matter what secondary metaphors are used to fill out further what Christ means for Jesus, an apparent constant is that Jesus is always the Christ of God. I say "apparent constant," because every time the interpretation of God shifts, so does the meaning of "God's Christ."

In our Christian scriptures, *there are shifts* in the meaning of God—of this we are sure, because there are shifts in the metaphors that shape God's appearing and working in human history and our interpretations of God's historical presence. I want to track with three and a half meanings of God as these are accessible to us in foundational metaphors of God invoked in early Christological faith in Jesus.

The first of these metaphorical narratives involves *Ruach*/Breath/Wind/Spirit and its coordinate *Dabhar*/Word/Deed/Act/Fact. In the second and third chapters I will explore a cluster of metaphors in the early Hebrew narrative that provide a larger context of Hebrew religious anthropology. In the fourth chapter I will focus upon the assumptive religious world in which *Ruach* is a key metaphor for Yahweh's active presence, and in the fifth chapter I will do the same for *Dabhar*. *Ruach* and *Dabhar* are primal metaphors for the Hebrew experience of God, whose Christological potential the final volume will address.

Sophia/Wisdom is the second metaphor. Perhaps in the fifth century B.C.E. and surely in the fourth, the *Sophia*/Wisdom tradition begins to infiltrate Jewish religious sensibilities. This influence is first felt as a literary style that gathers proverb-like wise sayings. In a more developed form, *Sophia* is a personification of God's own wisdom, with God before all ages, and through whom the world is first created, then ordered and saved. The *Sophia* metaphor more or less replaces the language of *Ruach* and *Dabhar*, not by eliminating them entirely (they do, however, recede), but by attributing their dual functions to the single figure of *Sophia*. The *Sophia* metaphor has more points of contact with the *Ruach* metaphor than with *Dabhar*, but reaches into *Dabhar* as well.

John 1:14 says that the *Logos*/Word became flesh and pitched a tent in our midst. This verse from the Christian scriptures has had more influence upon the shape of Christian belief than any other verse. It may even be fair to suggest that it has had more influence than all the other verses combined as a seminal hermeneutical influence. That massive impact is not only from this particular Johannine interpretation of Jesus, but from early and abundant philosophical reinterpretations of the Johannine interpretation.

I tend to count *Logos* as one and a half metaphors because of at least two major layers of meaning for this one metaphor/word. The two layers are not utterly disparate, they are not two separate metaphors. It is widely recognized in biblical studies that John's gospel is very different in character than the synoptics, and post-dates them all (is later than Mark by a full generation). Ever since the quest for the historical Jesus got underway, debate has ensued about how Greek a reading to give John, or how Jewish a reading. More recent assessments suggest that a lot of meanings implied in the Johannine *Logos* are influenced by the *Sophia* metaphor. Earlier assessments often felt that the thought of Philo was evident in the Johannine text. These two assessments indicate the layers to which I alluded above. Even when one has assessed whether John tilts toward a more Jewish *Sophia* or a more Greek Philonic *Logos,* it remains the case that what John interprets about Jesus is not reducible to either. He is creating new meaning that does not simply coincide with either of those motifs.

I tend to see *Sophia* meanings in John's gospel. However, the fact that he chooses *Logos* and not *Sophia* for incarnation suggests to me the cultural availability of *Logos* as a metaphor, and perhaps its greater cultural viability as well. Regardless of how Greek John's *Logos* was or was not, from very early on those who elaborated the meaning (and added to and transformed it) were very much influenced by Platonic and Stoic thought, as was Philo when he set to interpret his Jewish faith. If these writers, the apologist and the fathers, have not read Philo's thought, they at least matriculated in the same schools of thought as Philo.

Philo of Alexandria, a highly educated, articulate, religious Jew, is a contemporary of Jesus. In the many works in which Philo interprets Jewish faith, he regularly works from Stoic thought, and introduces Greek meanings into the very soul of Jewish being. But there are worlds of difference between Alexandria and Galilee in Jesus' time. And no matter how the Johannine community may have understood *Logos,* there is general consensus that these notions were not ready-to-hand in the Galilee of Jesus, and were certainly not part of Jesus' self-understanding.

In the seventh chapter of this volume I will be attending to one and a half *Logos* interpretations of God, and how they impact upon the meaning of Jesus as the Christ of God.

I stress again one of the major methodological points from the opening chapter of the first volume: there is no such thing ever as an uninterpreted fact. We experience only and always from the conditioned perspectives of our personal and collective histories. Thus, the interpreter always shows up in some way *inside* the interpreted fact.

One of the principal ways in which we interpreters contribute to the facts we experience is through the metaphors that shape our understandings—not after the arising of knowledge, but as concomitant with and partly constitutive of our knowledge. This is the case whether we experience shoes and ships and sealing wax, cabbages and kings, and even God, or especially God!

Thus I have been speaking about the metaphors of God, and how shifts in those metaphors cause Christological meaning shifts in Jesus as God's Christ. For those who do not move beyond the popular notion of metaphor as ornament, this might sound like a reductionist way of attending to the titles of Jesus, treating them, as it were, as "mere" metaphors. And for those whose bent is the long tradition of philosophical theology, metaphor does not cut the ontological mustard that philosophical categories cut, i.e. metaphors might be expressive or decorative, but they are not as serviceable to ontology as rational categories.

Since metaphor plays such a critical role in the analysis and constructions that I am about, I want to return to this concern which I have already addressed initially in *The Galilean Jewishness of Jesus*.[1] There I leaned heavily upon Paul Ricoeur's theory of metaphor,[2] and Sally McFague's theological appropriation of it.[3] In much of what follows, I am particularly indebted to a detailed analysis of the *Metaphoric Process* by Mary Gerhart and Allan Russell.[4]

Metaphors

> . . . metaphor, far from being limited to a linguistic artifact, is characterized by its epistemological function of discovering new meanings. What is at stake is still knowing in process but considered in its nascent moment. In this sense, metaphor is a thought process before being a language process (Paul Ricoeur).[5]

Metaphor as a linguistic artifact is both legitimate and worthy. It belongs to the *métier* of the poets, novelists and dramatists. My primary concern, however, is with the epistemological function of metaphor, the role it plays in the origination of knowing. In this capacity, metaphor midwifes experience. It is in attendance at the nascent moment. The poet may indeed reinvoke the metaphor, as may the philosopher or theologian. The nearer poetry, philosophy and theology are to the metaphors of the nascent moment, the safer communicators they are in the arts and skills of analysis.

In the reflections that follow, I will discuss metaphor from a number of inter-related perspectives: their tensive character, their epistemological and ontological functions, their role as makers of meaning (how we are to be in the world), and, finally, the fragility of the metaphoric process. Throughout my discussion of the metaphors of God, these are the senses of metaphor that I always have in mind.

Metaphor as Tensive

Imagine a pained and dejected Hebrew shepherd three thousand years ago, who, in a moment of religious encounter, experiences being cared for by Yahweh with great tenderness and specificity. His realization of being cared for is disclosed in his beholding of God as a shepherd, himself as a sheep on the edges of the herd, perhaps on the edges of life. He does not first experience being cared for and then understand the caring to be shepherd-like. Rather, shepherd is the appearing of Yahweh's caring. "Divine shepherd" *is* the manifestation of Yahweh to this Hebrew herder of long ago. "The Lord is my shepherd," sings the psalmist. But he does not make up the metaphor for his psalm; he incorporates it from experience into his lyrics of praise. The metaphor of the nascent moment makes later appearances in the herder's grateful and lyrical reflection.

The shepherd knows who Yahweh is. Yahweh has already appeared as Warrior on Israel's side, as King above all kings, as Creator of the world. The shepherd also knows very well of course what a shepherd is. He is aware that the herder is not known only as a trustworthy caretaker of sheep. Shepherds also have the reputation of being rogues. So untrustworthy is the shepherd in ancient Israel that his testimony is not allowed in court.[6] Presumably, therefore, Yahweh is not in all ways a shepherd. The shepherd meanings have to be squeezed around as they mediate our knowing.

Gerhart/Russell offer a visual model for explaining how a metaphor works. Imagine two fields of meaning on a plane side by side. With all their differences, something in the first field is related to something in the second field by a beholder of both. One has to ignore a lot of differences to focus upon the connection. Some of the differences (like the shepherd as rogue) would veil rather than disclose the being of Yahweh. Imagine, then, that the first field of meaning is folded over the second field of meaning and pressed and cajoled into shape until the similarities are juxtaposed and at the center of focus. "The metaphorical relationship arises when we *insist* that the relationship between 'already knowns' is analogical. The effect of this insisting is to warp, distort, fold, spindle, and perhaps mutilate our world of meanings."[7] More simply, tension is created by the forced analogy. The connection fits, of course, but it doesn't fit perfectly. But even the imperfect fit discloses something that could not be disclosed in any other way. The imperfect fit together with the experience of powerful disclosure: these together illustrate the tensive character of a metaphor.

This is true of all the metaphors of God: *ruach, dabhar,* etc. Fidelity to the original disclosive appearance of Yahweh requires not losing entirely the metaphor's tensive quality. This applies equally and doubly to Christological reflection upon Jesus as the Christ of a God both of whom, Jesus and the Father, we meet in the metaphors of nascent moments of religious experience.

The Metaphoric Process of Knowing

The expressive, descriptive and ornamental uses of metaphor are altogether legitimate, worthy metaphorical functions. But these belong to a later moment of articulation and not to the nascent moment when the process of knowing is itself occurring. In the nascent moment, metaphor is not even primarily a sculptor of language; rather, as Gerhart/ Russell say, "the metaphoric process is the primary sculptor of our *thinking* territory."[8] They are suggesting that Ricoeur's conviction that thinking rises up out of symbol-making[9] can be further understood in respect to metaphor, a development which Ricoeur cites and approves in his foreword to their book. Metaphors may help to elaborate an idea, but they also pertain to the invention of an idea,[10] and that is our concern here.

That there is no uninterpreted "fact" means also that there is no such thing as totally "objective" knowledge which bears no imprint from the subjectivity of the knower. Yet it is important to affirm in this context that something is indeed truly making its appearance. Being really appears, even if always an interpreted appearing. Affirming that all fact is interpreted does not exclude genuine referentiality in the interpreting.

A metaphor participates in the unveiling of being, and we ourselves are collaborators in the making of the metaphor. The appearing of something that happens in the metaphoric process is a true disclosure of reality. Some*thing* or some*one* becomes present. The metaphoric process, therefore, truly presences being and is ontologically based. That *Ruach, Dabhar, Sophia* and *Logos* all presence God is testified to by believers in the canonization of texts that carry these metaphors along from lived experience to lived experience to lived experience.

Not only that, the tensive function of the metaphor is integral to the disclosure of being that occurs. Ricoeur insists that if one thing is like another in every metaphor, there is always a secret "is not like." The tensive character of a metaphor has to do with forcing the connection between likes, notwithstanding the not-likes. But "not-like" begins where "like" ends, and therefore actually frames the disclosing.

Metaphor as Meaning-Maker

We turn now to metaphor as a creator of meanings out of which people are to live. Once shepherd is a metaphor for Yahweh, the meaning of Yahweh is changed from what it was before. We cannot know God in the same identical way as both shepherd and not shepherd. Equally, if shepherd is stabilized culturally as a metaphor for God, we have also impinged on the meanings of shepherds in the fields tending their flocks. Shepherd meanings shape our experience of Yahweh and Yahweh meanings shape our experience of shepherd. The metaphoric process impacts upon all the fields of meaning that it touches. Since Luke 2:18, "In the countryside close by there were shepherds out in the fields keeping guard over their sheep in the watches of the night," Christians cannot ever again behold the shepherd only as a bucolic occupation. Through shepherds the world first receives the news of its Savior.

I share Gadamer's and Ricoeur's sense that when we are interpreting we are also engaged in construction work. We are not just apprehending what is there, but *making* meaning out in front of both us and what is there. One metaphor out of many possible metaphors actually mediates my understanding. And this metaphor spawns a different behavioral response than any of the others would have. One of the most obvious examples is the difference *in us* between God as Father and God-dess as Mother. Christians, by and large, hear pagan construction over and against Jewish-Christian meanings at the word "goddess," because the father metaphor has built such a formidable construction. When and to the extent that feminine metaphors significantly and communally mediate the Christ event, the behavioral texture of Christian life and Christian prayer will take some very, very new turns. Not the least among the turns will be meanings that attend upon the functions of power, for father and mother provoke contrasting authority models in every culture.

Ruach and *Dabhar* each make meaning out of the human experience of God differently than do *Sophia* and *Logos*. And *Logos* itself makes different meaning as the primary language of religious experience in the Johannine community than it does when it has been ontologized by the Stoic meaning-makers of the patristic period. It is not easy to get back into the other side of the Stoically metaphysicalized *logos,* for the Johannine community *Logos* was a metaphor in the knowing of Jesus and God and the inextricable connection between them in the Johannine faith experience. That "Jesus is the human face of God" is not simply interchangeable with a *Logos*-knowing of Jesus/God, but they reach into similar apprehensions: that the phenomenality of Jesus is also, in faith, the phenomenality of God.

In this current study the underlying presupposition is that Jesus must be experienced as being all that he was/is entirely within the framework of first century Galilean Judaism if we are to hear the original voice that gave us Christians our beginnings. While the meaning we make of Jesus must and does exceed the original voice on its original horizon, it still may not neglect nor contravene nor violate Jesus' historical Jewishness.

The underlying question, given the presupposition and conviction just named, is: Which of the Christological metaphors will be most helpful in jumping back over the chasm dug by Greek metaphysics? Some may object that "chasm" overdoes it; but when I behold that discontinuity between Christianity and Judaism that has dishonored the Jewishness of Christian origins, I think "chasm" might be gentle. And while there are many social and political causes at work as well, the recurrent Stoic language and conceptuality of early Christian belief must never be underestimated in its power to construct a divide. The rabbinic option for Aramaic and Hebrew is a divide-constructing device as well.

Overcoming Metaphysics

> . . . it must be possible to recall the later dogmatic language to [its] foundations in experience, to a language in immediate interplay with experience, a language of naming rather than one of definition. It is at this level that the sense of the terms "Father," "Son," and "Spirit" is lodged and every effort at definition will lose that sense unless constantly checked against the original biblical naming. . . . The step back out of metaphysical theology is a step towards the Jewish matrix of all our theology (Joseph O'Leary).[11]

"The Overcoming of Metaphysics in Christian Theology" is the subtitle of Joseph O'Leary's careful post-modern essay on Christian theology. I agree with the task of overcoming metaphysics. But first I want to indicate what "metaphysics" means when I speak of its needing to be overcome. Then I want to say why I think it *must* be overcome. There is a post-modernist reason for the "must." I also want to indicate a faith reason why metaphysics *should* be overcome. There is a metaphoric reason for the "should." I would like to share, then, where in process/relational modes of thought the relativization of metaphysics began to occur for me. And, finally, I want to call attention to the ideological biases that always operate in everyone's thinking and speaking. When a system of thought is perennialized, so is its ideology. It is the "meta-" of metaphysics that encourages the perennializing, at least as Aristotle's metaphysics has often been interpreted.

The "Meta-" of Metaphysics

What has come to be known as Aristotle's *Metaphysics* was not designated as such by Aristotle. It was a later editor who so named it because it was placed after (*meta* = "after" or "beyond" in Greek) Aristotle's work on the physical sciences.[12] However, *meta* has picked up a different meaning in the philosophical tradition of the West, namely, *timeless* first principles concerning the nature of being. The expression "perennial philosophy" reflects this sense of timelessness. These articulated philosophical intuitions are thought to be valid articulations for any time and any place, i.e. meta-historical and meta-cultural.

Whatever understandings of metaphysics there are that presume timelessness, these are the meanings that must be overcome. There is no fault-finding in this conclusion, because the untenability of timelessness as a characteristic of human thought and human articulation is a general conclusion that follows upon the rise of historical consciousness. Our age is surely not the first in which people have recognized that we are conditioned by our relationships and our experience. But it does appear to be a characteristic of our age that the irreducible contingency of human concepts, the radical historicality of human articulations, are widespread data of western consciousness.

Timebound humanity must recognize that no interpretation from one time, place and language is ever translatable without remainder into another time, place and language. No past can ever be reconstructed in a new time, for its capacity far outweighs the partial insights we might have.[13] My quest for a Jewish Jesus has these limitations as well. The different conclusions at which different people, engaged in this same quest, arrive is proof enough of the complexity and limited results of historical retrieval. That doesn't mean it shouldn't be tried!

For all the same reasons that preclude a timeless metaphysics, all understandings and articulations of Christian faith are radically contingent. We always speak out of a particular community with a particular history. We can never escape our particularity in our interpretation. However, today as we try to respond to the rise of historical consciousness, we bear the burden of many centuries in which faith has sought understanding in the categories of timeless metaphysics. "The metaphysical structuration of faith causes it to forget its finitude, giving it a discourse for all times and places, rendered autonomous in regard to the community and its praxis."[14]

It is certainly not my position that our doctrinal traditions have not caught the truth of faith's experience. They have indeed, often splendidly. But they have not done so in timeless ways that can for all generations continue to mediate and transmit the experience and tradition of faith with the same adequacy as in their first moment of truth. Indeed, for all of their original power, in a later community of experience they can obscure rather than disclose. While no living community can escape the issue of normativeness, and should not even try, how that normativeness functions must be very different as we own our finitude and embrace contingency as our character.

It is, therefore, the timebound nature of all human activity that requires the overcoming of classical metaphysical understandings, and of classical meta-theological and meta-doctrinal understandings. I mean overcoming all the "metas" that presume historically conditioned understandings and articulations as normatively transferable across eras and cultures.

Roman Catholics today cannot but wonder at Rome's new Universal Catechism, precisely because "universal" is a "meta." How can Europe adequately think a faith for all Africa or all China, for all ages, or even men adequately think a faith for all women. We are creatures of finitude, and that is who we are before God and from God. The overcoming of meta- is also, or has the potential to be, a religious reclamation of finitude.

The "Meta-" of Metaphor

The "meta-" of metaphor refers to understanding that is transferred "over" from one thing to another, the transfer of meaning "beyond" the first to the second. The "meta-" of metaphor has never picked up the transcultural or transhistorical valences that the "meta-" of metaphysics has sometimes claimed. There is an irony in this because metaphors, if they are rooted in common human experiences, like water and wind, like eating, like giving birth and dying, are preeminently durable—more so than metaphysics. Metaphors are still not timeless, since how we experience these things does vary from culture to culture, and age to age. Water for a desert inhabitant has a different power than for the rain forest dweller. But the problem with metaphor and metaphysics is other than that.

The epistemological function of metaphor is based upon a similitude between one thing and another. This "is like" feature that one item shares with another is what enables the metaphor to mediate experience, notwithstanding the fact that to match some shared reality, we must sometimes first distort, bend, fold and spindle to fashion the functional analogy. All of the cognitive, emotive, communicative and evocative powers of metaphor are based upon the "is like."

The two are of course not identical; there is also the element of "is not like." The "is not like" is also implicated in the construction of meaning in which interpretation is engaged. God is also not like wind and word, not like wisdom, and not like the order of the *Logos*. The "is not like" is regularly a secret. If we were forever attending to the "is not like" the "is like" would not be able to get on with it. We usually treat the "is not like" like a repressed secret: we sort of know it, but choose not to remember what we sort of know. But if the "is not like" is totally eclipsed, we have an ontological naiveté: the "is not like" is no longer sharing in the construction of meaning, and the positive parts of the meaning become crass, and they can even lie.

As Ricoeur and others propose, a proposition I accept, religious thought arises out of the metaphor and symbols that mediate our knowing of God. Metaphor belongs to the primary thinking of religion. Faith has often put metaphysics (the timeless version) to work in its quest for understanding. As the "handmaid of theology" in this task, philosophy has often been invoked to help illustrate the plausibility and intelligibility of faith claims by locating them within the very interpretation of being itself. What we seize upon with metaphysics are the "is like" features of our foundational religious metaphors. Once this happens, the "is not like" features are not simply secret, they are roundly repressed and delivered entirely from their constitutive role in making meaning.

In a later chapter of this volume, which addresses the metaphysicalizing of the *Logos* metaphor, I want to suggest that what some of the heterodoxies are fencing with, borderline or full-blown, are problems built into the ontologized metaphors that lost their secret "is not like." I think there is good reason to understand Arius this way, from an early century. And while not in the arena of heterodoxy, Piet Schoonenberg's Christological proposal ran into problems for quite the same reason.[15] Not Chalcedon itself, which is sparse in its affirmation, but the metaphysical elaborations of Chalcedon, be it Leontius of Byzantium or contemporary reflection, have lost reference to that part of Christological meaning which only the metaphor's "is not like" can provide.

Simply, the metaphors of the primary language of religious experience lose vital control when the "is not like" is dispatched from their meaning world. Pressing metaphysics into the service of the "is like" is one of the surest ways of losing that necessary control. For reasons grounded in the rise of historical consciousness, I have suggested that metaphysics must be overcome. For reasons rooted in the nature of the metaphoric process, even apart from the other reason, metaphysics ought to be overcome for the maintenance of metaphor.

In a word, overcoming metaphysics is required by the nature of the metaphoric process of knowing. This is therefore an epistemological argument that places the classical metaphysical tradition under permanent suspicion.

Megaphysics and Process Thought

Roman Catholics who have become interested in process theology have often been attracted there as an alternative metaphysical system that does more justice to the contemporary experience of becoming. It was Pierre Teilhard de Chardin who said that the incessant becoming of the world is the primary datum of experience. Such was certainly my initial attraction to process modes of thought.

After the first fervor subsided, when I recognized that Berkeley, Locke and Hume, not Aristotle and Aquinas, were Whitehead's primary dialogic partners, I began to change my sense of the real nature of Whitehead's achievement. Let me note some of these, because they are relevant to the issue of metaphysics.

Though Whitehead could not have been conditioned by contemporary hermeneutical philosophy, from his scientific background he was keenly aware of the conditioned nature of anything and everything, and of the symbolic stratum with which knowing begins. Metaphysics takes on a different meaning for Whitehead, namely, it assumes a perpetually provisional status. "Metaphysical categories are not dogmatic statements about the obvious; they are tentative formulations of the ultimate generalities . . . progressive but never final. . . . [Philosophy's technical categories] remain metaphors mutely appealing for an imaginative leap."[16]

Having said all of that, Whitehead's quest for the best imaginative generalizations he can make is meticulous and formidable. He wants to formulate categories that necessarily apply, but the necessity is not *a priori,* it is a generalization and is fallible. So I would conclude that Whitehead tells a very large story, belonging fully to its time. But it is a mega-story and not a meta-story. Although Whitehead speaks of metaphysics, of course, he calls *Process and Reality* an essay in cosmology, i.e. it addresses the deliverances of experience in regard to a particular world. I believe that Whitehead has, by and large, understood better than Whiteheadians the finitude of philosophical systems.

I want to leave room for mega-stories and mega-physics, which deconstructionist post-modern theories tend to disallow. The challenge to a mega-story is how to let the "is not likes" of foundational metaphors keep a ghostly presence in the plot.

Perennializing Our Ideologies

Liturgy is a good place to see what difference metaphors make, for the way we describe God has ideological reverberations and behavioral implications.

Liturgy, among the many things it does, is an act of world-making. Worship constructs and maintains meaning for its participants. The psalms of the Jewish scriptures have liturgy as their setting. The psalms are a sort of collection of the most popular liturgical "hymns" over a long period of history.

As every sociologist knows, wherever world-making is afoot, social interests are operative. This is no less the case when liturgy is the world-making agent. In his book *Israel's Praise,* Walter Brueggemann notes that even our praising stands right on the edge of ideology.[17] Some of the psalms "sing up" and some "sing down." The psalms frequently call us to praise Yahweh, and then give the reasons why we should. Sometimes the reasons are historical remembrances of what Yahweh did for us in the past, and presumably will do again. It is the marginalized whose reasons for praising Yahweh "are marked by a primary impetus toward justice, equity, and righteousness."[18] These are songs from below, and they offer Yahweh's presences in history as the reason for the praise. They are sung by people who need justice, and praising God for God's justice helps make a just world. God's mercy and justice are frontmost.

Other psalms praise Yahweh as Creator of the heavens and the earth. Yahweh's splendor and power are evoked by the Temple which the king built and the king supports. Yahweh is praised for the cosmic order. History plays a smaller role in these psalms that the kings compose. The psalms are "sung down." Whether or not a reigning king actually composed them, they spring from a royal consciousness. From a human position of security they celebrate order, with Orderer as a metaphor for God. God's majesty is frontmost. Songs up and songs down created different meaning worlds.

Theologies, similarly, are done from below or from above (not to be confused with low and high Christology). They may proceed from a people's pain or a people's security. Those who sing from below commit to making a just world. Those who sing from above commit to making an orderly world. Songs up and songs down create different meaning worlds from which to live.

It is an educated social class that engages in metaphysical speculation. They have the resources and the leisure to ponder the wonder of being in the complex categories of being. Therefore, I am suggesting that philosophical theology is sung down. The perennial cast of philosophical theology, in the classical mode, also perennializes the ideological biases of the social class that engages in and is shaped by metaphysical theology.

The *Logos* interpretive metaphor is early pressed into the service of the Christological tradition, and almost just as early attracts the Stoic tradition as a philosophical interpretation of a foundational metaphor. The great theological debates of the early Councils do not impinge upon justice issues at all as far as I can discern. The hungry would not have been affected had Arius and Nestorius won the debate, except insofar as the outcome of the debate also affected the shape of empires.

There is something profoundly and inescapably historical about the operation of the *Dabhar*/Word of God and its most frequent appearance in the mouth of the prophet. *Dabhar* has an ideological bias in favor of singing up. Thus far, *Dabhar* Christology has not generated a widespread philosophical theology. If it had, we would perhaps then also have a perennialized Christology sung up from the pain of history. Liberation theology is probably the nearest we come to *dabhar* theology sung from below in the music of the marginalized. It is structured by devices of social critique and not by metaphysics. I tend to think that transcendental Thomism, in both of its best contemporary expressions, are theologies sung from above, as is process theology. I love them both, have lived in them both, and as an insider I feel their range and their limitations.

We are to be holy as God is holy. The moral texture of that holiness is unquestionably in Yahweh's justice and mercy. I think precisely because these commitments have not been the dominant theological motif of western Christianity I find myself tilting Christologically in their favor. But the full chorale of praise for Yahweh must be sung up and sung down. Brueggemann's advice is cogent: we must maintain a dialectic that is able

> to imagine and invoke a world of utter majesty and transformative mercy. . . . Yahweh as *a God of majesty* governs in royal splendor befitting the best-established imperial power. Yahweh as *a God of mercy* is peculiarly attentive to the cries of pain and wretchedness among slaves, peasants, and all those who are marginal in society. This deep polarity of God must not be reduced in either direction. . . .[19]

I am making two interrelated comments. First, there is the reminder that all interpretation proceeds from a social situation and reflects the ideologies of that situation, just as do, therefore, theologies sung up and theologies sung down. Every interpreter comes from a history, a social situation, a social class, a set of vested interests. What Jürgen Habermas has added as a corrective to interpretation theory is the reminder that all positions have ideological biases and must be subject to ideology critique.[20]

My second reflection in this section is a reminder that if the interpretation makes a claim to a status as perennial, then the concomitant ideology becomes perennial as well. Because of its metaphysical connections, western Christology has tended to be sung perennially from above. Any dialectic theology sung from below has been at best muted, and often inaudible. The contemporary cacophony between Latin America and the Vatican is in great part the cacophony of power songs and pain songs still awaiting difficult orchestration within the same symphony. Among composers, Charles Ives would be a better candidate for this orchestral challenge than Antonio Vivaldi. Which is to say, the U.S. cultural experience of encompassing pluralism may know something important for Christian existence.

Reprise

This book is about the metaphors of God that have been used in Christological reflection upon Jesus as the Christ of God. Shifts in God-metaphors, therefore, represent shifts in Jesus-meanings. I have stressed that the metaphors of God are not ornamental, primarily, but have sculptured our very experiencing of God even before the experience finds voice. These metaphors belong to the process of knowing itself.

Second, I have stressed that the being-disclosure which metaphors mediate depends as much upon the "is not like" component as upon the "is like" component. There is a tendency in the excitement of the disclosure to forget completely the "is not" instead of guarding it as an important but well-kept secret. The metaphysicalizing of a metaphor, of which Stoic reflection upon the Johannine *Logos* is an example, is one of the surest ways of losing the truth mediation of a metaphor's "is not like" factor.

Third, in several ways I have named and agreed with the post-modernist conviction that metaphysics, in the classical "meta-" sense, must be overcome, because "meta-" belies the timebound nature of all human reflection. The quest for perennial apprehensions of major truths, even the truths of our faith experience, is not legitimate. The spirituality of the theologian must be content with our creaturely finitude.

Fourth, I made the suggestion that mega-physics, the large systematized insight, is legitimate so long as we understand that the organization has much to do with the interpreter's free construction. We must not suppose we have discovered the essential inner logic once and for all. I must confess that I do not see clearly what mega-physics or mega-narratives must look like to facilitate a large disclosure and yet not fall prey to the "meta-" temptation.

Lastly, thinking analogously of Walter Brueggemann's reflection upon Israel's praises, I have stressed that all theologies exist on the edge of ideology, and that the metaphors that mediate our experience of God are also ideologically laden. That is neither good nor bad in itself, it just is the human case. It is important that theologies sung from below and theologies sung from above have a workable even if hectic relationship.

Now we will begin to explore the metaphors of God.

Notes

1. Bernard J. Lee, *The Galilean Jewishness of Jesus: Retrieving the Jewish Origins of Christianity* (New York: Paulist Press. A Stimulus Book, 1988), pp. 36–40.

2. Paul Ricoeur, *The Rule of Metaphor* (Toronto: Univ. of Toronto, 1979).

3. Sally McFague, *Metaphorical Theology* (Philadelphia: Fortress, 1982).

4. Mary Gerhart and Allan Russell, *Metaphoric Process: The Creation of Scientific and Religious Understanding* (Fort Worth: Texas Christian Univ., 1984).

5. Gerhart/Russell, 1984, p. xii.

6. David Miller, *Christs* (New York: Seabury, 1981), pp. 8–14.

7. Gerhart/Russell, 1984, p. 114.

8. Gerhart/Russell, 1984, p. 132, emphasis added.

9. Paul Ricoeur, *The Symbolism of Evil* (Boston: Beacon, 1967), pp. 347–357.

10. Gerhart/Russell, 1984, p. 108.

11. Joseph O'Leary, *Questioning Back: The Overcoming of Metaphysics in Christian Theology* (Minneapolis: Winston, 1985), p. 128.

12. Sir David Ross, *Aristotle* (London: Methuen, 1960), p. 13.

13. O'Leary, 1985, p. 118.

14. O'Leary, 1985, p. 133.

15. Piet Schoonenberg, *The Christ* (New York: Seabury, 1971), esp. pp. 50–105.

16. Alfred North Whitehead, *Process and Reality,* corrected edition (New York: Macmillan Free Press, 1978), p. 4.

17. Walter Brueggemann, *Israel's Praise* (Philadelphia: Fortress, 1988), chapter 3, "Doxology at the Edge of Ideology: The King of Majesty and Mercy", pp. 55–87.

18. Brueggemann, 1988, p. 74.

19. Brueggemann, 1988, pp. 65, 73.

20. Jürgen Habermas, *Knowledge and Human Interests* (Boston: Beacon, 1979).

2
The Narrative Structure of Hebrew Experience
Part I: Yahweh, Covenants, Father

Introduction

A culture's symbolic code (its symbols and rituals) are embedded in and expressive of its narrative structure. There is a coherence among the many parts. It is never a perfect coherence, however. There is a relentless metamorphosis that goes with being alive. The fabric of life always has some frayed edges where new fabric is woven. Granted, therefore, that we never have a flawlessly coherent narrative, in these next two chapters I want to describe some of the major strands that are in the warp and the woof of the Jewish deep story to which belongs the life of Jesus.

Let us Christians, then, walk on the less traveled road as we continue here our quest for the Jewishness of Christian origins by exploring the Jewish story out of which Jesus lived and out of which the first Christian communities forged their new existence. In Chapters 2 and 3 we are concerned especially with those elements of the ancient Hebrew interpretation of religious experience that form the backdrop for *Ruach*/Spirit and *Dabhar*/Word. Then follow Chapters 4 and 5 on *Ruach* and *Dabhar,* 6 on *Sophia* and 7 and 8 on *Logos.*

I feel some kinship with the *annaliste* historian's interpretation of an historical era's *mentalité.* Carolyn Walker Bynum has shown the value of this approach in her work on the spirituality of the high middle ages, in which she concentrates on the many images with which religious people recounted their religious experience.[1] While one may overdepend upon the value of any single image, she suggests that

> if we trace the networks of images built up by [these] authors and
> locate those networks in the psyches and social experiences of those
> who create or use them, we find that they reveal to us what the writers
> cared about most deeply themselves and what they felt it necessary to
> present or justify to others . . . the emotional significance of a[n
> older] word or image (even very common words) cannot be inferred

from its modern meaning but must be established by a careful study of the other images and phrases among which it occurs in a text.[2]

This present chapter rummages around for a narrative structure among the multiple images and ideas of the earlier scriptures, as the backdrop for the *Ruach/Dabhar* metaphor discussion in later chapters.

I am using the expression "narrative structure" in the way it was developed in the first volume of this trilogy. It names a kind of deep story that a people lives out of in all its particular stories—the way that being French is different from being German, the way the U.S. cultural story differs from that of Great Britain, even though both speak English. No one can really tell the deep story. We have to look at historical particulars as

> allusive expressions of [deep] stories that cannot be fully told, because they live, so to speak, in the arms and legs and bellies of the celebrants. These stories lie too deep in the consciousness of a people to be directly told. . . . [Sacred stories] are subject to change, but not by conscious reflection. People do not sit down on a cool afternoon and think themselves up a sacred story. They awaken to a sacred story, and their most significant mundane stories are told in the effort, never fully successful, to articulate it. For the sacred story does not transpire within a conscious world. It forms the very consciousness that projects a total world horizon, and therefore informs the intentions by which actions are projected into that world.[3]

The formative metaphors in the life of any culture help us interpret the deep story of that culture. As I have been repeating already, I believe that the *Logos* metaphor for divine reality and its presence in history has dominated the unfolding of Christian faith in the west, even though it would not have been effective in Jesus' own sense of God. But *Ruach* and *Dabhar* would have been familiar furnishings in his house of being. I am interested in the way in which *Ruach*/Spirit and *Dabhar*/ Word describe the redemptive presence of God in history, and how they might be far more fully appropriated by Christians to interpret the experience and the meaning of Jesus. Since Spirit and Word belong to a system of interrelated meanings—to a narrative structure—they must be situated thus.

The deep story which nurtured the identity of Jesus, his relation to God and the world, his sense of vocation and destiny, was thoroughly Jewish. Thorlief Boman's *Hebrew Thought Compared with Greek* makes dramatically clear how different are the deep stories of the Hebrews and the Greeks.[4] I want to respect the importance of those differences without seeming to pit them against one another. Jewish and Greek elements together have given western culture much of its configuration. Jewish communities in diaspora had long been engaged in Jewish/Greek syncretism by the time of Jesus. In Christian experience the Greek has tended to swallow up the Jewish, and we have lost much of the Jewishness that belonged to the immediate world of Jesus and his followers— hence, it has been very difficult to hear the life of Jesus on its own ground.

All the early records of the Jesus-event are in Greek, even though the spoken word of Jesus and his followers was Aramaic. The gospels (especially the synoptics) and Paul retain the trademarks of both Jewish and Greek life. But soon the Jewish elements are largely eclipsed. Those people who "wrote" the western Christian story, e.g. Nicea and Chalcedon, were people with a Greek deep story. It's a different dance to Pan's pipe than to David's harp.

In the remainder of this chapter I will be examining major components of the Hebrew deep story. I am focusing upon those elements which are essential to the elucidation of *Ruach*/Spirit and *Dabhar*/ Word—as these are understood in the context of Metaphor One. This means that I have not included materials that emerged from the latter centuries B.C.E. when the Greek influences became more marked, e.g. the Wisdom figure. Basically, then, I will not be paying much attention to the foundations for Metaphor Two. The Wisdom Figure is important Christologically, but seems unlikely to have been part of the deep story within which the religious awareness of Jesus was incubated. The Wisdom Figure was part of the deep story to which many very early Christian communities quickened, but that already marks the turn toward Athens, or more accurately, toward Alexandria. I am interested in that less traveled road.

In turn I will be treating in this chapter the Hebrew understanding of Yahweh God, especially the emergence of a strong monotheistic commitment. Then I will address covenant as a root metaphor, the basic motif that mediated the Hebrew people's understanding of how Ultimacy trafficked with their immediacy. I will be paying attention to the successive evolutions of covenantal understandings. It is in the evolution of covenant that God comes to be known/disclosed as Father, with Hebrew kings and Hebrew people experiencing themselves, correspondingly, as sons of God. After looking at the covenant experience, I will turn to the name "father" as directly used for God, and as implied. Following this, I will be examining two aspects of Hebrew anthropology. The first is the notion of corporate personality, a social conception of human experience very different from our own. Then I will focus upon "heart" as the seat of personal existence, again an understanding that is very different from our rational approach to life.

Then in the next two chapters I will treat somewhat in detail two major motifs for describing how God was experienced as being at work transforming the historical experience of the Hebrews: the Spirit of God, and the Word of God. I want to propose that Spirit and Word are closely coordinated presences of God in Hebrew experience. They are not two models of divine immanence, but each is half of the same model. This entire exploration of particular elements of the Hebrew story is an attempt to sound the depths of the deep story.

I hope to remain faithful to the empirical/historicist commitment I described at length in the opening chapter of Volume 1. I do not want to make any claims about the nature and character of God that are not grounded in the immediate lived experience of the Hebrew people, where all God's names are redolent with history. I will be primarily concerned to describe the experience of God in the language of the earlier scriptures, and to note evolution and development in the Hebrew experience of both self and God.

An empirical method requires examining the *experiences* in which the immanence of God is named Father, or Covenant Maker, or Spirit, or Word, etc. I will attempt at some points to generalize the experiences. I am mindful of Whitehead's sense of philosophical generalizations, that they are metaphors mutely appealing for an imaginative leap. The leap is the attempt to discern the narrative structure—the interrelatedness— of the many metaphors in a system. I will move from parts to whole. As the deep story comes into view, its art form is that of mosaic.

Yahweh—God

In our own personal lives, what the word "God" means undergoes many transformations. There are large differences between what God is for a six year old and a sixty year old, for someone riding the crest of ecstasy and someone crawling through despair, uncertain whether the next moment deserves to be lived. Similarly, there are marked transformations in Israel's understanding of God. Some changes are deep purifications, some are responses to the vicissitudes of history. The most important of all the developments is the move from polytheism through henotheism to monotheism.

Israel emerges out of and departs from the polytheism of most of the Near East. But there are vestiges of polytheism in the earlier scriptures themselves. The book of Judges recounts that the Israelites displease Yahweh because they serve the gods of Aram, Sidon, and other places. These are not named as false gods, only as other gods than Yahweh. Yahweh allows Israel to be ravished by these other nations, and in his anger says to his people who ask his help: "But it is you who have forsaken me and served other gods; and so I shall rescue you no more. Go and cry to the gods you have chosen. Let them rescue you in your time of trouble" (Jgs 10:13–14). Israel gives up the foreign gods and Yahweh relents. The Israelites then recall Jephthah, whom they had earlier exiled, to return from the land of Tob and be their leader. Jephthah agrees to do so, and enters into negotiation with the king of the Ammonites to seek a peaceful settlement. The Ammonite king argues that the Israelites have no right to the land they occupy; they took it away from someone else. Jephthah reminds the king that the Ammonites got their land in the very same way: "Will you not keep as your possession whatever Chemosh, your god, has given you? And just the same, we shall keep whatever Yahweh, our God, has given us . . . ." (Jgs 11:24). It is presumed that there are other gods besides Yahweh.

Henotheism is an intermediate stage between polytheism and monotheism. While there is not a clear confession that there is only one God who exists, there is a solid conviction that there is only one God who finally matters, and that God is in the ascendency. Yahweh has earned that ascendent position by what he has done for the Israelites. When Moses proclaims the great commandments, he begins with an account of the covenant which Yahweh made "with us who are here, all living today" (Dt 5:3). The first of the commandments which Yahweh gave is: "I am Yahweh your God who brought you out of Egypt, out of the place of slave-labor. You shall have no gods except me" (Dt 5:6–7). In the context of henotheistic faith, Chemos, the god of the Ammonites, would not get the same treatment that he got from Jephthah in his arguments with the king.

It is in the post-exilic period that absolute monotheism takes shape and becomes Israel's faith forevermore. A particularly clear statement of this faith is in Deutero-Isaiah:

You yourselves are my witnesses, declares Yahweh,
and the servant whom I have chosen,
so that you may know and believe me
and understand that it is I.
No God was formed before me,
nor will be after me.
I, I am Yahweh,
there is no other Saviour but me.
I have revealed, have saved, and have proclaimed,
not some foreigner among you.
You are my witness, declares Yahweh,
I am God, yes, from eternity I am.
No one can deliver from my hand,
when I act, who can thwart me?
Thus says Yahweh,
your redeemer, the Holy One of Israel . . . (Is 43:10–14a).

This is an absolute monotheism. There is only one God! There never was another! There never will be another.

In Volume 1 I spoke to the issue of particularism versus universalism in the Judeo-Christian tradition. We confront this issue here in Jewish monotheism. If there's only one God, then that God is everybody's God. But that God takes sides by sending an army against Babylon. That same God elects one nation for special treatment, and unspecial nations pay for it. Although the notion of election and concomitantly that of special treatment are thematic in the Hebrew experience of its election and its covenant, we do find testimony in Amos, for example, against special treatment for Israel: "Are not you and the Cushites all the same to me, children of Israel?—declares Yahweh. Did I not bring Israel up from Egypt and the Philistines from Caphtor, and the Aramaeans from Kir?" (Am 9:7). When Isaiah predicts universal peace in the days to come, it will be because Yahweh's authority is over all nations. Since there is only one God whose same authority reaches all nations, war makes no sense. Thus the logic of the prophecy: "Then he will judge between the nations and arbitrate between many peoples. They will hammer their swords into ploughshares, their spears into sickles. Nation will not lift sword against nation. No longer will they learn how to make war" (Is 2:4). Both Judaism and Christianity have continued to experience the tension between tribalized and universalized deity. That tension remains a challenge for each of the major religions of the world.

I cannot stress strongly enough that what emerged in Hebrew faith was an absolutely uncompromising monotheism: there is one God only. Among the deepest wedges between Jewish faith and Christian faith are understandings of Trinity that seem to compromise monotheism. [Unitarian belief is not interchangeable with monotheistic faith, although unitarianism is indeed a reaction to a trinitarian faith felt to compromise the one only God.] Christian faith has from early on been a trinitarian faith. Christians cannot but be monotheists. But Christian history has yet to find a way to do justice to its experience of the threeness of Father, Son and Spirit. The great amount of attention to trinitarian theology in recent decades testifies to the unfinished business. We are still taut somewhere on the tightwire, strung between a merely accidental threeness and an outright tritheism.

The kind of empirical historicism I have talked about in Volume 1, citing the work of James, Whitehead, Derrida, Dean, and others, is an entirely recent undertaking, post-modern in many ways. The Hebrews cannot properly be called empiricists or historicists. But this temperament is congenial to the Hebrew experience of the earlier scriptures because of their incredible concreteness. Whatever the Hebrews know about God they learn from those places in their history where Ultimacy traffics with immediacy. All talk about God is noisy with the sound of that traffic. "I am Yahweh your God who brought you out of the Land of Egypt" (Ex 20:2). Yahweh's linkage with historical experience is profound and pervasive. This is the God of Abraham, the God of Isaac, the God of Jacob. Whatever is known about who God is, is learned through what God does. There is no other source of information than that. There is an otherness of God that outstrips God's witness with us. But if we know anything about the otherness, it is only by means of what God's witness evokes and suggests. What Yahweh might have been like before creation, if there was a before, or in God's Self without creation—these things we cannot know. The only God we know is the God who is with us in history.

In the tension between particularism and universalism, the confession that God is Creator is the most universalist confession about Yahweh. God made everything, the stars, the heavens, the earth, and all that is in it. The Genesis accounts of creation are not and were never intended to be cosmological, in the Greek sense of that term. They are religious affirmation about the debt of gratitude that all beings owe to God. They are an act of faith in the providence of God, from start to finish, as it were. They affirm our dependence upon God. The preoccupation of the earlier scriptures, however, is not with Yahweh as Creator, that is, as "first" or "initial" Creator. It is with Yahweh who relentlessly reCreates, who reMakes over and over and over.

Yahweh has entered human history and is remaking human life. The corners that are busiest with the traffic between Ultimacy and immediacy are the moments when Jewish history undergoes creative transformation. Yahweh finds *a people* that is like any other people. But gradually and painfully, with partial successes and partial failures, Yahweh transforms *a people* into *Yahweh's people*. It is above all in this process of creative transformation that Yahweh is experienced, known, named, praised, loved, and, yes, even resented (what human life that takes God on seriously doesn't sometimes encounter God as the enemy!).

"Covenant" is the metaphor and motif which for the Hebrews best names those busiest of corners where Ultimacy and immediacy traffic. That is the next piece of mosaic to put in place.

The Covenants

The Latin root of our word "religion" means "tying together" or "bonding." Religion is the human response to the experience of being "really related" to deity. Different religious traditions have various key metaphors for interpreting the character of that bonding. Those metaphors will be meanings stretched from daily, ordinary experiences of bonding. The bonding between wife and husband, for example, serves to illustrate the relationship between the Hebrew people and their God (in Hosea). While this and other images (creator/creation; potter/pot) mediate Hebrew religious experience, the motif of covenant is not just "a" key, but "the" key to both the earlier and later scriptures. Or to switch images, if my approach in this chapter is to construct a mosaic, covenant is the master design that suggests where all the pieces fit. Or perhaps differently in respect to the mosaic: covenant is the mortar that holds the pieces together in their relationship to each other, and there is some mortar all the way around every piece. Covenant wraps around every piece of the mosaic. Covenant is different from some of the other images, such as Israel as the spouse of Yahweh. Covenant is experienced as historical. The treaty contract is written down and kept in the ark. It dates to particular times and particular people. However, no safe deposit vault holds a marriage certificate for Yahweh and Israel. Covenant is interpreted as an historical event with Yahweh, in a way that spousehood is not.

Let us look at the covenant meaning before it gets stretched into religious signification. Even a superficial reading of the earlier scriptures makes clear how constant is the intrigue between tribes and nations, how often life is disrupted, how often boundary lines are redrawn. In these scriptures we are witnesses to a period of history which marks some fundamental development in the structures of civilization.

We move from relatively self-contained villages and a rather simple life style to towns that interact with other towns and have a life style of greater complexity. This means that townspeople use and need products that are only available from other towns. Towns, tribes, nations have to learn to relate to each other in ways that allow life to carry on. There must be some dependability. And treaties are that form of dependability that norms their relationships.

The treaty, then, becomes a critical instrument in the creation and support of bonding that serves new modes of human civilization in the Near East. The stability of daily life requires effective treaty making, along with sufficient power to enforce the treaty stipulations. As I indicated just above, when we look for images to help us understand and process our bonding with deity, we have recourse to important experiences of bonding in our daily lives. The treaty/covenant patterns of Near Eastern life are at hand and are important; they provide the motif which becomes the key metaphor from early on. It would be my surmise that treaty or covenant is not primarily a metaphor of embellishment or clarification, but a metaphor of knowing. Covenant is how Yahweh comes to be known.

Discoveries from archaeology have helped us understand the evolution and patterns of treaty agreements. Such achievements as radio carbon dating have greatly improved our ability to place materials accurately within a time frame. Texts and inscriptions have been uncovered in digs and found in caves which give us a far fuller and more accurate picture of what life was like in those days when the events of the scriptures transpired and were later written about.

In 1954, J.B. Pritchard published a very important collection of ancient texts that elucidate biblical materials, *Ancient Near Eastern Texts Relating to the Old Testament.*[5] Among these texts are translations of significant treaties that existed in biblical times. Since then additional treaty materials have been found. It soon became evident to biblical scholars that the successive transformations of the covenant idea in the earlier scriptures reflect transformation in treaty forms of the ancient Near East. I do not want to suggest that every development of the covenant idea is metaphorically nip and tuck with changes in treaty forms, or that the development of either trajectory is purely linear. But that there is an intimate relation between development of the religious idea of covenant and the development of political treaty forms seems indisputable.

The discovery of Near Eastern treaty texts occasioned significant new studies of the biblical convenant metaphor.[6] The two resources upon which I most depend in my presentation below are the article on "*berit*" in the *Theological Dictionary of the Old Testament*[7] (sometimes also transliterated as *berith*), and Delbert Hillers' *Covenant: The History of a Biblical Idea.*[8] Hillers traces the development of the religious notion of covenant in tandem with the political movements in the Near East, and especially in the political and economic life of Israel. Because we go to important places in our daily experiences to find analogical bases for religious experience, there is a profound relationship between cult and culture at all levels. Thus, for example, Hillers observes: "If we can discover the principles and practices connected with concluding legally binding pacts in ancient Israel and her neighbors, we will probably have the foundation for grasping the sense of the pact with God."[9]

The word covenant/*berith* occurs more frequently in the later than in the earlier prophets. But even when the word covenant is not used, legal treaty language comes into play. For example, the Hebrew word *yada,* which means to know, to understand, and to have sexual intercourse, also has a legal treaty meaning. In that context, *yada* means that parties to a treaty recognize each other in terms of the treaty. In a Hittite treaty, the Sun (the king) says: "And you, Huquanas, *know* only the Sun regarding Lordship. Moreover, do not *know* another Lord. . . . I, the Sun, will *know* only you."[10] Thus, in Amos Yahweh says: "You alone have I known [entered into covenant with] of all the families of the earth, that is why I shall punish you for all your wrong doings" (Am 3:2). And Hosea says: "Israelites, hear what Yahweh says, for Yahweh indicts [takes into court for treaty failure] the citizen of the country: there is no loyalty, no faithful love, no *knowing* of God [behaving toward God as covenant partner] in the country . . ." (Hos 4:1–2a). In this passage we find not only treaty use of know/*yada,* but court language as well. In Micah 6 also, Yahweh, as it were, puts his people on trial for their infidelity, calling on the mountains and hills to be his witnesses. *Yada* is but one more example of a religious metaphor. A treaty meaning located in the immediacy of lived experience provides a fundamental religious metaphor for the experiencing of God. A basic political act, covenant, is stretched to name the Jewish experience of Ultimacy.

Following Hillers, I will trace a development in the religious notion of covenant, and mark the variations in treaty forms of the Near East with which covenant changes are often more or less concomitant. This procedure raises a vital question. Are we to understand the developments of the idea of covenant in terms of an evolution in human awareness about what Yahweh is doing? Or are we rather to attribute the development to a changing pattern in the kinds of initiatives which Yahweh is taking in history? The answer is yes to both questions. It's not either/or; it's both/and. It is a scholastic dictum that "whatever is received is received according to the nature of the receiver." If I want to address a friend at a great distance, and the friend has only a short wave receiver, it does me no good to speak into the telephone. God's initiatives are always incarnated in the operational modes of those for whom he cares. The caring of God is an actual event, and like all events, it has a structure. The caring of God is partly determined by God's own free decisions about the ways in which God will bestow love. But it is also determined by the historical configurations of those who are to be the recipients of that love.

Thus, developments in the character of covenant are not *entirely* the result of changes in the symbolic structure of those who experience God's transforming presence. Nor are they *entirely* the result of the ways in which God's caring changes and then is renamed by us accordingly. The character of the relational event known as covenant evolves under the pressures of both of those dynamics. There is a symbiotic relationship between religious experience and cultural experience in which the knowing of God is mediated through metaphors drawn from the culture.

William James has spoken of a conversion experience as a relocation of the "hot place" in consciousness.[11] The "hot place" is the habitual center of personal energy. "Hot place" names the values which become the object of our higher energies. The "spot" is "hot" precisely because all the energy directed there warms it up. "Hot place" is central to the constitution of a person's identity. The same point can be made about a community's life. The notion of covenant is the more or less habitual center of corporate identity for Israel. But successively different notions of what covenant means give Israel's identity different textures. Different notions of covenant convert Israel in a series of on-going transformations.

While we cannot enter into the subjectivity of God, it is interesting to speculate that God does covenantal caring according to the "imposed obligation" model of treaty when that is the best of the models historically available. When a more elaborate lord/vassal model becomes part of Israel's experience, the covenant care of God evolves accordingly. When the richer royal/grant model emerges culturally, God capitalizes, as it were, upon that progression and cares accordingly. When it is recognized that there are resonances between that model and the patriarchal testament of a father with his sons, the deep story of God's care begins to assume a parental structure. The fatherhood of God becomes a new theme. "Father" is an important metaphor for God, even though in the earlier scriptures it is not the covenantal "hot spot." There are only some dozen or so instances when God is explicitly called Father in the earlier scriptures.

As I indicated above, the Hebrew word for covenant is *berith*. Its most likely derivation is from the Akkadian word *biritu* which means a clasp or a bond. The earliest covenant-related meaning in Hebrew seems to be not so much a contract between two people, but an obligation imposed by one party upon another. More developed meanings stress obligations that exist on both sides. As the making of treaties becomes politically important in the Near East, a treaty form develops. Not every treaty follows this model in exact detail, nor weights the different parts in the same way. Yet there are enough similarities so that the treaty form can be generalized:

(a) The preamble is a short introductory statement. Often the parties to the treaty are identified.

(b) Then there is an historical prologue. Details of past history between the treaty parties are given, or the history of the treaty maker might be indicated.

(c) Following this, the actual components of the treaty obligations are given.

(d) The treaty then indicates where the document is to be kept, and stipulates ritual readings of it so that all parties to the treaty are regularly reminded of it.

(e) Gods are called upon to witness the treaty, and their names are given.

(f) Finally, there is a list of the blessings that will come to those who are faithful, and of the curses that will fall upon the unfaithful.

The impact of this treaty form upon the religious rites that surround the Hebrew experience of covenant is quite clear, no matter which particular understanding of covenant is the operative metaphor.

I will indicate the development of the covenant experience in four stages. The first is the "royal grant" model which is exemplified in the covenants with Noah and with Abraham. The second is the "suzerain" model which the Mosaic covenant typifies. Then there is a significant shift in the configuration of Israel's own polity when the nation gets its first king, a move from theocracy to kingship. Adjustments of the covenant notion are required. There is a combination of the two earlier models (some elements from each), with the addition of the notion that the king is God's son. The notion of God's Fatherhood is a component of this third covenant form. The fourth form is the transformation that occurs under the prophetic movement, when covenant is interiorized—written on hearts and not on tablets of stone. This development is not an orderly, purely linear development. Biblical texts that are later in composition may reflect an earlier oral or written tradition. The four stages I am indicating represent a generalization whose intent is to indicate three things: that there is a continual development of the key covenant motif; that ordinary daily experience (here the political experience of treaties in the Near East) provides a metaphoric structure for religious meaning; and, finally, that one vital aspect of the Fatherhood of God is that it names the character of the covenantal bonding between Yahweh and Yahweh's people.

Chronologically (i.e. of periods of history, not the temporal sequence in which biblical texts were composed), we begin with the covenants with Noah, and then with Abraham. In both cases, Yahweh makes a covenant in which all of the obligation is upon God. There is no exact parallel in Near Eastern materials uncovered thus far. The nearest in character (and there are differences as well) is the royal grant treaty which the following Ugaritic text exemplifies: "From this day forward Niqmaddu son of Ammistamru king of Ugarit has taken the house of Pabeya [. . .] which is in Ullami, and given it to Nuriyani and his descendants forever. Seal of the King."[12] The details of the covenant with Noah are in Genesis 9:1–17. "I give you everything. . . . Be fruitful, multiply, teem over the earth and be Lord of it. . . . See, I establish my covenant (*berith*) with you and with your descendants after you. . . . Here is the sign of the covenant I make between myself and you and every living creature with you for all generations: I set my bow in the clouds and it shall be a sign of the covenant between me and the earth." All of the initiative is from God. The agreement is binding for all time, for it is made with Noah and his descendants for all time. The covenant is in no way dependent upon Noah's fidelity—it is made "regardless."

The account of the covenant with Abraham is given in Genesis 15. "I am Yahweh [preamble] who brought you out of Ur of the Chaldeans [historical prologue] to give you this country as your possession [content of agreement]. . . . Look up at the sky and count the stars if you can. Just so will your descendants be" (Gn 15:7,5). Then, in a fashion customary to treaty making in the Near East, the treaty is validated by cutting animals in half, and making a path between the halves through which the treaty makers pass. This symbolizes ritually the fate that will befall anyone unfaithful to the treaty. The guilty party will suffer the fate of the cut-in-two victim. As soon as the sun sets, a smoking furnace and a firebrand (symbol of Yahweh) pass between the halves. In this "J" account of the covenant, no obligation is imposed upon Abraham.

Two chapters later, in Genesis 17, a second narration of the covenant is given, this time the "P" tradition. Yahweh says:

> For my part, this is my covenant with you: you will become the father of many nations. . . . I shall make you exceedingly fertile. I shall make you into nations, and your issue will be kings. I shall maintain my covenant between myself and you, and your descendants after you, generation after generation, as a covenant in perpetuity, to be your God and the God of your descendants after you. And to you and your descendants after you, I shall give the country where you are now immigrants, the entire land of Canaan, to own in perpetuity, and I will be their God. God further said to Abraham, You for your part must keep my covenant, yourself and your descendants after you, generation after generation . . . every one of your males must be circumcised. You must circumcise the flesh of your foreskin, and that will be the sign of the covenant between myself and you. . . . My covenant must be marked in your flesh as a covenant in perpetuity (Gn 17:4–13).

While there are no details as to what Abraham must do, he is enjoined to maintain the covenant and to ritualize circumcision. However there is no threat that the agreement might be terminated if he doesn't. There is no treaty provision that the "text" must be ritually and periodically read. However—and perhaps analogously—the rainbow and the circumcised male genital are enduring reminders of the covenant's presence.

Of all the covenant forms, the Mosaic covenant is the most fully elaborated. There are several important passages in which the covenant is detailed, especially Exodus 20 and parts of Exodus 24. The treaty pattern here is the Suzerain (also called the Lord-vassal) model. The king or lord or suzerain makes a treaty with a people. Although the initiative comes from the king and the treaty is more or less imposed, there are agreements on both sides. The king is to be honored and served. Military service might be required, or taxes might have to be paid. But the protection of the people/vassals is guaranteed.

The following materials are taken from Exodus 20:1–21, and 24:3–11. God speaks: "I am Yahweh your God [preamble] who brought you out of Egypt, where you lived as slaves [historical prologue]" (Ex 20:1–2). Then the first three covenant requirements are given, which require loyalty to God, a jealous God who will not tolerate flirtations with other gods. The remaining seven precepts or commandments govern the mutual behaviors of those placed under covenant. There are precedents for this in the Near Eastern treaty patterns, i.e. separate peoples treatied with the same king then have obligations toward each other. A Hittite king made the same treaty with three different vassals. That treaty not only related each vassal to the king, but required of the vassals certain behaviors toward each other:

> Behold, within my land are three noblemen: you, O Targashnallis, Mashhuiluwas, and Manappa-Dattas. . . . The one of you is not to fall out with the other, and one should not seek to kill the other, or capture the other. And if you, Targashnallis, do evil against them, I will take their part, and you will be my enemy. But if they fall out with you, then I will take your part, and they shall be my enemies.[13]

In the covenant tradition of the Hebrews these mutuality requirements blossom into a fierce ethic of justice.

The last seven commandments detail how parties to the covenant with Yahweh must comport themselves with one another. Moses reads all the commands of Yahweh. The reading and responses also follow treaty rituals in which the lord or suzerain says "You shall . . ." or "You shall not . . ." and the people respond "We shall . . ." or "we shall not . . ." Then there is the ritual slaughter of animals, and afterward the covenant terms are read. Then "Moses took the blood and cast it toward the people. 'This,' he said, 'is the blood of the covenant that Yahweh has made with you, containing all these rules.' "

What follows is a stunningly beautiful scene: "Moses went up with Aaron, Nadab and Abihu, and seventy elders of Israel. They saw the

God of Israel beneath whose feet there was, it seemed, a sapphire pavement pure as the heavens themselves. He laid no hand on these notables of the sons of Israel: They gazed on God. They ate and they drank." In the ancient Near East, one of the most important ritual ways of celebrating a concluded treaty was for the treaty partners to eat together ceremonially. That practice is still retained among the bedouins of the Negev and Sinai deserts.

Many more details of the covenant are spelled out in the first five books of the earlier scriptures, the Torah or Pentateuch. The ark of the covenant is the place where the sacred covenant texts are kept. The regular reading of these texts becomes a central feature of Jewish ritual. Deuteronomy in particular is itself a large, expansive document of the covenant. The whole of Deuteronomy 28 is a listing of blessings and curses. The sound of them certainly "encourages" fidelity! For those faithful: "You will be blessed in the town and blessed in the countryside; blessed, the offspring of your body, the yield of your soil, the yield of your livestock, the young of your cattle, the increase of your flocks; blessed, your basket and your kneading trough. You will be blessed in coming home and blessed in going out" (Dt 28:3–6). Not bad! But if you are unfaithful: "Yahweh will strike you down with Egyptian ulcers, with swellings in the groin, with scurvy and the itch, for which you will find no cure. . . . Get engaged to a woman, and another man will have her; build a house, you will not live in it; plant a vineyard, you will not gather its first-fruits" (Dt 28:27,30). And there are many more curses to discourage infidelity!

The Mosaic covenant, then, represents a considerable development from the early ones with Noah and Abraham. It differs not only in its much greater detail, but in its structure. The suzerain model is clearly visible in the Mosaic covenant, and not in the earlier version. However, what both of these have in common is that Yahweh is the ruler who executes a covenant with his people. Israel is a theocracy, and God is King. The transition from Israel as theocracy to Israel as kingdom marks the next development.

The tribes of Israel are suddenly calling for a king. Israel had for a long time been a very loose kind of federation of tribes. We are not given the reasons for this new desire, but there are clues in Samuel's protests against this development. As the nations around Israel become more complex and more organized, for both economic and political reasons Israel is clearly at a disadvantage. A king can raise monies and raise an army, pulling all the resources together that are available. A kingdom can have a unified foreign policy and the ability to enforce it. Israel needs a king to "keep up with the Joneses," perhaps even to the point of survival. The people say to Samuel: "So give us a king to judge us, like other nations" (1 Sam 8:5). When Samuel lists the disadvantages of having a king (1 Sam 8:10–18), he is probably naming exactly the reasons why the people want a king: he will raise armies, and will get you organized economically. Samuel is dismayed. He feels personally rejected, and recognizes as well what such a change would mean for Israel's relation with Yahweh. So he prays to Yahweh who replies that it is not Samuel, but he, Yahweh, who is being rejected, and that Samuel should accede to the people's wishes. Saul was anointed first king, although it is principally under David that Israel begins to function in a more full-fledged way as a kingdom.

The kingship in Israel creates a new problem: how to fit a king into the religious picture. Previously there were but two parties, Yahweh and Israel. What is to be done with this new third element, the king? The Mosaic covenant, reflecting the suzerain treaty model, is so deeply engrained in the structures of worship and law that it may be transformed (and only with difficulty), but cannot be replaced without destroying the people it created. The early covenant had been related to Israel's progeny and national destiny through individuals (e.g. Abraham). But these earlier covenants with Noah and Abraham had long since been functionally eclipsed by the Mosaic covenant. What the earlier covenants have that the Mosaic covenant lacks are promises to *individuals* (e.g. Abraham) about their being chosen by God, and that the covenant relationship will be transmitted through their descendants. The language is now reintroduced, particularly in respect to David and his son Solomon. Let us return to Saul, the first king.

Saul is privately consecrated by Samuel (1 Sam 10:1). In the same chapter (perhaps simply an alternative version) Samuel calls a convocation of the people, notes their infidelity in wanting a king, but then says that through the lots that were drawn Saul is "the man Yahweh has chosen" (1 Sam 10:24). The people of Israel are accustomed to the text of the Mosaic covenant being a foundational document for their covenant. After the people acclaim Saul as king, Samuel explains the new constitution for the new kingdom, has it inscribed in a book, and places it before Yahweh. He does this in front of the people, then dismisses them.

Because of Saul's misbehavior, Yahweh instructs Samuel to anoint David as king even while Saul is still living. However, it is only after

Saul's suicide when David and his family move to Hebron that he is publicly anointed king of Judah (2 Sam 2:1). At a later time, all the tribes of Israel came to David at Hebron, and he is anointed king of Israel as well as king of Judah. "David was thirty years old when he became king, and he reigned for forty years. In Hebron he reigned over Judah for seven years and six months; then he reigned in Jerusalem over all Israel and Judah for thirty-three years" (2 Sam 5:4–5). David's choice of a new city as a center for Hebrew identity, at the very time that kingship is introduced, is a stroke of political and religious genius. The symbolic move facilitates Israel's religious adjustment to its new political configuration.

However, the really new element that is introduced into Israel's story at this juncture is that the king begins to be called God's son. That a king is understood as a son of God is not uncommon in the Near East, but Israel (as I shall discuss later in more detail) seems to have skirted calling God "Father" because of how often in the Near Eastern mythologies this has the idea of sexual procreation. However, the expression "son of . . ." became a literary device in Hebrew for indicating someone who did something especially well. Sons resemble fathers, so whatever one is a son of, one resembles. It is a metaphor. "Son of a liar" means the biggest and best liar of them all. "Sons of thunder" would be among the noisiest, most cantankerous people you'd find (as were the argumentative brothers, James and John, among Jesus' disciples). A "son of God" is someone who is drawn into a very special relationship with God and is closely associated with God's designs in history. The Fatherhood of God, correspondingly, names a special relationship of choice or election that brings someone into a privileged relationship with God. Thus, in Psalm 2, a later text that remembers the Davidic kingship, Yahweh says to the messianic king: "You are my son, today I have fathered you. Ask of me, and I shall give you the nations as your birthright, the whole wide world as your possession" (Ps 2:7–8).

David recognizes what a discrepancy there is between his house of cedar and the tent in which the ark rests. He resolves to build a temple for the ark. Through the prophet Nathan, David is informed that not he but his son will be the one to build the temple:

> And when your days are over, and you fall asleep with your ancestors, I shall appoint your heir, your own son to succeed you (and I shall make his sovereignty secure. He will build a temple for my name) and I shall make his royal throne secure for ever. I shall be a father to him

and he a son to me; if he does wrong, I shall punish him with a rod such as human beings use, with blows such as they give. But my faithful love will never be withdrawn from him. . . . Your dynasty and your sovereignty will stand ever firm before me and your throne be secure for ever (2 Sam 7:12–16).

This new covenant form, then, is interpreted in part with the introduction of the metaphor of divine Fatherhood.

The third major development in the experience of covenant has come with the transformation of a theocratic league of tribes into a kingdom. The choice of Yahweh must be understood to fall upon the king in order to accommodate this new political reality to the Mosaic covenant, in which there was no third party in between Yahweh and his covenant partner, Israel, for in theory, at least, the judges were adjudicators and not rulers. The Noah/Abraham covenants offer a precedent for the function of an individual figure and his descendants in respect to the transmission of the covenant from age to age. The king becomes this individual figure beginning with the Saul-David-Solomon trajectory. With David the kingship becomes dynastic. With Solomon the notion of the king as son and God as Father further accommodates the kingship role into the covenant story of the Hebrew people. The next great transformation occurs under the prophets.

The third configuration of covenant was an evolution in the context of a vital development in the political structure of the Jewish people. The transformation of the covenant in the time of the prophets is an evolution in the context of events that are widespread in the civilized world. This transformation is a response to a shift, as wide as it is deep, in the very structures of being human, the structures that give human nature its identity. In an earlier chapter I alluded in passing to what Karl Jaspers has called "the axial period" in human history. The prophetic period, in which the narrative structure of Hebrew experience undergoes telling development, must be seen in the context of the axial period. The Pharisaic movement must likewise be seen as a continuing response to that same drift in the human spirit. And so must the teaching of Jesus and the structure of Christian experience. Because of the importance of the axial period, I want to summarize the judgment of Jaspers.[14]

The axial period, centering on 500 B.C.E., actually extends from 800–200 B.C.E. Developments of a similar nature occur in China, India, Persia, Greece and Palestine. When Jaspers speaks of the events of the west, he includes the Hebrew prophetic movement as part of that movement, given the huge role that Jewish experience played, along with Greek experience, in giving the western soul its character. I will cite Jaspers' generalization of the axial transformation, then indicate several specific developments. Then I will return to the prophets, and to the change in covenant that takes place.

The axial period is a time when people's lives leave behind the character of "being played out" in the world; they become self-conscious "players." There is a new kind of relation to a past, and to a future over which human decisions have some control. In short, the human person begins to live in a more fully historicized way, and faces "meaning" questions for the first time. Jaspers writes:

> What is new about this age . . . is that man becomes conscious of Being as a whole, of himself and his limitations. He experiences the terror of the world and his own powerlessness. He asks radical questions. Face to face with the void he strives for liberation and redemption. By consciously recognizing his limits he sets himself the highest goals. He experiences absoluteness in the depths of selfhood and in the lucidity of transcendence.[15]

Jaspers notes the specific qualities of the soul that emerge in the west in the axial period.[16] The human spirit in the axial period becomes aware that it can make decisions that influence destiny. It also recognizes that it lives in a world which cannot be circumvented. That world places us and our freedom under requirement and opens us to the void. With this new experience of self as a free self there comes a new sense of the self as a responsible self, a personal ethical self. There is a desire to inquire and understand: a search for order. Especially noteworthy is that a "*conscious inwardness of personal selfhood*" is achieved "with a decisive absoluteness."[17]

Precisely that conscious inwardness of personal selfhood is what we see emerging in the prophets and reshaping how God and his people shall henceforth be together in covenant. I will address that reshaping of covenant; but I also want to indicate that the consequences of the axial transformation will be addressed further when I treat the notion of Israel's "corporate personality" in a later section of this chapter. And, as I indicated in my discussion of the Pharisees in Volume 1, I believe that the Pharisees continue the evolution of individual existence upon which the prophetic existence embarked. In the final volume, I shall also be indicating my conclusion that Jesus' teaching furthers still again the axial evolution of individual existence, but with a radical affirmation of the individual's social matrix.

Our transformations are seldom if ever the result of some brand new element suddenly occupying a first place in the structure of our experience. Both personal and societal transformations are normally a restructuring of our patterns of experience in which whatever element occupied the "hot place," as James calls it, is displaced by some other element that was already there, but was peripheral. Something is called to come up from a lower place to a higher place in the structure of personal identity. We will see how in Jeremiah the covenant is transformed when an element already available in the tradition, but not central to covenant, takes a higher place. That element is heart. I will use Jeremiah as an instance of the axial transformation of covenant.

It was already the case before Jeremiah that the heart was understood to play a function in fidelity to the covenant. Circumcision became a sign of the Abrahamic covenant. The Deuteronomic code, an expression of the Mosaic covenant, notes that hearts must be circumcised as well as genitals (Dt 10:16). Jeremiah speaks for Yahweh: "Circumcise yourselves for Yahweh; off with the foreskins of your hearts . . ." (Jer 4:4a). With Jeremiah, heart moves from a cooler place into a "hot spot":

> See, the days are coming—it is Yahweh who speaks—when I will make a new covenant with the House of Israel (and the House of Judah), but not like the one I made with your ancestors on the day I took them by the hand to bring them out of the land of Egypt. They broke that covenant of mine, so I had to show them who was master. It is Yahweh who speaks. No, this is the covenant I will make with the House of Israel when those days arrive—it is Yahweh who speaks. Deep within them I will plant my law, writing it on their hearts. Then I will be their God and they shall be my people (Jer 31:31–33).

The law is no longer written on tablets of stone, but on the heart, inside each individual person. It is with the rise of axial individuality that covenant is internalized so deeply in the later prophets. Each person must appropriate covenant deep within. From out of that interiorization, each will instinctively know how to live. It is a gentler, if you will, more personal and tender approach to covenant.

A basic instigating factor for the last transformation is the emergence of the experience of individual personality in the axial period of human civilization. Both "*leb*-heart" language and "*Ruach*-Spirit" language have a far more defining presence from here on. Yahweh does not stop interacting with Israel as an entity and interacts only with individuals in a covenant arrangement. But what is different is that the destinies of the nation and the individual are not tied so inextricably together.

We have looked now at successive developments in the Hebrew experience of themselves as related to God in this formal manner of covenant. For the ancient Jews, covenant is a metaphorical way of knowing who God is for them, and who they are with God. The literal, first meaning of covenant is a secular meaning reflecting treaties between nations. The Hebrew relationship with God "is like" those treaties. Since covenant is a metaphor, there are also, of course, aspects of the Hebrew relationship with God that are not like the treaty form.

Treaty/covenant does not "merely" describe the relationship with Yahweh after the fact, but has the epistemological function of mediating the direct experience of Yahweh. Since the literal meaning of treaty supplies the "is like" basis of the metaphoric process, when that literal meaning shifts its character, so does the experience of God. When the treaty shape changes, the metaphorical valences change, and shifts occur in covenantal experience between Yahweh and his people. A change in metaphor is a change in knowing and living.

The story line is simple. Yahweh starts with a people who is not any more special to him than any other people, but freely chooses to make them his elect, and to transform their history through their special relationship with him. Although covenant has a lot of different faces, it is the basic framework for the Hebrew experience of God's transforming presence in their life. It is the root metaphor and it writes a sacred story. It is the religious deep story out of which this people lives. They live into it and they live out of it. Each of the successive forms of the covenant is a particular story which is a version of the cultic deep story. Covenant may be the deep story, but there's no such thing as a generic deep story. There are only particular instances, and it is these successively transformed instances that disclose the deep story. Covenant, with all its variations of plot and subplot, remains the religious and cultic deep story of the Hebrew people.

God as Father

It appears strange that Israel seems almost intentionally and for a long time to have avoided calling God its "Father."

In Near Eastern religions when a god is called father, the implication is regularly that of procreation. The gods sexually beget the world's people. Israel's understanding of God as Creator differs so fundamentally from the reproductive nation of parent that the Hebrew people assiduously avoided "father" terminology until there was sufficient historical space between them and those early procreator versions of divine Fatherhood. The notions of Father and Creator combined only twice (Dt 32:6 and Mal 2:10) in the earlier scriptures, but there is no hint of procreation.

However, when Israel does introduce this understanding into the structure of its faith, something new happens in the history of religion. What is extraordinary about God as Father in the earlier scriptures, as Joachim Jeremias has remarked, is that Israel uses the motif of adoption to combine God's Fatherhood with an historical action:[18] "I am Yahweh. I shall free you from the forced labor of the Egyptians; I shall rescue you from their slavery and I shall redeem you with outstretched arm and mighty acts of judgment. I shall adopt you as my people and I shall be your God" (Ex 6:6). God's electing/adopting love manifests itself in the exodus from Egypt. There is no single action of God in Jewish history that becomes as paradigmatic of covenantal love as that one. "Who led you out of Egypt" almost becomes Yahweh's family name.

Though God is not explicitly named Father, his Fatherhood is clearly implied in the words Moses addresses to the pharaoh: "This is what Yahweh says: Israel is my first-born son. I told you: let my son go and worship me; but since you refused to let him go, well then! I shall put your first-born son to death" (Ex 4:22–23). As the Jews leave Egypt, the blood of the lamb upon the doorpost signals to the avenging angel to pass over that household as he goes about killing the first-born of the Egyptians. After the sons of Yahweh leave Egypt, the Father's care continues: "You have seen him in the desert too: Yahweh your God continued to support you, as a man supports his son, all along the road you followed until you arrived here" (Dt 1:31).

I have already indicated the place which God's Fatherhood plays in the revision of covenant once Israel has a king. And I have noted how Yahweh becomes Father through adoption. I will turn, therefore, to the prophets, for it is there that we find the most explicit presentation of the Fatherhood of God. Malachi, for example, reproaches the priests for their behavior toward God, their Father: "The son honors his father, the slave stands in awe of his master. But if I am indeed Father, where is the honor due to me?" (Mal 1:6). Chapters 63–64 of Isaiah contain a long and beautiful song of praise to Yahweh's goodness. One of the most poignant passages of the song speaks of God as Father:

> Look down from heaven and see
> from your holy and glorious dwelling.
> Where is your zeal and your might?
> Are your deepest feelings,
> your mercy to me, to be restrained?
> After all, you are our father.
> If Abraham will not own us,
> if Israel will not acknowledge us,
> you, Yahweh, yourself are our Father.
> "Our redeemer" is your ancient name (Is 63:15–16).

In the Fatherhood of God texts in Jeremiah, there is some extraordinary pathos. Let me first cite one that is a reproach. It is notable because the reproach is of a father to a harlot daughter: "And you maintained a prostitute's bold front, never thinking to blush. Even then you did not cry to me, 'My Father!' " (Jer 3:4–5). Some verses later, we catch the sadness of God who, on beholding the infidelity of his people, seems to fantasize how it might have been:

> And I was thinking:
> How am I to rank you as my children?
> I shall give you a country of delights,
> the fairest heritage of all the nations!
> I thought: you will call me Father
> and will never cease to follow me (Jer 3:19).

In this passage of great tenderness, Israel is lured into God's Fatherhood. A splendid thing happens in Jeremiah 31, the great new covenant passage. Yahweh lets his freely chosen Fatherhood of Israel impose obligations upon him, in what Joachim Jeremias has called the final word about divine fatherhood. The final word is a divine "must":

> Is Ephraim, then, so dear a son to me,
> a child so favored,
> that after each threat of mine
> I *MUST* still remember him,
> and let my tenderness yearn over him,
> Yahweh declares. (Jer 31:20).

"God's incomprehensible mercy and forgiveness *must* be exercised."[19]
And this is the deep story that is played out without interruption in the
Judeo-Christian scriptures: caring—insistent, relentless caring from our
God. Even anger is sooner or later assuaged by mercy, by Yahweh's
care.

We must also note that there are two parenthood-of-God texts in
Isaiah in which Yahweh's caring is described in images of motherhood:

> Zion was saying, Yahweh has abandoned me,
> the Lord has forgotten me.
>
> Can a woman forget her baby at the breast,
> feel no pity for the child she has borne?
> Even if these were to forget,
> I shall not forget you. (Is 49:15).
>
> Rejoice with Jerusalem . . .
> so that you may be suckled and satisfied
> from her consoling breast,
> that you might drink with deep delight
> from her generous nipple. . . .
> As a mother comforts a child,
> so shall I comfort you;
> You will be comforted in Jerusalem (Is 66:10–13).

I must also note an androgynous image of God, although it occurs
but once. "You forget the Rock who begot you, unmindful of the God
who gave you birth" (Dt 32:18). English translations sometimes do not
catch the androgyny. The JB English text says rather, "You forgot the
Rock who fathered you." The two verbs in the two clauses are a very
close parallel with Jeremiah 16:3 which speaks of fathers who beget and
mothers who give birth. God is metaphored by both the siring father and
the birthing mother.

I have cited these feminine and androgynous metaphors of God at
the end of my discussion of the Fatherhood of God because, even
though they are not thematic in any major way, they recognize the
importance of the femininity of God. There is something true about the
covenant, and correspondingly about a God who makes such a covenant, that requires the metaphor of woman: God's womb, her consoling
breast, her savorous breast, her glorious breasts. There is some "it is" of

God that needs to be experienced and interpreted by the "it is" of woman in order to be understood.

While there remain titillating but tiny recollections of goddess metaphors, the patriarchal stratum of the cultural deep story of the Hebrew people is sufficiently assertive to preclude any substantial development of the Motherhood of God. But given that patriarchal assertiveness in the bowels of the deep story, the presence of Mother-God talk is a crucial, if begrudging, affirmation that the Fatherhood of God is not a self-sufficient metaphor.

To generalize, then, from historical particulars: the Fatherhood of God is metaphorically disclosed in the history of God's covenant with the Hebrew people. The Fatherhood results from God's free decision *to adopt* a people as his children. There was a time before the adoption when God was God, but not God the Parent. The adoption is experienced as an historical event, as a result of which Yahweh *becomes* Father/Parent, and the Hebrew people *become* God's children. The father-patriarch of any Hebrew family gives his blessing and the inheritance to the first-born son. Israel is not any one of God's children, but the first-born son. We have here an inheritance image of covenant. The gift is irrevocable. But permanency and constancy, which also accrue under the royal grant covenant pattern, are not the whole story. For there is forgiveness, mercy, tenderness, compassion, offered in the context of parental caring. If there is scolding—and there is—it springs from the heart of parental love bent upon "bringing children up right" because the children are dearly loved.

Although God as Father is never really a dominant motif in the Hebrew people's structure of religious experience in the earlier scriptures, "father" does begin to emerge as a significant clue to the nature of the story that Yahweh is creating with his people. To call God a "Father" in the earlier scriptures is to name what he has become in his relationship to the people of the covenant. Evidence from the Mishnah suggests that by Jesus' time, praying to God as "Our Father and our King" is becoming ritually commonplace.

The Fatherhood of God, as briefly characterized here, would have belonged to the assumptive world of Jesus. The Father metaphor made its major entry into that assumptive world through the experience of covenant. Father is not God's name, as McFague insists. Rather, it is one of the many images for God that have tumbled out of people's experience, "not meant *to describe God* so much as *to suggest the new quality of relationship* being offered to them [by God]."[20] To say that this is the Father meaning that functioned in the religious world of Jesus is not to suggest that his relationship to that Father is but another instance of the meanings given him by his religious world. No concrete particular is simply an instance of the general. Each instance adds to the experiential data base on which the generalization is made, and sometimes requires movement toward a still larger generalization in order to accept the new experience. The central importance of God as Father in the narrative structure of Christian experience originates in its centrality in the being of Jesus and in the formation of his identity and mission. The history of Christian doctrine may be seen as a relentless response to the appeal of the Father(/Son) metaphor for imaginative leaps.

The reconstruction of Christian religious metaphor under the feminist critique and with a feminist hermeneutic is one of the major projects—perhaps the major project—of our day. The male metaphor both issued from and reinforced the patriarchal models of power that have put the earth in danger. The biblically recognized insufficiency of the father metaphor stands to be moved from a minor reminder to a major reshaper. Not the least of the values in such a reconstruction is remodeling the functions of power. The servant model easily and authentically lends itself to such a redemptive reconstruction. A much fuller discussion of this issue I reserve for the volume that follows.

If the "is like" part of a metaphor is essential to a metaphor's mediation of experience, the "is not like" part also tells the truth. As I indicated above, when the literal daily meaning of treaty/covenant shifted, so did the "is likes" and "is not likes" through which the covenant metaphor mediated the knowing of Yahweh. When the cultural sense of a metaphor's first, literal meaning shifts, not only does the "is like" shift, but so does the "is not like." As the feminist movement in this country reshapes relationships, perceptions, meanings, behaviors, and especially language, the cultural meaning of fatherhood is transformed. This transformation also reshapes what father cannot and can interpret about God. For contemporary cultural reasons, the very meanings once named by father are hidden for many people by exactly the same word (I confess that is often true for me).

Replacing Father with Mother creates an insufficiency in the other direction. Using both names is awkward, though it is a fuller metaphorical interpreter of meaning. The ideological weight of Mother, as either a replacement or an addition, disturbs the ideologies of the systems shaped by the patriarchal underpinnings of the metaphorical base of

Father. It places power structures under radical suspicion. "Parent" is a more neutral word which tells a lot of true "it is's"; but it lacks the emotional power of either Mother or Father and is unable so far to conjure up the affective richness of Mother and Father.

Our debt to the gift of religious experience is to ransack culture once again to find the best way to name, as Tillich has said so marvelously, the God beyond God. So long as we are ardently and experientially engaged in a search, it should not embarrass us to have been unable thus far to find compelling and appropriate replacement religious language for patriarchal fatherhood, for we have not found a cultural solution either. As a male, I often feel the extreme awkwardness of speaking and writing without a ready language to say what is to be said. I suspect this widespread cultural awkwardness is a holy one, and that resistance to the awkwardness of the search is a failure against the essential mystery of God—not to mention against sociological statespersonship, as Whitehead has observed:

> A continuous process of pruning, and of adaptation to a future ever requiring new forms of expression, is a necessary function in every society. The successful adaptation of old symbols to changes of social structure is the final mark of wisdom in sociological statesmanship. Also an occasional revolution in symbolism is required.[21]

Whenever I use Father/God and God/he language in this book, it is not an ideological choice. It is my empirical commitment to the materials that are described and generalized in the scriptures and the interpretive traditions with which I deal. Today's sociological wisdom will have to prune and adapt as Spirit moves it.

We continue, in the chapter that follows, our historical/empirical examination of Hebrew interpretations of religious experience. We will look at a notion, strange to our cultural ears, of corporate personality. We will then see the centrality of "heart" to ancient Hebrew self-understanding. Finally, we will attend to the moral qualities of Yahweh's reality: justice and mercy as seen from below, majesty as seen from above.

Notes

1. Carolyn Walker Bynum, *Jesus as Mother: Studies in the Spirituality of the High Middle Ages* (Berkeley: Univ. of California, 1984), p. 6.

2. Bynum, 1984, p. 7.

3. Stephen Crites, "The Narrative Quality of Experience," *Journal of the American Academy of Religion,* 39(1971), pp. 296–297.

4. Thorlief Boman, *Hebrew Thought Compared with Greek* (Philadelphia: Westminster, 1960), p. 17.

5. J.B. Pritchard, ed., *Ancient Near Eastern Texts Relating to the Old Testament* (Princeton: Princeton Univ., 1954).

6. Very important, for example, are: George Mendenhall, *Law and Covenant in Israel and the Ancient Near East* (Pittsburgh: The Biblical Colloquium, 1955); and D.J. McCarthy, *Treaty and Covenant* (Rome: Pontifical Biblical Institute, 1963).

7. G. Johannes Botterweck and Hilmer Ringgren, eds., *Theological Dictionary of the Old Testament,* Vol. III, (Grand Rapids: Wm. B. Eerdman's, 1990).

8. Delbert R. Hillers, *Covenant: The History of a Biblical Idea* (Baltimore: Johns Hopkins, 1969).

9. Hillers, 1969, p. 5.

10. Hillers, 1969, p. 121.

11. William James, *Varieties of Religious Experience* (N.Y.: Mentor, 1958), p. 162.

12. Hillers, 1969, p. 105.

13. Hillers, 1969, pp. 50–51.

14. Jaspers, 1953, esp. chapters 1, 5, and 6.

15. Jaspers, 1953, p. 2.

16. Jaspers, 1953, pp. 61–66.

17. Jaspers, 1953, p. 63, emphasis his.

18. Joachim Jeremias, *The Prayers of Jesus* (Philadelphia: Fortress, 1978), p. 13.

19. Jeremias, 1978, p. 15.

20. McFague, 1982, p. 166.

21. Alfred North Whitehead, *Symbolism* (N.Y.: Capricorn, 1959), p. 61.

3
The Narrative Structure
of Hebrew Experience
Part II: Corporate Personality, Heart, Justice

Introduction

Two people listening to each other and hearing accurately is a human feat worthy of honor. Listening across cultures and hearing accurately is among the harder things people are asked to do. In the first instance, the task is less complex though still a steep challenge, presuming that the two people inhabit the same cultural world of meaning. In the second instance, when basic presumptions about the human condition are not shared, the asceticism needed to listen is worthy of sainthood!

A keen sense of the irreducibility of pluralism is one of the characteristics of post-modern sensibilities. We are coming to recognize that unlike the fox and the swallow, we do not enter a world where the meaning of being a fox or a bird is quite closed and located biologically in the genes. Human being, unlike fox being, is unfinished. It is the "nature" of the human being to produce a human world and to finish her/his being. "One can only say," writes Peter Berger, that it is " 'the nature of man' to produce a world. What appears in any particular historical moment as 'human nature' is itself a product of man's world-building activity."[1] To understate the case considerably, the worlds made by ancient Hebrews and contemporary Americans do not coincide with great regularity.

Really hearing Jesus is quite a call. That is why our best efforts at retrieving Jewish social constructions of meaning from Jesus' world are so important. The two worlds cannot be so fully bridged that their boundaries are dissolved entirely. Maximum accuracy still retains a residue of minimum pluralism. Describing *The Human Condition,* Hannah Arendt observes that "plurality is the condition of human action because we are all the same, that is, human, in such a way that nobody is ever the same as anyone else who ever lived, lives, or will live."[2] It is not hopeless to want to understand. Real understanding happens, even though always in limited ways.

In all of this I am saying in different words things I have named before, but as introduction to the three discussions that follow. The ancient Hebrew social sense of self contrasts so deeply with our more individualized sense of self that we have to work very hard indeed to sympathize into the experience of corporate personality. It is not just a naive idea that conditions the axial burgeoning of individual consciousness. It is cultural history that must be presupposed when one hears Jesus or Paul. Today's world surely needs a deepened, if not mystical, sense of our corporate existence in a world that is either ours together, or perhaps not at all.

The heart motif is equally elusive. Pascal observed that *"le coeur a ses raîsons que la raîson ne connaît pas,"* but that has never been an operative western social construction of reality (not even in western romanticism). We might own with Pascal that every now and then the heart has some valid reasons that human reason cannot quite comprehend, but we have not constructed a selfhood with heart at the center. Heart is the second of our considerations in this chapter.

Finally, a people's moral direction is always charted on the larger map of that people's social imagination, i.e. their social construction of their relational webs. The meaning of justice, so central to the Hebrew moral intuition, is best presented after the discussion of corporate personality and heart, even though it has appeared in my reflections along the way.

Corporate Personality

For ancient Israel, causal interdependency between individual and group is so fierce that the very notion of individual as we know it in our culture is functionally non-existent. For us who have been raised in the western world, it is very difficult to take seriously the notion of corporate personality. We are apt to presume that it is nothing more than either a very primitive, though not very accurate, perception of "how things really are," or else just a figure of speech to help us take relationships seriously.

Boethius' often-cited philosophical description of a human being catches the western deep story quite well—that part of our deep story that makes access to parts of the Hebrew deep story arduous at best, and often simply inaccessible. A human being, he says, is an individual substance of a rational nature. "Substance" is a key Aristotelian category: something is what it is, but also has some "accidental" configurations. A human individual is the same human individual whether she or he is tall or short, dark or light, has many relationships or few. The human self is an autonomous self; it first exists and then enters into relationships. The relationships may change, but the individual, autonomous self remains fundamentally the same self. Accordingly, the philosophical category of "relation" is a philosophical "accidental." It is undoubtedly this deep conviction about the individual, autonomous self that has promoted such superb Greek reflection upon freedom. Aristotle defines a human being as "a political animal," but that still means an individual who always functions politically, not an individual whose very existence presupposes and is constituted out of a body politic.

Further, when Boethius defines a human being as an individual substance of a *rational* nature, he reflects the judgment that rationality is our most accurate generalization of what it means to be human. Reason is the seat of human personhood. This model for understanding what it means to be human stresses the primacy of individual experience and finds the glory of human existence in rational intelligence.

The Greek model, to which we are especially accustomed, contrasts therefore in two very fundamental ways with the Hebrew model. First, in the Hebrew cultural deep story, the corporate or social aspect of reality has a primacy over the individual aspect. That primacy is most obvious in the earlier Hebrew experience. But even as individuality emerges in the axial/prophetic period, the notion of individuality is set upon social and corporate moorings, and thus continues to contrast significantly with the Greek model. While Paul's interpretation of the body of Christ is not merely a repetition of corporate personality, I believe that Paul's ontic sense of the organic unity of Christ as a single body is unthinkable without his Hebrew background.

Secondly, the Hebrew experience contrasts with the Greek in the ascendency of the heart metaphor over any "head-bound," rational interpretations of human experience. It was my own encounter with process/relational modes of thought that helped me see and take seriously these two aspects of Hebrew experience. For Whitehead, every individual is an emergent from relationships. The individual makes decisions, of course, about how to give shape to its derivation, and how to add novelty to it. But that derivation is not just an original, once and for all derivation. As my colleague Michael Cowan has often observed, the relational web is the perpetual womb of our becoming. The umbilical connection between individual and community is never severed. But unlike the womb metaphor, individuals in their turn birth society. It is a reciprocal parent-child creation.

Corporate personality presumes some kind of similar interpretation. Whitehead uses the category of "feeling" to name the primordial contact that one entity has with another, i.e. the sheer physical feeling that another entity is "there." Only secondarily do we interpret what is there with conceptual feelings. In Whitehead's imaginative interpretation of experience, these physical feeling-prehensions underlie the pervasive causal relations between individuals. I don't want to overdraw the analogy between the ascendency of heart in the Hebrew sense of human experience and Whitehead's theory of feeling, or between corporate personality and Whitehead's theory of prehensions. But I would note that these two aspects of process thought are especially congenial to the Hebrew interpretation of human experience—enough so to encourage me not to think of heart, for example, as just a different location for rationality, but as a different construction of human meaning.

In his work on *The Interpretation of Cultures,* Clifford Geertz speaks about these cultural patterns as models in a double sense. They are "models of" in that they reflect the way a people experiences itself. But the same cultural understandings also provide "models for," that is, they provide a template for the construction of new experience.[3] The Hebrew "model of" and "model for" what it means to be human lays a heavy stress upon the primacy of social and relational considerations, and locates the psychic center in human affect. Because of the central role of affect in Hebrew anthropology, "the heart" is a recurring theme in the earlier scriptures (and in Paul as well in the later scriptures).

It is one of the strange but understandable ironies that while the Hebrew "model of" and "model for" human experience almost certainly provided the meaning construct for all that Jesus was and did and said, when his good news was disseminated throughout the western world, a starkly contrasting "model of" and "model for" structure of meaning and experience was the medium of understanding, formulation, and articulation. Christian scriptures themselves have their feet in both worlds. In no small measure, that model-rift accounts for the destructive friction that arose so early between Jews and Christians. There were some Jewish religious thinkers of the first century C.E. who toyed with the similar Greek philosophical models that Christian *Logos* theology used. They were experienced as tampering with monotheism, and were pronounced guilty of the "Two Powers" heresy.

I want to recount a fable from Volume 1 in this study. In eastern lore, the world rests upon the back of a big elephant, whose feet are upon a still larger world, which rests again on the back of a still larger elephant. There is finally a bottom elephant whose feet do not rest upon anything! That is, every system of thought finally gets back to presuppositions that are not provable—they just "are." Often in the early centuries, the real joust between very Jewish Christians and very Hellenized Christians may have been less between truth and falsehood, and more between little herds of "bottom elephants," i.e. between root metaphors and the narrative structures those metaphors generated. Without the benefit of culturally relativized historical criticism, Christians and Jews early in the common era could not have apprehended the relativity of their social constructions of reality. In his recent book on Jewish-Christian dialogue, Michael Goldberg reminds us that "virtually all our rock-ribbed beliefs about our lives are grounded in some bedrock story," and that "convictional claims all find their origin and intelligibility in each community's central narrative."[4] The metaphorical/narrative distance between Jerusalem and Athens is certainly not the only reason for the painful and destructive distance between Christian and Jews, but it should never be underplayed either.

It is commonplace to talk about the relationship between early Christianity and Judaism in terms of the relationship between Athens and Jerusalem—between the cultural forces of Hellenization and those of Hebraization. But, as I shall lay out later in the book, the true "places" of polarization are in fact the Greek option of Alexandria (for Christians) and the Hebrew/Aramaic option of Usha in Galilee. That's where the respective shapes of post-second temple Christianity and Judaism are socially constructed.

Our awareness of the cultural and historical conditioning of all our models still taxes us fiercely when we run into a model that calls into question what we have always presumed simply to be the case. Geertz observes, for example, that our western understanding of an individual "as a bounded, unique, more or less integrated motivational and cognitive universe, a dynamic center of awareness, emotion, judgment and action organized into a distinctive whole and set contrastively both against other such wholes and against its social and natural background, is, however incorrigible it may seem to us, a rather peculiar idea within the context of the world's cultures."[5] Yet it is an idea that we take for granted.

In the discussion of both the social and affective character of Hebrew anthropology, I am especially grateful to the seminal studies of H. Wheeler Robinson.[6] It may be the strangeness of such an anthropology, or perhaps even a supposed primitiveness that we have now gotten beyond, that has prevented these understandings from helping us Christians reappraise some basic Christological positions. To try to understand Paul's "mystical body" or "faith of the heart" without the Hebrew "model of" and "for" is probably to miss him almost entirely. Let us examine in turn the notion of corporate personality, and then the centrality of heart to Hebrew anthropology.

The notion of corporate personality is clearest in Hebrew history before the axial period of human civilization. And for the period of the earlier scriptures, that means basically pre-exilic history. Yahweh makes a covenant with a body of persons, not with individuals. Even the king is a figure through whom Yahweh's promises and guarantees are directed to his people. The king is called Yahweh's son, but Yahweh's son is also what the nation is called in Hosea 11:1. *The relation of individuals to Yahweh is mediated through the corporate personality of the nation. The relation of Yahweh to individuals is mediated through the corporate personality of the nation.* The functional consequences of the idea of corporate personality will become clearer through some examples.

The corporateness of the family unit can be seen in both burial practices and the Levirite marriage law. To die is to be reunited to the family clan. Yahweh promises Abraham: "For your part, you will join your ancestors in peace; you will be buried at a happy old age" (Gn 15:15). Then, when Abraham had breathed his last, dying at a happy ripe age, old and full of years, "he was gathered to his people" (Gn 25:8). It is a corporate existence after death as well.

Jacob's death is similarly a remarkable passage:

> Then Jacob gave them these instructions, "I am about to be gathered to my people. Bury me with my ancestors, in the cave that is in the field of Ephron the Hittite, in the cave in the field at Machpelah, facing Mamre, in Canaan, which Abraham bought from Ephron the Hittite as a burial site of his own. There Abraham and his wife Sarah were buried. There Isaac and his wife Rebekah were buried; and there I buried Leah—the field and the cave in it which were bought from the Hittites." When Jacob had finished giving his instructions to his sons, he drew his feet up into the bed, and breathing his last was gathered to his people (Gn 49:29–33).

Ezekiel the prophet, as we shall see, makes a very strong plea for individual responsibility for one's actions. Parents' sins are not visited upon their children. There is individual, not corporate guilt for an individual wrongdoing. Yet even so, different nations in Sheol are depicted there as being in corporate groups gathered around their corporate graves (Ez 32:17–32).

If corporate identity extended backward to include the dead, it also went forward to offspring. To die without a male heir to carry on the family name/reality is a great curse:

> If brothers live together and one of them dies childless, the dead man's wife must not marry a stranger outside the family. Her husband's brother must come to her and, exercising his levirite [his duty as brother], make her his wife, and the first son she bears must assume the dead brother's name; by this means his name will not be obliterated from Israel (Dt 25:5–6).

Robinson cites the following passage from Robertson Smith, and suggests that the living group can be extended both before and after:

> A kin was a group of persons whose lives were so bound up together, in what must be called a physical unity, that they could be treated as parts of one common life. The members of one kindred looked upon themselves as one living whole, a single animated mass of blood, flesh and bones, of which no member could be touched without all the members suffering.[7]

The tragic story of Achan in Joshua 6 and 7 is a classic illustration of the corporate personality understanding at work. When Joshua storms Jericho, he gives two orders. First, no one is to take plunder in the city. Second, Rahab, the whore who hid the men Joshua sent to reconnoiter Jericho, is to be spared for what she did. But because a family and a household is a corporate unit, not only Rahab, but all who belong to her, and her father's household as well, are spared and given a home with Israel. Achan, one of Joshua's men, took some forbidden plunder. Because of the action of this one individual, scripture judges that "the Israelites were unfaithful," and "the anger of Yahweh was aroused against the Israelites" (Jos 7:1). Because of this, Joshua's army fails miserably in its battle to take the town of Ai. In prayer, Joshua asks Yahweh why this happened. Yahweh says it is because *Israel* has sinned, because Israel has violated the covenant (Jos 7:11). But remember, it was the single individual Achan who took proscribed booty!—but Israel sins in Achan: "They have violated the covenant which I imposed on them. *They* have gone so far as to take what was under the curse . . . they have stolen it . . . they have hidden it . . . Israel you will not be able to stand up to your foes" (Jos 7:10–13, passim).

When Achan is identified, this "corporate" Achan is led to the valley of Achor—that is, Achan, his sons and daughters, his oxen and sheep, his tent and everything that belonged to him. *All Israel* went along to the valley of Achor, and *all Israel* stoned him (Jos 7:24).

We who live out of a quite different deep story must be careful not to replace this corporate understanding of person with our own notion of a mere collective. We must be reluctant as well to understand this kind of talk as some form of literary personification. Corporate being is a realism in Hebrew anthropology. Although the Hebrews would never have explained it so abstractly, in our categories we would have to affirm corporate personality as being something ontological if we are to catch the earnestness of the Hebrew perception of the social nature of reality.

Further, in my opinion, we must remain open to the possibility that this is an accurate ontological perception that can offer a corrective to western individualism, with the U.S. American version as perhaps the most needful of correction.

In Ezekiel and Jeremiah we hear a really new sense of individuality sounding through. As I listen to the following passage in Ezekiel, I imagine Achan's family saying, "Why didn't somebody come up with this sooner!" Ezekiel says:

> The word of Yahweh was addressed to me as follows, "Why do you keep repeating this proverb in the land of Israel: The parents have eaten unripe grapes; and the children's teeth are set on edge? As I live—declares the Lord Yahweh—you will have no further cause to repeat this proverb in Israel. Look, all life belongs to me; the father's life and the son's life, both alike belong to me. The one who has sinned is the one to die" (Ez 18:1–4).

This new development does not replace the model of corporate personality, but modifies it. Ezekiel continues to affirm as well the corporate character of the covenant, even in its renewed form after the exile: "I shall give them a single heart and I shall put a new spirit in them" (Ez 11:18).

Robinson treats the emergence of the Hebrew sense of individuality as a product, in great part, of the experience of individuality that emerged in the prophets themselves, especially Jeremiah. As the pained and tearful prophet sees himself over and against the people to whom he proclaims Yahweh's new covenant, his own awareness of self is strengthened. The prophetic tradition gradually nourishes the larger cultural tradition, and this results in a transmutation of the deep story. The notion of corporate personality is modified but not surrendered. Individuals have their own moral centers and assume individual responsibility, yet one people has a single heart, and even in death there are tribal gatherings in Sheol.

This transformation must be placed in the larger context of what seems to be happening in many places in human civilization, that is, in the context of what Jaspers is calling the axial period. It almost seems as if a new human experience of individual personhood accumulates to the point of critical mass, and is then available broadly, whether in India, Persia, Greece or Israel. In Israel the prophets catch the fever of "the individual" and transmit it to their people.

Sometimes shifts in the cultural deep story generate shifts in the religious deep story. It is plausible that the prophets feel the axial shift in their own persons, ingest it into their own religious deep stories, and introduce this transmutation into the deep story of the nation. Shifts in the religious deep story of significant individuals generate shifts in the cultural deep story. The prophets catch the new experience of individuality and introduce it into the character of the covenant. Slowly, the cultural deep story of Israel assimilates the axial shift, but retains in its social construction of individuality a profoundly social nature. We do not encounter the autonomous individual.

It is difficult to find referents in contemporary experience to help us relate to the notion of corporate personality. The nearest analogy I can find is with ecology. The root word is the Greek *oikos* which means home or dwelling. Literally, ecology is the science of our common home. We talk about an eco-system, by which we mean that we are so organically linked together that whatever happens to any part reverberates throughout the entire system to every single other part. And any slightest change in the system itself has effects upon every tiniest part. What you do to even the smallest, you do to me and to everyone else as well. There is no such thing as a purely private destiny, no purely private sin or purely private virtue, no purely private love or purely private hate; there is no purely private relationship with God, no purely personal spirituality. And my individual subjectivity is not any less real for it. Only it is not an autonomous self with accidental relationships. It is an individual reality whose actuality is an emergent from the relational web. We do not awake some morning and then decide to walk into the *oikos*. The *oikos,* our common home, is what we come out of. We have a communal home address before we ever wake up with consciousness.

Let us look now at a second feature of the Hebrew "model of" and "model for" the structure of human experience. Heart is at the very center of it.

Heart

Sometimes an omission can be as telling as an inclusion, and that is surely the case in the physiological psychic model that functioned in Hebrew anthropology. Some eighty parts of the body are mentioned in the literature of the earlier scriptures, and the brain is not one of them! Robinson concludes, rightly I think, that this omission means that for the Hebrews the center of consciousness does not lie in the head, that is, in the rational mind. Since psychic functions are so closely related to physiology in Hebrew anthropology, that omission is remarkable.

In this discussion of heart I will be calling attention to the Hebrew sense of affect as both a corporate and a personal center. I shall stress this perception because it differs so significantly from the model that westerners nearly always live out of. The only way to feel the difference is to encounter this deep story in instance after instance of its embodiment, and listen to its details on its own ground.

We are accustomed in the ordinary language of daily conversation to the distinction between head and heart in how we live. But we know far more about living out of the head than the heart (ask any therapist). We would do violence, however, to both head and heart if they are set up in opposition. So-called "faculty psychology" has treated mind, heart, and will as separate or discrete faculties. It is more accurate to understand that each of these is a particular way in which the entire person with all the energies of its being can attend. When I am asking whether something is true or false, I am attending especially in a head way. When I am asking whether something is to be done or not done, I am attending with will or decision. When I am asking whether something is lovable or detestable, I am attending in a heart way. It is obvious how much those concerns overlap, and therefore how partial the insight is. But that may help draw a few first strokes of a portrait of a heart-centered anthropology.

To begin with, the word we meet in Hebrew is *leb;* it is *kardia* in the Greek Septuagint. Of the four vital organs named and associated in some way with psychic functions, heart, kidney, liver and bowels, *leb/kardia* is by far the most significant. Bowels, *me'im,* for example, occurs nine times with reference to psychic functions: sexual love (Sg 5:4); religious affection (Ps 40:8); compassion and pity (Is 15:11); etc. *Leb/kardia* occurs 851 times. Although there is some arbitrariness to his generalizations, Robinson indicates five ways in which this word functions: (1) it is used simply to name the physical organ, or metaphorically to mean "in the midst of" 29 times; (2) it is used 257 times to refer to personality, inner life, or character in general; (3) 166 of the references are to emotional states ranging from intoxication and distress to joy and courage; (4) there are 204 uses that refer to what, in our anthropology, we would probably call "intellectual" activities such as attention and reflection; and (5) 195 times this word has the sense of volition or purpose.[8] What is clear is that heart is the principal word for the innermost parts of the human psyche—heart is where you get closest to WHO someone really is.

What I find widespread but unsupportable is the frequently made judgment that in Hebrew anthropology the heart is the seat of rational activity. For example, in the Kittel-edited *Theological Dictionary of the New Testament,* when the article on *kardia* traces its Old Testament usage, we find the judgment that the heart is the seat of rational functions.[9] In his *Anthropology of the Old Testament,* Hans Walter Wolff writes that "we must guard against the false impression that biblical man is more determined by feeling than reason. This mistaken anthropological direction is all too easily derived from an undifferentiated rendering of *leb.*"[10] It is the case that in the sapiential literature, under the strong influence of Hellenistic rational centered anthropology, heart does begin to take on more rational hues. But that is not the case in the texts that pre-date sapiential literature.

Reflective activity alone does not necessarily mean rationally dominated activity. There is a lot of difference between pondering in my heart some experienced tenderness, and meditatively questioning with Socrates and his friends at the Symposium what is the nature of love. Both are reflective, of course.

In Hebrew anthropology, heart is where what I ultimately stand for resides, and is consequently where WHO I am is defined. I may say things that are discordant with my heart and do things that are unfaithful to my heart, but if my heart is in the right place I am capable of remorse.

Heart is not emotion in the more ordinary sense of the word, though that is included. Heart refers to the valuational structure whence flow the loves and the hates that define me. It is not the fluctuating emotions of the hour that yield my character, but the abiding sense of where preciousness lies for me. As we sometimes say, "Home is where the heart is." We will examine some pieces of the heart story to observe how Hebrew people interpret and construct experience.

Yahweh sends Samuel to Bethlehem, telling him that one of Jesse's sons is to be the next king. When Samuel arrives at Jesse's home and catches sight of the son Eliab, he concludes that this is the next king because he is tall and imposing. But Yahweh tells him: "Take no notice of his appearance or his height, for I have rejected him; God does not see as human beings see; they look at appearances, but Yahweh looks at the heart" (1 Sam 16:7). Because who we are is so intimately bound up with what our hearts are like, Yahweh who knows us perfectly knows our hearts.

When the ark is brought to the temple which Solomon has built, Yahweh's presence will be there. Solomon prays that the temple will be a center of piety and that Yahweh's care will come out from there. "[When anyone beseeches you], listen from heaven where you reside; forgive, and since you know what is in the heart, deal with each as their conduct deserves, for you alone know what is in every human heart" (1 Kgs 8:38–39). Yahweh then assures Solomon that he will be present to his people through the temple, that he will see and hear, that he will forgive. He will be attentive to prayer that is offered there. Describing his presence there, Yahweh says to Solomon: "Now and for the future I have chosen and consecrated this house for my name to be there for-ever; my eyes and my heart will be there forever" (2 Chr 7:16). Yahweh will not be superficially there in the temple as at an outpost. His heart will be there looking at other hearts. In the temple the WHO of God meets the Who of us.

When God's presence to us is a deeply transforming presence, the transformation occurs in the heart. When Samuel anoints Saul, he says that God will change him into a different kind of person. And indeed, as soon as Saul turns to walk away from Samuel, "God changed his heart" (1 Sam 10:9). Saul then "went home to Gibeah and with him went the mighty men whose hearts God had touched" (1 Sam 10:26).

Saul is the first of the kings, but thereafter they are often judged according to their qualities of heart. King "Jehu did not faithfully and wholeheartedly follow the law of Yahweh" (2 Kgs 10:31). During his illness, Hezekiah prays: "Ah, Yahweh, remember, I beg you, how I have behaved faithfully and with sincerity of heart in your presence and done what you regard as right" (2 Kgs 20:3). There is high praise for Josiah: "No king before him turned to Yahweh as he did, with all his heart, all his soul, all his strength, in perfect loyalty to the law of Moses; nor did any king like him arise again" (2 Kgs 23:25). The blind prophet Ahijah scolds Jeroboam through his wife: "Yahweh, God of Israel, says this: I raised you from the people and made you leader of my people Israel. I tore the kingdom from the House of David, and gave it to you. But you have not been like my servant David who kept my commandments and followed me with all his heart, doing only what I regard as right" (1 Kgs 14:7–8). And we hear about Jehoshaphat that "his heart advanced in the ways of Yahweh" (2 Chr 17:6). On the other hand, King Rehoboam "did wrong in not setting his heart on seeking Yahweh" (2 Chr 12:14).

David is sometimes held up as a model. History gets romanticized: many of David's machinations are hardly exemplary. But even at his worst, his heart seems to have been fixed upon Yahweh with enough ardor that he can be called back to fidelity. The perception is that in the final analysis David was a splendid king, and was so because of his heart. One can do right things, but they are not pleasing if they are not backed up by a right heart. Thus King Amaziah is praised but with reserve: "He did what Yahweh regards as right, though not wholeheartedly" (2 Chr 25:2). Amaziah's external behaviors were proper, but he lacked heart.

The *Baltimore Catechism's* description of mortal sin was consistent with the western deep story: something must be seriously wrong in itself, you must know that it is wrong, and then choose the deed regardless. Affect is not mentioned because it is not understood to enter into the essence of a truly human act. True, our affective state may alter our actual responsibility for our actions, sometimes increasing it and sometimes decreasing it. Purposes and goals are formulated in our rational consciousness. The long list of anathemas that Christian history has accumulated are attached to wrong ways of thinking. To some extent, it is a function of the western deep story that Arius, Martin Luther, George Tyrrell, and Leonard Feeney were excommunicated, and Hitler was not.

In the Jewish deep story, the ultimate infidelity is to be wrong-hearted, not wrong-headed. I do not want to caricature the difference to the point of absurdity, but the contrast between the Hebrew and the western understanding of the nature of being human, i.e. of human being, is a very strong one. When we hear ancient Jews talk about purpose in respect to heart, they are not simply attributing what we mean by purpose to the heart instead of the mind. They are naming valuational intuition as the source of purposiveness. (The "emotive ethics" of Max Scheler is perhaps the nearest any western thinker has come to sensing heart as the seat of personal existence—and there are still significant differences.)

Whether a Hebrew named it or not, there were undoubtedly times when he or she did what we call "making up our minds." Whether a western person knows it or not, unquestionably there are times when western people follow the lead of the heart. I know, however, that I would far rather hear from someone in a significant relationship with me, "I am following my heart in my decision to be your friend," than "I have fully made up my mind to be your friend." Not only are those two individual experiences differently textured, but imagine the difference between lives that habitually center themselves in the one way rather than the other. What's at stake in a major way is a style of being human, an identity engendering style. Listen to David's prayer. Although he knows his son Solomon will build the temple and not he, he has asked the people to contribute their resources for the temple, and they have responded magnanimously.

> . . . they had presented their free will offerings *wholeheartedly* to Yahweh. King David too was filled with joy. Hence, in the presence of the whole assembly, David blessed Yahweh. David said: "May you be blessed, Yahweh, God of Israel our ancestor, for ever and for ever! Yours, Yahweh, is the greatness, the power, splendor, length of days, glory. . . . Yahweh our God, all this wealth, which we have provided to build a house for your holy name, has come from you and all belongs to you. Knowing, my God, how you search *the heart,* I know, and how you delight in *honesty of heart* I have willingly given all this; and now with joy I have seen your people here offer you their gifts willingly. Yahweh, God of Abraham, Isaac, and Israel our ancestors, watch over this for ever, *shape the purpose of your people's heart,* and *direct their hearts* to you, and give an *undivided heart* to Solomon my son to keep your commandments, your decrees, and your statutes, to put them all into effect, and to build the palace for which I have made provision" (1 Chr 29:9–19).

When the temple is built and the ark is put in place, Solomon addresses the people, and recalls: "My father David had set his heart on building a temple for the name of Yahweh . . ." (1 Kgs 8:17). The heart is the place where purpose/intention is framed. It is also where discernment occurs, and where understanding happens. Over and over, heart refers to the precious center of humanhood. Thus far we have examined texts that come principally from the six historical books of Samuel, Kings and Chronicles. Most of the heart meanings throughout the earlier scriptures are typified in these materials. And now we must turn briefly to the prophets.

The use of heart occurs but once in Amos. In Hosea, heart is used eleven times. One is a fairly literal/physical usage. In another, Yahweh says that he could not treat Israel like Admah or Zeboiim: "My heart within me is overwhelmed, fever grips my inmost being. I will not give reign to my fierce anger, I will not destroy Ephraim again" (Hos 11:8–9). All of the other nine references are to the heart of Israel, that is, to Israel's essential being.

With the classical prophets, heart emerges with great importance (and here we are more into the axial period of human consciousness). Heart occurs thirty-six times in Isaiah, forty in Ezekiel, and fifty-two in Jeremiah. None of the uses of heart in the prophets is brand-new, except for the clear relocation of the covenant "text," as it were, in the heart rather than on tablets of stone. This is not a matter of new heart meanings, but of a new way of putting the older meanings to work in a new understanding of covenant. This transformation of covenant is contemporaneous with the evolving sense of individuality in the Hebrew souls. Heart/covenant is a way of expressing a profound new experience of interiority. But as the seat of personality in Hebrew anthropology, this covenant use of heart loses none of its affective weight. The emphasis in Paul's writings upon the heart as the locus of faith is in a direct line of inheritance with the reconstitution of covenant in the prophetic period.

Another difference in the later prophets—again, not a new use but a new emphasis—is that in Isaiah, Jeremiah and Ezekiel heart language refers far more often to individuals, and not just to the corporate heart of a people. As we shall see in the discussion of Spirit in the next chapter, this is also the time when *Ruach*/Spirit emerges into prominence, and the affinity of Spirit for heart also becomes marked. In the discussion of covenant, I cited Jeremiah's description of the new heart-centered covenant. Let us look now at the place of heart in Ezekiel's announcement of a new covenant:

> I am going to display the holiness of my great name, which has been profaned among the nations, which you have profaned among them.

And the nations will know that I am Yahweh—declares the Lord
Yahweh—when in you I display my holiness before their eyes. For I
shall take you from among the nations and gather you back from all
the countries, and bring you home to your own country. I shall pour
clean water over you and you will be cleansed; I shall cleanse you of
all your filth and of all your foul idols. I shall give you a new heart,
and put a new spirit in you; I shall remove the heart of stone from
your bodies and give you a heart of flesh instead. I shall put my Spirit
in you, and make you keep my laws and respect and practice my
judgments. You will live in the country which I gave your ancestors.
You will be my people and I shall be your God (Ez 36:23–28).

Most of the studies of the use of heart in Hebrew anthropology do
some cataloging of uses. Many uses of heart language are like our own;
they refer to emotional states: joy and suffering, hope and despair,
courage and cowardice, etc. Not unlike our usage, heart is also used to
describe fundamental attitudes: no one wants to get too close to a "hard-
hearted" person, whereas a "softie" is an easy touch. Frequently, as I
pointed out earlier, interpreters seem to presume that a Hebrew experience of being human is roughly interchangeable with our experience of
being human, and that "heart" is just a different way of talking about
what we mean by other words, such as mind or reason.

Translations of the Hebrew or Greek scriptures into English often
betray what I consider to be a very inadequate understanding of the
difference between two social constructions of human being. I tend to
choose the Jerusalem Bible (JB) English text because it is a very satisfying and flowing prose, but often adjustments must be made. The JB's
woe to false prophets is to those "who follow their own spirit" [*leb/
kardia*], whereas the New English Bible (NEB) speaks more accurately
of those "who prophesy out of their own hearts" (Ez 13:13). Even more
remarkably, four verses later, JB refers to false prophets "who make up
prophecies out of their own heads (sic!)," while NEB correctly says out
of their own "hearts."

Heart and mind and spirit are simply not interchangeable words for
the same function; they name different humanities. The two humanities
obviously share as well some defining structures, but their substantial
variations are critical to an understanding of a biblical faith of the heart.
Western Christianity has been preoccupied with faith of the mind. Neither emphasis is exclusive, but their respective priorities structure human life according to seriously contrasting systems of virtue.

Reprise on Heart

There are two generalizations I want to underline. The first is that the role of heart in Hebrew anthropology suggests that the Hebrew experience of being-human is structurally different from the western experience of being-human. Heart points to feeling, not only as our fluctuating emotions, but as affect in the sense of a felt structure of valuational responsiveness that constitutes the most immediate grasp of anything and everything, anyone and everyone, God included. Heart is the "hot spot" in the structure of Hebrew experience, and it is around this hot spot that all the other "spots," from warm to cool, constellate.

The second generalization is by way of noting that without losing its sense of human being as affect-centered, there is a development in the Hebrew sense of person. The development is principally in terms of an emerging experience of being not just clanspersons with clan-tied destinies, but clan-individuals with individual destinies. Personal transformation does not replace corporate transformation, but there is a new kind of mutual immanence between the individual and the relational web.

Working out of empirical historicist commitments, I have tried to make my generalized interpretations of Hebrew experience of "heart" respect a multitude of typical individual interpretations of experience. In the tumble of story there is not the same logical consistency that one is accustomed to look for in a systematic treatise. However, I feel that by and large, the meanings I have treated do constellate in the ways I have suggested. That does not mean that some individual uses of a word here or there do not depart from my generalization. But I do posit enough consistency to deduce a narrative structure, a mega-story, along the lines I am recommending.

Justice—Metaphor for the Character of Yahweh

Whatever people finally say God is like must be based upon what they know of God from God's "worldly" presence to them, and from their interpretation of those events that "presence" God. God's truth is never exhausted by our interpreted experience, but whatever we do understand originates there. Revelation always includes the human interpreting of the divine initiatives, whether the small daily ones or the large canonical ones.

It is not simple. There are collisions in human history when the

metaphors for God collide, as they do when justice and mercy metaphors come face to face with majesty metaphors; that is when those from
the underside of history pray for help from the same God whom the
secure ask to maintain the settled order that nurtures them. In such
collisions, the partiality of all our metaphors is disclosed alongside our
tendency to worship them instead of the One whose presence they mediate. Consider the contrast between the following passage from Isaiah
which imagines God's reign in terms of a voluptuous banquet, and the
passage from Exodus in which each has enough, but barely enough, and
only enough:

> On this mountain for all peoples,
> Yahweh Sabaoth is preparing a banquet of rich food,
> a banquet of fine wines,
> of succulent food, of fine wines (Is 25:6).

> [In the desert] they collected [the manna], some more and some less.
> When they measured it what they had collected by the *omer,* no one
> who had collected more had too much, no one who collected less had
> too little. Each had collected as much as he needed (Ex 16:17–18).

We see in these passages two aspects of God. The first is God's intention
for people to enjoy the earth and its abundance. In tasting how sweet the
succulent food and fine strained wines are one can also taste and experience how sweet is God. True but tricky! Probably no other religious
tradition knows as poignantly as the Jewish tradition that idolatry is the
easiest and foulest infidelity—easiest because the sweet earth can easily
be enjoyed instead of the sweet God, and foulest because the most
essential ingredient in historical construction, God's holiness, is then
preempted, and history inevitably befouled. Nonetheless, it is clear that
Yahweh would rather Yahweh's children have plenty than too little, and
that plenitude is a discloser of divine lavishness, even if we are too
quickly beguiled and seduced by it.

The Exodus passage makes two things clear, the first in the passage
itself, the second in the larger context of the passage. First, plenitude for
anyone is out of range until sufficiency for everyone is assured. Surplus,
contrary to U.S. policy, is not more than enough for one person, or more
than enough in terms of an economic system, but rather what might be
left over after all human need is satisfied.

The second message of the Exodus event is that even if food is poorer in the desert than it was in Egypt, freedom in the desert is more precious than slavery in Egypt. In contemporary language, participation in the processes that determine life is also an essential justice ingredient, and the lack of it constitutes slavery.

In a word, the messianic world of Isaiah presumes the just world of Exodus. But that is almost too mathematical and legal. What is at stake here is the way in which the holiness of God is experienced in the non-negotiability of God's justice. Justice is not merely legal. It is the most fundamental expression of God's goodness. Justice is our best insight into the character of God. It's who God is. When justice is brought into play in making history, God is brought into play. When justice is excluded, God is excluded. Abraham Heschel sees that the presence of justice and the presence of Yahweh are so linked that when justice is absent, God is left alone in the world and discarded.[11] Sometimes the prophet is angry at the lonely exile we have imposed on God.

Justice, then, is not one of the issues that appear on the horizon. Justice is the horizon. Salvation history appears on it.

Royal and Prophetic Consciousness

When we attempt to interpret the experience and the words of others, it helps greatly to know from what social and economic class they come, and to know as well how our own class conditions us. Biblical scholars have for some time reckoned with this ideology critique in observing two biblical mindsets, rooted in socio-economic differences. People in power judge differently than people out of power. Those in power speak (to use the biblical language) from a royal consciousness. Those from history's underside speak from a prophetic consciousness.

In *Israel's Praise,* Walter Brueggemann holds that we can often tell from what socio-economic class a particular liturgical song (psalm) comes.[12] Psalms generally praise Yahweh. As soon as they call for praise they give reasons why we should praise. There are royal reasons and prophetic reasons. First the royal reasons.

Some psalms praise Yahweh as Creator of everything, earth and sky, stars, sun and moon, as the one in whom the order of the universe originates. These, Brueggemann recommends, are the praises of those in power (the palace people). They affirm order, and they mean present order. The singers of these songs do not have a long walk between the temple and the palace:

> Sing a new song to Yahweh!
> Sing to Yahweh, all the earth,
> Sing to Yahweh, bless his name . . .
> Declare his glory among the peoples . . .
> It was Yahweh who made the heavens;
> in his presence are splendor and majesty,
> in his sanctuary power and beauty. . . .
> Adore Yahweh in the splendor of his holiness.
> Tremble before him, all the earth. . . .
> Say among the nations, "Yahweh is king." . . .
> Let the heavens rejoice and the earth be glad. . . .
> He will judge the earth with saving justice
> and the nations with constancy (Ps 96 passim).

The psalm ends with praise for Yahweh's justice, but nothing suggests that justice does not already obtain.

The out-of-power people praise Yahweh for different reasons. They cry for help, and when they praise Yahweh, it is for the help he has given in the past and will give yet again. Psalm 59 is a prayer of the beleaguered:

> Rescue me from my enemies, my God,
> be my stronghold from my assailants,
> rescue me from evil doers. . . .
> Wake up, stand by me and keep watch,
> Yahweh, God of Sabaoth, God of Israel. . . .
> Do not annihilate them, or my people may forget . . .
> shake them in your power, bring them low,
> Lord, our shield. . . .
> And so I will sing of your strength,
> in the morning acclaim your faithful love. . . .
> My strength, I will make music for you,
> for my stronghold is my God,
> the God who loves me faithfully (Ps 59 passim).

It is clearly from oppression that this psalmist's voice is raised.

Liturgy (and Theology) and the Social Construction of Reality

Brueggemann makes the point that social interest is audible in these psalm-songs, and is audible therefore in the liturgies in which they were sung. Liturgy is not innocent of politics, because it engages in world-making. "Praise," he says, "is a bold political act."[13] People pray for the world they want, and they praise the aspects of God they feel will help them make that world, the presumption being that the world they want corresponds to God's intentions. Liturgy creates the moods and motivations that facilitate world-making. I want to cite Brueggemann a bit more at length, with the analogy in mind that theology and doctrine are also world-making activities and therefore political acts:

> Our premise is that praise is in fact world-making. What kind of praise is practiced goes far to determine what kind of world Israel will make and live in. We have seen that Israel's primal act of praise and therefore Israel's proper world are marked by a revolutionary impetus toward justice, equity, and righteousness. Israel engages in praise of the God who acts for justice, equity and righteousness, and Israel commits itself to the ordering and maintenance of just such a world. The narrative in the liturgy is for the sake of the social world to which Yahweh and Israel are committed.[14]

Mutatis mutandis, theology as well names God and names our historical bent vis-à-vis such a God. The deeper a tradition's theological penchant (the ancient Hebrews had none), the more effective a world-maker it is. Thus, a Jesus who is the Christ of a God of the exodus makes a different world than Jesus who is Christ of a God of majesty (this is Christ the King).

Now the point is not that majesty is wrong and justice is right. Each consciousness, royal and prophetic, knows something true. I agree with Brueggemann's judgment that this deep polarity is there in the person of God, and we must not reduce it in either direction.[15] The ancient ideal would have been a Davidic kingdom in which God's justice abounds. But this is not an ideal world, so the tensive character of God's own polarity translates into a continuous dialectic between the songs of majesty and the chants of mercy. The two musics may both be necessary, but they are not without priority.

The Prophetic Tilt

The prophet's primal scream against "the secret obscenity of sheer unfairness"[16] is continuous with the rage of the ancient Hebrews against their Egyptian enslavement and the Maccabean revolt against the implantation of Greek culture in the Jewish soul. It is a protest against all domination, and above all to the dominated destitute. "Prophecy is the voice that God has lent . . . to the plundered poor, to the profaned riches of the world. . . . The prophets take us to the slums."[17]

I want to name a conclusion now, the details of which will be laid out in the following two chapters on the spirit and word of God. It is this: if you track with all the times in the earlier scriptures that *Ruach/* Spirit and *Dabhar/*Word are used to interpret the historical experience of God, you will find that their relationship to prophets and prophecy is preponderant.

Because the roots of injustice are so often imbedded in the royal system, Bernhard Anderson observes that "prophecy was intimately associated with politics from the very first moment of its appearance in Israel."[18] The task of prophecy is precisely to empower human beings to become subjects of history—historical change agents—to cooperate with Yahweh in remaking the world according to Yahweh's intentions. If there is a single word that is a best clue to Yahweh's intentions, it is surely *sadeq/*justice. *Sadeq* is the character of God's holiness as well as of any social world that has made itself holy like God. The creation of new social reality is a Christological meaning of Jesus profoundly and radically resourced in the narrative structure of Hebrew experience in which the conscience of Jesus was incubated.

Notes

1. Peter L. Berger, *The Sacred Canopy* (Garden City: Doubleday, 1967), p. 7.

2. Hannah Arendt, *The Human Condition* (Chicago: Univ. of Chicago, 1971), p. 8.

3. Clifford Geertz, *The Interpretation of Culture* (NY: Harper, 1973), p. 93.

4. Michael Goldberg, *Jews and Christians: Getting Our Stories Straight* (Nashville: Abingdon, 1985), pp. 13, 14–15.

5. Clifford Geertz, "On the Native's Point of View," in Keith Basso and Henry Selby, eds., *Meaning and Anthropology* (Albuquerque: Univ. of New Mexico, 1976).

6. H. Wheeler Robinson, *The Christian Doctrine of Man* (Edinburgh: T. & T. Clarke, 1958); *Corporate Personality in Ancient Israel* (Philadelphia: Fortress, 1964); *The Religious Ideas of the Old Testament* (London: Duckworth, 1964).

7. Robinson, 1964, p. 4.

8. Robinson, 1958, p. 22.

9. Gerhard Kittel, ed., G.W. Bromley, tr., *Theological Dictionary of the New Testament,* Vol. III (Grand Rapids: Eerdsman, 1965), p. 606.

10. Hans Walter Wolff, *Anthropology of the Old Testament* (Philadelphia: Westminster, 1981), p. 42.

11. Abraham Joshua Heschel, *The Prophets,* Vol. I (New York: Harper, 1962), p. 15.

12. Walter Brueggemann, *Israel's Praise* (Philadelphia: Fortress, 1988).

13. Brueggemann, 1988, p. 2.

14. Brueggemann, 1988, p. 74.

15. Brueggemann, 1988, p. 63.

16. Heschel, 1962, I, p. 9.

17. Heschel, 1962, I, pp. 5, 3.

18. Bernhard Anderson, *Understanding the Old Testament* (Englewood Cliffs: Prentice-Hall, 1986), p. 252.

4
The Narrative Structure
of Hebrew Experience
Part III: God's *Ruach*/Spirit

Introduction

Covenant is the masterplot of the Hebrew story, and all the rest is commentary. Covenant is the religious metaphor that mediates how this ancient as well as this contemporary people comes to know Yahweh. Covenant is what Yahweh is forever and again up to.

The greatness and majesty of Yahweh are beyond question and beyond all telling. The splendor of Yahweh is disclosed above all in Yahweh's intentions for human history, and in all the experiences of Yahweh wherein those intentions are encountered. The valuational structure, if we may use that awkward language, of Yahweh's historical intentions is named in many ways, but the themes of justice and mercy clearly tell us the most about the overall cast of Yahweh's heart.

Yahweh's transforming presences in Hebrew history are promoted with a special poignancy in the prophets who feel the world around them with the feelings of God. The moral quality of Yahweh's heart is specified relentlessly in terms of justice and mercy. Because of the greatness of Yahweh, praise and thanksgiving are our religious duty. But the nature of Yahweh's majesty is so essentially bound up with justice that if justice is violated worship is simply absurd. And if worship does not help build a just world, its object must be some other god than Yahweh.

The privileged descriptions of this transforming presence are Spirit and Word. They are metaphors. They not only sculpt language about Yahweh in the praise of Israel. Long before that, they sculpt the experience itself. The power of these metaphors is not only that they are immensely effective after the fact but that they help constitute the fact. I will take each up in turn.

The Volatile, Elusive **Ruach**

In the Judeo-Christian tradition, to speak about God's Spirit with any degree of lively consciousness is to be near the very heart of religious experience—a place disproportionately enticing and scary. There is something so elemental about the Spirit experience of deity that we have recourse to the most elemental thing about life to understand it: human breath; and to the most elemental forces and resources we encounter on the face of the earth: wind, fire and water. Wind: it is gentle, cool and soothing; it is terrifying, fierce, dangerous; it may be like weather's wind, full of mystery because we know not whence it came or whither it goes—and it cannot be tamed; or it may even be the artificial wind of the winnowing fan that separates wheat from chaff, that is, it judges. Fire: it is hot like human passion—no commitment made to Ultimacy is adequate if it is not radical, and total, and wholehearted. And that means passionate. Fire imagery can be in the form of an enkindled heart expressed in tendernesses beyond telling; it can be a furnace's fire that clears the dross and exposes the splendor; it can warm a hearth, and even make survival a gift stolen from the icy chill; it can rage out of control and destroy. Water: it surrounds us in the womb; living things must have it; it cleanses; it floods; it drowns; it is necessary and friendly; it is uncontrollable and vicious. Those are the places we are when we address the matter of God's Spirit. Theo-logizing, as the word says, is our attempt to put order into our God-experience. No wonder that the undomesticatable Spirit of God so eludes theo-logic.

There are three Hebrew words for what is often translated as "spirit" in English. I will focus principally upon *Ruach*. Probably the most basic experience described by this Hebrew Spirit word is that of "moved air." As such, the word literally means both "breath" and "wind." No English word in religious use is able to say precisely those two same things at once. As any translator of scripture knows, it is sometimes impossible to know which English word to choose: wind, breath, spirit with a small "s," or Spirit with a large "S." Whatever word is chosen, finally, is chosen on the basis of an interpretation. Whichever choice is made, the other notations are eliminated, and often what else is eliminated is the polyvalent meaning of the original Hebrew word which better respects the mystery of spirit (or is it Spirit, or is it Life-breath, or was it just a wind we heard?).

Ruach: *The Livingness of God*

The same word that means wind and breath is also one of the most important Hebrew words for the life principle. Hebrew psychology is a physiological psychology. Psychological functions are named in connection with parts of the body or body functions. The names are metaphorical. To understand this psychology, we must try to understand how breath was a metaphor for life, i.e. for what theologians have also called soul. For the Hebrews, breath sometimes seems almost not a metaphor for life but a literal equivalence. Breath is life. No breath, no life. Take clay, shape it like a human being, give it breath and it's a living being. Take dry bones, reassemble them, add muscle, sinew, and skin, give breath and it's alive. So when we speak of God's Spirit in some way we are naming the very Livingness of God that breaks into the livingness of history, a transforming presence that touches us in a principle (not principal) way.

The "Worldly" Ruach

There is still another factor that roadblocks our access to the Hebrew experience of God which we name Spirit. There's a long trail of history behind every word, and when any word is used in any present moment it has many of its ancestors on its back, and they are all screaming. Words have ancestral voices that cannot be drowned out. One of the most powerful ancestral voices for Spirit in our English usage is that spirit contrasts with matter. Not only that, it contrasts favorably with matter. We have a long history of uneasiness with the so-called material aspect of reality. Again, spirit evokes a contrast with body—how often have we heard the expression "body and spirit" to evoke a sense of the "whole person." Here again, spirit has a lot better reputation than body, especially if you introduce the flesh word "carnal."

If you told someone that you received a spiritual phone call last night, he or she would probably conclude that you and whoever called talked about "holy things." But if you said to someone that you received a breathy phone call, he or she would probably conclude that you hung up the phone immediately and reported harassment to the phone company. However, the breathy phone call is probably closer to what is called Spirit of God, a very visceral entry of God into the innards of history.

Carl Jung said that the Catholic Church's definition of the assumption of Mary was probably the most important religious event since the reformation. His reason was that this dogma at the level of mythic instinct takes a stand against "spiritualism" (there are those ancestral voices again). The assumption of Mary, suggests Jung, guarantees that the fullest way of being with God is a bodily way. There is no way that we English-speakers can fully over-ride the ancestral voices of our word "spirit" that say something very different about God than did the Hebrew use of the word. Perhaps it is enough to be aware of some instinctual limitations upon our access to Hebrew religious experience. It is not my intention to canonize Hebrew religious experience, or celebrate its superiority to any other. Let me simply reiterate my desire to develop a clear sense of Hebrew religious experience because that's where Jesus came from, and this work is a struggling attempt to meet Jesus again on his own ground, and imagine where Christological reflection might have gone had a doctrinal tradition wandered up that road.

Historicized Interpreting

History—that harborer of the enworlded appearances of God—is the basis of our experience and knowledge of God. Not all history is equally numinous. For the Hebrew people, the most numinous places are those in which transformation is afoot. Covenant becomes the foundational metaphor that mediates Ultimacy's traffic with Hebrew immediacy—heavy traffic whose portage carries qualitative increment into life. As this people unfolds its experience of covenant, "Spirit of God" and "Word of God" emerge as two of the most used ways of telling who God is to them and of how Yahweh's transforming presences effect what they do. I speak of "presences" in the plural, because the existence of two ways of speaking suggests that there were two kinds of experience of Yahweh's efficacy, with objectively experienceable differences—different enough to require different linguistic formulations. Efficacy means effects. So we are talking about two different kinds of effects. Effects are detected in events. Theological empiricism suggests examining events in which Spirit is named as efficacious, and attempting to make a descriptive generalization.

The next step is to do the same for Word texts. If Spirit and Word are so often transformatively at work, it will help to know what each seems to be up to, and then to ponder what kind of coordination between them there might be. Even though the Hebrew mind is certainly neither abstract nor intentionally systematic, there must have been some consistency in experience at the base of some consistency in how the transforming and efficacious presence of Yahweh is described. It would be foolhardy to believe that *all* the Spirit texts will have some common elements that promote a generalization without exceptions. We are not dealing with that kind of systematic mind. The same is true for Word texts.

These significantly consistent uses of Spirit and Word language do suggest, I am convinced, that some basic meaning, some fundamental sense of things, constellates around each of these words. I will propose such a constellated understanding for both Spirit and Word. I will then suggest how they are co-ordinate with each other in God's creative transformation of human history. Clues to the coordination are in the effects of God which are experienced and named as *Ruach* or *Dabhar*.

Lest the important obvious go unsaid, I simply want to note my awareness that I am not simply "naming fact," but am interpreting an ancient experience from a contemporary viewing place. The interpreter and the interpreter's world always edge their way into the facts. I want to honor the ancient experience of Yahweh, but any fusion of horizons will be different from the original horizon. That is inevitable. Interpretation theory says that texts themselves are "unstable" since their meaning is never simply what is there in the fixed words, but that it emerges out in front of text and interpreter. History itself, then, is also an unstable text. When I proposed constellated meanings for *Ruach* and *Dabhar* those are meanings out in front of both me and the ancient texts; they are not simply "dug out" of the texts.

In the procedures which follow, I will first pay some attention to the several Hebrew words for spirit. Second, it will be important to see what that word means in Hebrew anthropology, for that is the more literal and immediate experience upon which religious symbolism is constructed. The religious meaning has a necessary meaning bond with the first, literal meaning. Then comes a look at events wherein the efficacy of Spirit is named. In order to get more concrete about events, I will be asking who are the people that the Spirit goes after—and here I will invoke an interpretive schema. Fourth, I will examine the principal metaphors that go with Spirit: wind, fire and water. These are poetic ways of naming effects, and effects are what we want to understand. Finally, I will suggest my understanding of the constellated meaning of Spirit. That, then, will be the meaning of Spirit that I call up Christologically in the second half of the book.

"Spirit" Words

There are three Hebrew words used for spirit, soul, or life principle: *neshamah, nephesh,* and *ruach*.[1] *Neshamah* is used 24 times in the earlier scriptures. Of these, nine uses refer to the life principle. In the account of Elijah's restoration of the Zarephath widow's son to life, we find that "the son of the mistress of the house fell sick; his illness was so severe that in the end no *neshamah* was left in him" (1 Kgs 17:17). That is typical of the use of *neshamah*.

The spirit word *nephesh* occurs 754 times in a large variety of ways, almost like heart. Robinson classifies 282 usages of *nephesh* as referring to the life principle. There are numerous psychical usages as well. "The term may also denote the whole inner life of thought and feeling, as when the law is said to restore *nephesh*"[2]—e.g. "The law of Yahweh is perfect, refreshment for the *nephesh*" (Ps 19:7). But the word we are most interested in is *Ruach*.

Ruach occurs 378 times. Let me give Robinson's classification of its usages, recalling that there is some unavoidable arbitrariness in anyone's classification.[3] We do, nonetheless, get a sense of the word from its range of use and its frequency. *Ruach* refers to wind in either natural or figurative ways 131 times. It names the principle of life 39 times, none of which occurs in a pre-exilic text. It refers to psychic functions 74 times. It names the effective influence of God 134 times. *Ruach* and *Nephesh* are similar to *Leb*/heart in that they refer to the interior regions of life and therefore to the interior regions of the human spirit and its psychical functions. A difference, however, is that breath is like wind—it moves, it can be felt. It can go from here to there, from Moses to seventy new leaders, from Elijah to Elisha. *Ruach* has a literal meaning that makes it a better word than heart for describing how the depths of one person might reach the depths of another. *Ruach*/breath and *Leb*/heart do get connected later in the prophetic tradition. Since the Spirit of God gets to us in our interior depths, we will hear heart become a locus of the effects of God's Spirit.

Spirit for Community

Recall that covenant is the transformative story that the Hebrew *people* are called to live—not individuals one by one collectively, but a *people* corporately. Covenant happens to individuals derivatively when they belong to the people that is covenanted. Even when corporate destiny is not tied so seriously to individual destiny, it never stops being the case that covenant only belongs to the individual who belongs to the covenanted people. In this context, the first generalization I suggest about the events that name God's efficacy as Spirit is that Spirit is never a gift for the sake of an individual, but comes to individuals who play important roles in the formation of God's people. The hymn of praise in

Isaiah 63:7–14 presents Yahweh's Spirit as the director of sacred history. When this people is unfaithful, it causes God's Holy Spirit (spirit?) to grieve (v 10). Yahweh endowed Moses with his Spirit and went to work in history at Moses' right hand (vv 11–12). Yahweh leads his people through the desert to a place of rest (vv 13–14). The prophetic text then praises Yahweh, saying: "This was how you guided your people to win yourself glorious renown" (v 14). The Spirit directs history.

The Spirit is about the transformation of a community. We are talking, therefore, about events in the life of a community. If God is transforming the life of a community, then he must be addressing that community in its decision making processes. The people have a corporate personality, a common "spirit" that animates the group, a shared deep story. But a corporate personality does not have a subjectivity of its own. Only individuals are subjects, some of whom are in positions such that their decisions have an impact on the decisions that others make; they are thus in a critical position to shape the common destiny. In Israel, these key people are, first, the political leaders—the patriarchs, the judges, the kings; second, the priests; third, the prophets. We will look first at the leaders (kings, judges, etc.), then the prophets, and finally, the priests to see what the Spirit is up to in these lives.

The Spirit and the Kings

The gift of God's Spirit to Israel's leaders is clear. Moses complains that the burden of leadership is too heavy for him alone. He begs Yahweh for help in carrying this great weight. Moses distributes the leadership tasks among seventy elders. Then "Yahweh took some of the Spirit that was on him [Moses], and put it on the seventy elders" (Num 11:25). Spirit clearly goes with office. Later, when Yahweh let Moses know that he would not be the one to lead the people into the promised land, Moses said to Yahweh: "May Yahweh, God of the spirits that give life to all living creatures, appoint a leader for this community. . . . Yahweh answered Moses, 'Take Joshua, son of Nun, a man in whom the Spirit dwells, and lay your hand on him' " (Num 27:18).

Recall that when Pharaoh had a perplexing dream, it was Joseph who was able to give him an interpretation.

> Pharaoh and all his ministers approved of what Joseph had said. Then Pharaoh asked his ministers, "Can we find any one else endowed with the Spirit of God like him?" So Pharaoh said to Joseph, "Since God

has given you knowledge of all this, there can be no one as intelligent and wise as you. . . . I hereby make you governor of the whole of Egypt" (Gn 41:37–39,41).

Two things are to be noted about this event. The obvious one is that having the Spirit of God fits Joseph for a leadership role. The second item to note carefully is that Joseph's accurate insight into the dream world, the unconscious, the non-rational (not = irrational!), is the clue to the Spirit's presence.

The book of Judges is the record of rather charismatic leadership in the Hebrew community, and again the presence of the Spirit of Yahweh is a critical factor. "The Spirit of Yahweh was upon Othniel; he became judge in Israel . . ." (Jgs 3:10). And again, "The Spirit of Yahweh was upon Jephthah" (Jgs 11:29). And still again: "The woman gave birth to a son and called him Samson. The child grew, and Yahweh blessed him. And the Spirit of Yahweh began to stir him in the Camp of Dan between Zorah and Eshtaol" (Jgs 13:24–25). We are certainly forced to conclude that the Spirit of God seeks out the leadership figures who play an absolutely vital role in guiding Israel's response to the covenant story to which Yahweh calls them. The pattern continues with kings as well.

In the context of covenant, I have already referred to the transition experience when Israel moves from theocracy and judge-leadership to a king. Samuel the prophet anoints Israel's first king with oil: "Samuel took a phial of oil and poured it on Saul's head; he then kissed him and said, 'Has not Yahweh anointed you as a leader over his people Israel? You are the one who is to govern Yahweh's people . . .' " (1 Sam 10:1). Samuel then promised a sign that would authenticate the anointing: "After this you will come to Gibeah of God (where the Philistine garrison is) and, when you are just outside the town, you will meet a group of prophets coming down from the high place, headed by lyre, tambourine, pipe and harp; they will be in a state of ecstasy. Then the Spirit of Yahweh will seize on you, and you will go into ecstasy with them, and be changed into another man" (1 Sam 10:5–7). "As soon as he turned his back to leave Samuel, God changed Saul's heart. And all these signs occurred that very day" (1 Sam 10:9).

Let us again make some notations. The gift of the Spirit is associated with ecstatic prophets, and Saul himself falls into ecstasy—and he is made into "another man." The radical transforming power of the Spirit is again associated with the non-rational, i.e. with ecstasy. Later in his career when Saul is chasing after David to kill him, Saul sends before him successively three advance groups of his own agents, and the same things happen to each: the Spirit of God seizes them and they fall into ecstasy. Finally Saul goes himself toward Ramah where Samuel and David are: "And the Spirit of God came on him too, and he went on his way in an ecstasy until he came to the huts at Ramah. He too stripped off his clothes and he too fell into an ecstasy in the presence of Samuel, and falling down lay there naked all that day and night" (1 Sam 19:23–24).

From this incident we conclude, first, that when the Spirit of God takes hold of the human spirit to make it readjust in radical ways, it shakes the human person to the core of his/her being. Second, we should note that music is associated with the prophets in whose company Saul is when the Spirit seizes on him—an "accompaniment" that is nonrational. Third, we should note that the way in which God's Spirit changed Saul into another man is by changing his heart. Heart is the affective seat of personhood, the "hot spot." The heart, therefore, is where the efficacy of the Spirit is directed. And, fourth, in this event we find the Spirit associated with anointing, pouring oil upon the head. We turn now to David.

Because Saul is unfaithful in his leadership (he takes banned booty), Samuel brings him the bad news: "Since you have rejected Yahweh's word, he has rejected you as king" (1 Sam 15:23). Yahweh then sends Samuel to Jesse's house in Bethlehem, indicating that one of Jesse's sons will be the next king. All are gathered for a meal at Jesse's except the youngest son who is in the fields tending sheep. "Then Samuel said to Jesse, 'Send for him, for we shall not sit down to eat until he arrives.' Jesse had him sent for; he had ruddy cheeks, with fine eyes and an attractive appearance. Yahweh said, 'Get up and anoint him: he is the one.' At this, Samuel took the horn of oil and anointed him, surrounded by his brothers; and the Spirit of Yahweh seized on David from that day forward" (1 Sam 16:11–13). David does not function as king until after Saul's death, but already God's spirit takes leave of Saul, and an evil spirit from God comes instead (see Montague's discussion of "evil spirit from God").[4] Saul's servants see that he has a bad spirit and go in search of a skilled harpist, for "when the evil spirit from God comes over you, he will play and it will do you good" (1 Sam 16:16). David is recruited, and "whenever the spirit from God came over Saul, David would take a harp and play; Saul would then be soothed; it would do him good, and the evil spirit would leave him" (1 Sam 16:23). Here again, the man of the Spirit has power over the troubled soul, and music is not a mere accompaniment, but the very instrument of power. In fact, in David's dying words he calls himself "the anointed of the God of Jacob, the singer of the songs of Israel," and acknowledges that "the Spirit of Yahweh speaks through me" (2 Sam 23:1–2).

Before we leave Saul and David, let us note that each is anointed and receives the Spirit. Once God's (good) Spirit takes leave of Saul and its opposite enters him, Saul's whole being is set against David. Over and over he tries to kill him. Saul, with three thousand men, goes after David who is near Engedi, on the shore of the Dead Sea. Saul has to relieve himself, and unknowingly enters the very cave where David is. David prays to Yahweh to restrain him from killing Saul, because Saul is "the anointed of Yahweh" (1 Sam 24:7). Saul puts his cloak aside as he relieves himself. David, without Saul's knowledge, cuts off the border of the cloak. Saul dresses again and leaves the cave. David follows after him and calls to him. He wants the fact that he could so easily have killed Saul but didn't to show his strong good will to Saul. David says to him, "This very day you have seen for yourself how Yahweh put you in my power in the cave and how, refusing to kill you, I spared you, saying 'I will not raise my hand against my Lord, since he is Yahweh's anointed' "—and as proof, David calls Saul's attention to the border of his cloak (1 Sam 24:11–12).

The item here to which I want to call attention is the expression "the anointed of Yahweh" or "the anointed of God." David respects Saul for that reason, and equally, on his deathbed, refers to himself in the same terms. The anglicized Hebrew word for "the anointed" is "Messiah." The anglicized Greek word for "the anointed" is "Christ." Lest the expression seem brand-new when we encounter it used of Jesus, let us note here that Saul and David each is called "the Christ of God." And in each case we are dealing with the one designated to lead God's people in its covenant relationship with him. Further, the efficacy of the Spirit is causally efficacious of the "christness" of both Saul and David. The Spirit of God does something in the interior of the human spirit that is constitutive in character, that is, it does something that is identity-creating: it makes judges and kings. It also makes prophets, the next figure we will be examining.

The Spirit and the Prophets

There are two senses in which the word prophecy is used. One is as a name for a highly excited state of religious fervor, often expressed in non-rational and even frenzied ways. The second sense of the word refers to the more archetypal figure who announces to his people the claims that a new age is making even now upon their lives. These two senses are not unrelated—for sometimes one must surrender, must learn abandonment, in order to "see" what God is up to and to respond. The surrender of our attachments to our own "spirit" can be a wrenching experience, an earthquake in the depths of personhood whose devastation is a prelude to being remade in a different spirit—a deconstruction before a reconstruction. In the materials that follow, I will be focusing upon the more archetypal prophet.

Balaam is the earliest instance of prophecy being attributed to the presence of the Spirit. Balak, the king of Moab, dispatched Balaam to place a curse upon the Hebrews. As a prelude to invoking the curse, Balak and Balaam offer holocausts to their Moabite deities. However,

> Balaam then saw that it pleased Yahweh to bless Israel. He did not go as before to seek omens but turned towards the desert. Raising his eyes Balaam saw Israel settled tribe by tribe; the Spirit of God came upon him, and he declaimed his poem as follows: "The oracle of Balaam . . . Balaam sees what Shaddai makes him see, receives the divine answer, and his eyes are opened. How fair are your tents, O Jacob! How fair your dwellings, O Israel! Blessed be those who bless you, and accursed be those who curse you!" (Num 24:1–4.9)

What are the effects of the Spirit? What is clear is that after the Spirit of God comes upon him, he "sees" differently than before. Instead of placing himself over and against the story of Yahweh's covenanted people, he celebrates what Yahweh has done with expressions of affectionate praise ("How fair! How fair!"). Finally, he reverses his original intention. He blesses instead of curses. The Spirit has turned him around!

During the time of the kings, the prophets did not seem to attribute their vocations specifically to the work of the Spirit in themselves. However, they were keenly aware of the power of the Spirit in the shaping of Israel's history. There is an interesting exchange of prophetic spirit that is related during the period of the monarchy (the reference is not to Yahweh's Spirit). Elisha asked Elijah for his spirit and received it. When Elijah approached, "the brotherhood of prophets saw him in the distance, and said, 'The spirit of Elijah has come to rest on Elisha' " (2 Kgs 2:15).

The preservation of the long messages of the prophets in written tradition begins in the eighth century. Among the pre-exilic prophets,

materials dealing with the Spirit are simply absent in Amos. Hosea is
impatient with priest and prophet alike (Hos 4:5). Yet he does call the
prophet a "man of the Spirit" (Hos 9:7). Micah, however, speaks of his
own prophecy explicitly in terms of the Spirit and its consequences:

> . . . I am full of strength
> (full of Yahweh's spirit)
> of justice and courage,
> to accuse Jacob of his crime
> and Israel of his sin (Mi 3:8).

The prophet identifies the Spirit as explanatory of his prophetic vocation. Further, we should note that judgment and justice are what the
prophet, full of the Spirit, is intent upon. Justice means far more in its
Hebrew context than in our current usage. For us, it tends to mean
giving each his or her due. But in the earlier scriptures, justice stands for
the essential rightness of things as God would have them. It is inclusive
of distributive justice, and insistent upon it, but larger in scope than
that. Justice names how history is to be ordered, because Yahweh is
righteous, and Yahweh calls history to order. Justice is in the deep story
of God. And because it is, it enters into the deep story to which God
invites history. God's Spirit in history, therefore, is vitally concerned
with issues of justice.

As we continue to look at particular events which are interpreted in
Spirit ways, we will consider First Isaiah and Jeremiah, and then look at
the prophets of the exile and the return, especially Ezekiel, and Second
and Third Isaiah.

First Isaiah never invokes the Spirit to explain his own vocation as a
prophet. But he does indeed have a theology of the Spirit. The prophet
is preoccupied with the age to come. When he speaks of the future
restoration of Israel, he relates *Ruach* to judgment and purification:
"When the Lord has washed away the filth of the daughter of Zion and
cleansed Jerusalem of the blood shed in her, with the *ruach*/spirit of
mishpat/judgment and the *ruach* of fire, [then] Yahweh will come and
rest on the whole stretch of Mount Zion . . ." (Is 4:4–5). In 26:6 Isaiah
speaks again of the Spirit of justice who sits in judgment, the *ruach
mishpat*. We see here his prophetic concern for justice as the story to be
told by Israel's history. Israel is to be a justice-people grounded in the
Spirit of Yahweh . The prophet calls Israel to listen to the justice-claim
of the age to come.

Isaiah also develops the water image of Spirit. In judgment against Syria, Yahweh's "lips are brimming with fury, his tongue is like a devouring fire, his *Ruach* is like a river in spate, coming up to the neck" (Is 30:28). Here we meet water as a symbol of fury. But water is benevolent as well, the source of life. In the age to come, "the *Ruach* is poured out on us from above, and the desert becomes productive ground, so productive you might take it for a forest. Justice will fix its home in the desert, and uprightness live in the productive ground, the effect of uprightness being quiet and security forever" (Is 32:15–16). Spirit is poured, like water; the sterile becomes the fertile. Justice reigns.

Isaiah also associates the Spirit with the leader of the age to come, a man from the line of Jesse/David: "A shoot will spring up from the stock of Jesse, a new shoot will grow from his roots. On him will rest the Spirit of Yahweh, the Spirit of wisdom and insight, the Spirit of counsel and power, the Spirit of knowledge and fear of Yahweh" (Is 11:1–2). Notice first that Isaiah connects the efficacy of the Spirit with (messianic) leadership. Second, while the Spirit does not generally say exactly what action is called for (as we shall see soon, this is more the role of God's Word), it gives the interior qualities that enable one to sense instinctively what Israel's deep story is like and what it requires. This, and the ethical characteristic of the kingdom (justice, integrity) which are also the consequences of Spirit, strongly suggest that what we are talking about at base is a valuational structure based on God's sense of order, which is instanced in the historical structure of covenant. Whoever leads the covenanted people must have a feel for that story. The leader's spirit must be shaped by God's Spirit, and this will happen, foretells the prophet.

It does not take long to talk about Jeremiah and Spirit/spirit. Jeremiah's tirades against false prophets make him leary of Spirit/talk, except with invective: "And the prophets? Nothing but *ruach* (here *ruach* just means wind), the Word is not in them" (Jer 5:13). For Jeremiah, the key is the Word of God; he frequently begins his prophecies saying, "The Word of Yahweh was addressed to me . . ." (Jer 2:1, and often). In Jeremiah's splendid description of the new covenant (Jer 31), he emphasizes this new interiorization by stressing the category of heart without reference to Spirit. It is with Ezekiel that we find a full flowering of Spirit understanding.

George Montague says that "with Ezekiel an entirely new 'wind' is blowing. . . . The spirit now appears everywhere."[5] Ezekiel's commissioning occurs in a vision. A voice says, " 'Son of man, get to your feet; I will speak to you.' As he said those words, the Spirit came into me and put me on my feet and I heard him speaking to me" (Ez 2:1–2).

Earlier in my discussion of "heart," I cited Ezekiel's prophecy of the new covenant. I want to return to three verses of that prophecy: "I shall pour clean water over you and you shall be cleansed . . . I shall give you a new heart and put a new spirit in you; I shall remove the heart of stone from your bodies and give you a heart of flesh instead . . . I shall put my Spirit in you, and make you keep my laws, and respect and practice my judgments" (Ez 36:25–27). There is an important synthetic constellation in these few verses. First we see *ruach* used for both Israel's spirit and God's Spirit. Second, the new spirit in Israel is an effect of Yahweh's Spirit having been put into Israel's Spirit. Third, the "place" of the new spirit is the heart, i.e. the seat of personhood, whether personal or corporate. The transformation worked by Spirit is in Israel's depths, where the deep story of covenant resides and creates Israel's identity as Yahweh's people. Fourth, the symbol of water helps clarify the nature of the effects of the immanence of God's Spirit in Israel's spirit: it purifies and cleanses. Fifth, a cleansing that amounts to a new heart means a transformation of the structure of Israel's valuational responses to history. The law used to be written on stone, but stone hearts are now replaced by flesh (i.e. "real") hearts. The law will be kept because of the desire and respect that characterize Israel's new heart. In these few verses a fairly comprehensive "theology" of God's Spirit is implied.

Incredible images of the work of the Spirit continue in the passages of Ezekiel which follow (chapter 37). The prophet says that the Spirit of Yahweh carried him and set him down in the middle of a valley strewn the whole length with dry, dead bones. Ezekiel is given the word to prophesy to the bones, that Yahweh will make his *Ruach* enter into them, and they shall live. There is a sound of clatter and the dry bones begin joining themselves together. That done, they become in turn covered with sinew, then flesh, then skin. And finally from the four winds there comes *Ruach* that enters them. *Ruach* at once evokes its multiple meanings: breath, wind, life principle, God's Spirit, Israel's spirit. The particular metaphoric structure of Hebrew discourse allows this, and the multivalent communication possible in Hebrew is simply not translatable. The bones come to life and stand on their feet. Tell that, Yahweh orders Ezekiel, to the House of Israel, a people who had been scattered in foreign captivity and who were "dead" as God's people:

> The Lord Yahweh says this: I am now going to open your graves; I shall raise you from your graves, my people, and lead you back to the soil of Israel. And you will know that I am Yahweh, when I open your graves, and raise you from your graves, my people, and put my *ruach* in you, and you revive . . . (Ez 37:12–14a).

In the first creation, a human being was fashioned from lifeless clay and breath was (*nephesh* in this case) breathed into it from God; it became the first live human being. In Ezekiel, Israel is metaphorically re-created from lifeless material into a living people of God. The wind/breath play on words is powerful: "Come from the four winds, *ruach;* breathe on these dead, let them live." It is painful to select an English word for *ruach,* for any choice surrenders the richness of the Hebrew puns. The breath that comes from the four winds is God's Spirit. It passes from God's depths into the inner part—the heart—of Israel with breathtaking intimacy. The innermost principle of God's livingness enters flesh and bones and is the innermost spirit of a new re-creation. Montague is certainly right that with Ezekiel a new wind blows. The prophet himself is a prophet because of the efficacy of the Spirit in his life. And what he proclaims is the transformative power of the Spirit in the depths of Israel's being.

In Second Isaiah (later material than the prophet Isaiah) a figure who is impossible to identify accurately is associated with the remaking of Israel. This is the first of what have come to be called the "servant songs" (Is 42). The servant's vocation is the result of the gift of Yahweh's Spirit (v 1); and the establishment of justice is the desired result of the servant's work in history (vv 1,4,6,7). The servant is called a teacher (v 4), and therefore is more likely understood as prophet than political leader. We have two breath/spirit words in the same verse: "Thus says God, Yahweh, who created the heavens and spread them out, who gave shape to the earth and what comes from it, who gave *nephesh* to its people and *ruach* to those who move on it" (v 5). As in Ezekiel, the Spirit is associated both with the prophetic figure who will teach Israel how to live so that a kingdom of justice exists, and with Israel's transformation into such a kingdom.

In Third Isaiah we find the eschatological prophet who will usher in the era of perfect justice. This prophet says, "The Spirit of the Lord Yahweh is on me for Yahweh has anointed me. He has sent me . . ." (Is 61:1). Anointing was first reserved for the high priest, and then extended to all priests. It was later extended as well to the kings. In Third

Isaiah, anointing by the Spirit is applied to the commissioning of the eschatological prophet. Anointing does not have an explicit reference to the Spirit in the case of priests, but that connection is quite clear in respect to kings and prophets.

A short summary about the prophets: Balaam is the first prophet whose prophesying is connected with the Spirit. In the pre-exilic prophets, there is concern for Spirit, but the prophet's vocation is not so much talked about in terms of the efficacy of the Spirit; the emphasis is rather upon the transformative power of the Spirit in the life of Israel. In Ezekiel and later Isaiah, there is bountiful indication that both the prophet's vocation and the transformation of Israel's own spirit is the work of God's Spirit. The prophet's vocation is precisely as an instrument in the transformation of Israel. The transformation, attributed to the efficacy of the Spirit, is a deeply interior one: it happens in the heart. And it is a radical one: the heart is so clear about its valuational operations that the law is now seen to be written in hearts, not on tablets of stone.

As I indicated earlier, kings, prophets and priests are the key figures who provide leadership, in one way or another, to Israel. These are the functional figures who have the most to do with Israel's decision making processes. We have examined the biblical sense of the role of the Spirit in respect to kings and prophets, and must ask now what priests and Spirit have to do with each other.

The Spirit and the Priests

Recall that we are looking at the relationship between the Spirit and the prophets, kings/leaders and priests because those are the people who play the most crucial role in the guidance of Israel's destiny. When we examined the leaders of Israel, we saw that the Spirit of God was often experienced as efficacious in their formation into leaders. Similarly, some of the prophets understood that God's Spirit came into them and made them prophets. The prophets also had a theology of the work of the Spirit in the creative transformation of the Hebrew people. What we do not find in the earlier scriptures is a sense of the priestly vocation as a result of the efficacious presence of the Spirit of God within a person. Priests are anointed; but in the earlier strata of tradition, anointing is not yet connected with the Spirit. Ezekiel is a priest as well as a prophet. But it is the prophetic vocation that dominates his texts, and the efficacy of the Spirit is connected to his prophetic, not his priestly vocation. We do, however, find a theology of Spirit in the priestly tradition. We must look at the reasons for the emergence of the priestly tradition, and the role of Spirit contained in it.

When the Hebrew people return home after the exile, they set about rebuilding their covenant community. The leadership for this rebuilding comes in large measure from the priests. They focus the long battered community upon the Torah, the law. (Here is still another excruciating translation problem: law is an incredibly impoverished rendering of Torah; there is no counterpart in our language because there is no counterpart in our experience.) In the Torah or Pentateuch, there is a lot of remembering where we came from, what made us in the first place. The composition of the Pentateuch very likely comes from this period, representing a collection of both very old traditions and new ones located backward into the times of origin, i.e. the creation. Montague observes "that the priestly theology is much more past-oriented than future-oriented. It thinks of the future in terms of regaining the past."[6] Having seen how active the Spirit is among the prophets who announce the claims of the age to come, it is not surprising that the Spirit is not seen to be at work among those who emphasize the claims of the past upon the present. Noting that the activity of the Spirit is rarely mentioned in the post-exilic period, Neve comments in a vein similar to Montague that "this is because in a community organized around the law, there is no longer the anticipation of the direct inspiration of the spirit, the unmediated guidance offered by Yahweh's *ruach*. The activity of the spirit is free and uncoerced, setting it in opposition to religious life organized on the basis of law."[7] Let us then see an example of the priestly understanding of God's Spirit.

Montague feels that even though the priestly tradition that appears in the Pentateuch deals with first things and beginnings, the Spirit theology of Ezekiel and Second Isaiah is a notable influence upon these texts. The creation account of Genesis 1 will provide our sample of the priestly understanding of the Spirit. The text runs:

> In the beginning God created heaven and earth. Now the earth was a formless void, there was darkness over the deep, with God's Spirit (*ruach elohim*) sweeping over the waters. God said, "Let there be light," and there was light (Gn 1:1–3).

Some scholars translate the *ruach elohim* as "a mighty wind," to which the text is susceptible (i.e. divine winds, or a divine storm). However, I am persuaded by Montague and others that what we have here at the beginning of creation is God's Spirit. We have already seen in the prophetic tradition that the Spirit works a deep interior, life-giving transformation that helps a people live out the story of covenant. In the creation story we begin with already existing "stuff" that is sheer chaos, a formless void. Montague comments about the chaos:

> That fact that it is unformed does not mean that it is evil. If it does not yet merit the epithet "good," it soon will. Because God's Spirit is hovering over it, chaos becomes promise. The *Spirit* of God thus disposes the chaos to hear in obedience the *word* of God. Because the chaos has been readied by the Spirit, when God says, "Let there be light," there *is* light. . . . The priestly creation story is a prototype for man's experience of order and chaos in his life and in this world.[8]

I want to underscore Montague's comments. In this creation account, the Spirit of God and the Word of God are collaborative. Each does something which the other needs for the full creative moment. There is the Spirit's role in disposing the chaos, and the Word's role in naming the particular configuration into which the chaos is to be transformed. After examining *dabhar* in more detail, I will continue this discussion of Spirit and Word as two halves of a whole "model" for experiencing and describing God's presence in history.

After looking singly at the Spirit in relation to prophets, priests and kings, I want to look at the relation between these dominant persons in Israel's history.

Prophet, Priest and King as Archetypes—and the Spirit

At this point I want to suggest an interpretation of the effects of God's Spirit in the transformation of Israel's history into the people of the covenant. In so doing I want to acknowledge at the outset a limitation upon the interpretation I will propose. My interpretation presupposes the clear temporal distinction between past, present, and future, such as the deep story embedded in the grammatical structure of Indo-European languages presumes. The fact that this grammatical structure does not exist in some other languages alerts us to its relativity. The grammar of the ancient Hebrew verb does not make distinctions analogous to our sense of time as past, present and future. In terms of theological empiricism, I am moving for a few moments from descriptive generalization to the imaginative use of an interpretive schema. If Yahweh is at work transforming a people, basically his efficacy must be directed to Israel's decision making processes. Because a community does not have a subjectivity of its own that can be addressed, the efficacy of God is directed above all to those persons who most influence the destiny of Israel: the prophets, priests and kings (leaders generally).

In an article on "Meland's Alternative in Ethics," John Spencer describes the kinds of claims that are levied upon a person whenever a decision is being made.[9] The temporal structure of those claims has suggested to me an understanding of the prophet/priest/king triad.

Every present moment, whether a moment of personal or communal life, represents a tensed relation with a remembered past, an anticipated future and a present which seeks to be a qualitatively satisfying present. Present moments are tensed in two ways. They are tensed in respect to temporal senses of past, present and future. And they are tensed also almost in the nervous sense, because past, present and future make claims that compete with each other, each with genuine justification: there is tension. Under pressure from this tension, the subject must become a negotiator, a "claims adjuster." There are "oughts" stemming from the past, the present and the future that impinge upon every new decision. The past levies claims upon all our decisions. Each present moment "is obliged to the given structures of the past which constitute its inheritance."[10]

That I have even arrived at this present moment I owe to the past, for better or for worse. My inheritance defines the present and sets for the present its task. Inheritance demands continuity between the old and the new. Nothing less than identity is at stake in that continuity. The principal obligation of a new moment to its inheritance is to take seriously the hopes that were incubated there. The claims of the past are strongly in the service of identity-maintenance. They try to see to it that goods that have been won are not lost. The oughts from the past are often able to evoke a ready obedience. There is a danger, however, should the claims of the past assume an apodictic authority; for that would generate a militant resistance to the new. In its quest for continuity, the past can be intolerant of the new since newness always foments discontinuity.

The future also lays claims upon all our decisions under the guise of both moral responsibility for the effects of our decisions, and as promise. Something "out front," i.e. promise, puts us under requirement. New worlds are in the making. We face an age to come. There is often a sense of a story that wants to get told, a configuration that seems to move from the future into the present like a red carpet unfurling toward us. The future requires of the present moment that it live forward, and take risks with the untried. There is an inevitable tension between the untried and the tried, between living forward and living faithfully with an inheritance. The claims of the future keep us alive and fresh. The oughts from the future have the power to elicit huge sacrifice in the service of a dream, a new world in-the-making. The claim of the ideal is a source of immense enthusiasm and energy. It is zesty in its consequences. But the future has a dark side as well. If its claims are given an exaggerated role, we quickly get out of touch with the concrete richness that has brought us to the present moment, and we may sell off far too cheaply what is worth great price. We can live very stupidly in the aftermath of jettisoned wisdom.

The present also levies claims upon all our decisions. Its claims are required for the goodness of the present moment. They try to provide for the quality of life. The goodness of the world, the goodness of life and the richness of our loves—these *deserve* to qualify any moment of experience. They have a right to be present now. We do not want to eat only leftovers. Nor do we want the pot always to be simmering for tomorrow's meal. The banquet *now* is the symbol of God's promises in a land that flows with milk and honey. The claims of the present try to make us provide for a high quality "now." Without the experience of present satisfaction the critical virtue of gratitude is not even possible; the impulse to praise languishes. The claims of the present have a dark side, however. If they are exaggerated, if they are not balanced with requests from the past and the future, then present enjoyment is shallow and fleeting. It has no roots and no reach. It is thin fare.

In the earlier scriptures, priests are usually the ones most vocal in behalf of inheritance. Ritual is essential to the maintenance and transmission of societal identity. Ritual is the province of priests. They think of the future in terms of regaining the past in all its fullness and splendor. The priest is the archetypal figure who represents the claims of the past. Every society has its priests who exercise this sociological function, though "priest" is seldom the name given. Each person has a little priest inside asserting the claims of inheritance. Not every individual priest in a religious culture may necessarily behave in this way—I am using priest as "type." The archetypal priest is the spokesperson for tradition.

King "types" normally possess administrative skills. They preside over the on-going daily life of a society. They try to satisfy as many people for as much of the time as possible. They are practical people who take practical account of the resources with which they have to work. They respect feasibility studies.

The king is the leader archetype. He was sometimes called a "judge" or one of the "fathers" (our father Abraham) in the earlier scriptures. She/he can be called president, or prime minister, or many other things. The king is the spokesperson for the claims of the present. The king must love past history and must provide a future for progeny. But the king's daily energies are directed toward trying to make the kingdom work well today. Tomorrow he will make it work well tomorrow, but only when tomorrow has become the new today. Each of us also has a little king inside, begging for a good today.

Now we turn to the prophet "type." God is always up to something in history. God is about the creative transformation of human experience. God is the source of promise, the call to newness, the lure into the future. In God's behalf, the prophets are the spokespersons for the age to come. They tell us how to live now so that the age to come will have a home among us. There is a future that will, no matter what, differ from all pasts. If we do not yield to the offer of new life, to the little prophet in each of us, the past will choke us as surely as we live and die.

Every decision which either a single individual or a group makes has claims levied on it from past, present and future. Priest, king and prophet are archetypal figures who represent these claims publicly, and perform a sociological function thereby. The names may be different, but every lively society has spokespersons for those claims. They may be in the form of political parties or lobby groups, or they may be persons with particular penchants for nostalgia, realism and idealism.

There is, I believe, a "preferred option" on God's part in the fact that the Spirit is portrayed as most active among the prophets and by the prophets. Next in importance is the activity of Spirit among the kings. In the earlier scriptures Spirit does not contribute efficacy to the making of the priest, though priests so formulate a kind of theology of the Spirit (embedded in myth). The extraordinary weight of the Torah (a priest-inspired production, where the priestly theology of Spirit is found) attests to the importance and continuing power of the past upon all our decisions, not least of all in guiding us into our successive futures. But in the final analysis, the location of the greatest activity of the Spirit seems to say that "living forward" is the God-given plot for our story. The supernumerary presence of God's Spirit to the risks of living forward is a guarantee that the unknown into which we are called will be benevolent and worth the risk.

Even if the claims of the age to come seem to have an edge over the other claims, all the claims are valid. But the uneasy truth is that not all of these valid claims can be *fully* responded to *simultaneously* in any present decision. There are inevitable conflicts. For example, the sacrifice which a burgeoning future demands cuts deep into present pleasure. Or sometimes the present need for decent human satisfaction makes the future wait a while. Or still again, the past wants to continue intact, but the future says to let go. The newness that must be accommodated nudges a former wisdom out of its privileged place. And so it goes. In any community the dialectic between the prophets, priests and kings is vital to the fullness of life. The richest decision for an individual or a community is the one which is a maximized response to claims that impinge from all three areas, with some necessary yielding in each area. The Hebrew people seem to have understood the importance of maintaining separation, for the most part, between prophet, priest and king, so as to promote a dialect between their vying claims. Samuel the prophet anointed Saul the king. Nathan the prophet scolded David the king. Joshua the leader had to go before Eliezar the priest. Prophet, priest and king are the primary actors in the drama of the Hebrew community's decision making.

Israel's history is a story of unremitting re-creations and transformations. The age to come places the present under relentless requirement to let itself be changed. Those processes of historical transformation constitute the history that is theophanous. Thus, it is not surprising to see the Spirit associated above all with the prophets who, among the archetypal figures, most pressure Israel's decisions so that this people will move forward. This is a covenant history in which God's people, by vocation, live into God's future for them. The weight of the Spirit is clearly upon living forward. To stress the future is to trust the More into which God ceaselessly calls the world. This stress does not denigrate the temporal oughts from past and present; they also make just claims upon Israel's decisions. Deprive a new flower of its roots and it dies. Fail to attend to its present needs and it dies. Fail to enjoy its present beauty and fragrance and its meaning is diminished. But when all is said and done, God is always up to something. What God is up to never loses its priority. The Spirit of Yahweh attends assiduously to that priority.

A brief hermeneutical excursus into Roman Catholic contemporary history may be in order. The important lesson of dialectic between prophet, priest and king has not been well heeded in the organizational structure of the Roman Catholic tradition (and in certain other Christian traditions, as well). One cannot occupy any official leadership position without ordination. The king structure has been priestified. Likewise, no one may officially address the community unless ordained (priest or deacon), or given permission by one ordained. (In the New Code of Canon Law, there is permission for lay preaching in extraordinary circumstances, but never the homily in eucharistic liturgy.) In recent years (though falling now into disuse), nothing dealing with religion was to be published unless approved with the *imprimatur* and *nihil obstat* from someone ordained. The clericalization of both leaders and proclaimers has tended to subsume the archetypal figures of king and prophet under the archetype of priest. The Spirit interpretation of priests may in part be Spirit that is "borrowed" from the kings and prophets who have been subsumed into priesthood. Because of that, the healthy dialectic that makes the claims of past, present and future inter-compete, inter-clash, and inter-correct occurs with great difficulty in the Roman tradition. The structural dominance of the priestly archetype tends to give the whole church the kind of bent that Montague ascribed to the priestly influence in the post-exilic period: constructing the future by regaining the past. It is worth noting that in the report of the Didache upon the practices of the early community, if a prophet visited a community, the prophet would supersede the local eucharistic president at the celebration of the eucharist.

We have examined the efficacy of God's Spirit first by a philological glance at the spirit words themselves. Then we inquired about the persons in whose lives the work of the Spirit was especially discerned. In keeping with the empirical mood of inquiry, I want to turn now to some of the images and metaphors that are used in connection with God's Spirit. Some of these images we have already seen and will simply be recalled. The images give further clues to the character of God's appearances as Spirit in the immediacies of Hebrew experience.

Images of Spirit

Paul Ricoeur's theory of symbol sets the stage for examining the images used symbolically for Spirit. A symbol has two meanings. There is a first, literal, obvious meaning, such as the fact that water cleans. Upon the first meaning a second is constructed which has a natural resemblance to the first: because Lady Macbeth's sin made her feel guilty to the point of madness, she feigned washing her hands over and over to cleanse herself. It's the first literal meaning that gives the second meaning away, and provides a basis for interpreting the second event.[11]

The most obvious double-meaning we have already observed in the breath/wind/moved air *ruach*—a double meaning so literally based on the physiological psychology of the Hebrew world that it should not be taken as just an image. *Ruach* means the deepest principle of life. It comes from the far reaches of interiority outward. As it comes out it can be noticed, it can even be communicated. Used of God, Spirit must indicate (and here we have moved symbolically) a self-communication from God coming from God's own depths. When God's Spirit enters the human spirit, it shakes us up at the level of our own inmost constitutive principle of life. It turns us around, changes how we feel, see and judge the world and its events. When God puts his own Spirit/breath into human beings, the Spirit almost seems to have its own objective existence there, and Yahweh worries about his reputation: "My Spirit/spirit cannot be indefinitely responsible for human beings, who are only flesh; let the time allowed to each be a hundred and twenty years" (Gn 6:3).

The Yahwist account of the creation of the human person is a vivid "breath" account of God's self-communication: "Yahweh God shaped man from the soil of the ground, and blew the *neshamah* of life into his nostrils, and man became a living being" (Gn 2:7). Translation should perhaps bear the strain of retaining the Hebrew word in passages like this, so that the polyvalence of *neshamah* need not be violated by deciding whether this is better rendered as "breath" or "spirit" or "Spirit." It's probably closer to "breath" in this instance, but those other meanings are breathing down the neck of "breath." In any event, breath/spirit are incredibly close as words for the most basic life principle.

Fire and water are similar in one of the literal uses of each. Fire literally cleanses dross from gold and bronze, and is to be used in processes of religious purification (cf. the prescriptions given in Num 31:23). Water literally cleanses, and is a source of religious purification as well (the rite of lustral water is given in Num 19:17–22).

In the prophet Isaiah, in a text previously cited, the cleansing of Jerusalem is done with a *ruach* of fire by God. In Ezekiel, also in a text previously cited, Yahweh pours fresh water on Israel to cleanse his people. He gives them a new heart and a new *ruach*. He puts his own *ruach* into them. The *ruach* is not said to be water in this case, but cleansing with water is clearly a gloss on the nature of the new spirit/

Spirit put into the people. What is the concrete immediate experience that gets interpreted? It is the experience of being cleansed and purified. The efficacy is attributed to the Spirit, and corresponds to the efficacy of both fire and water in different situations when dross is burned off and water washes soil away. The experience of God as Spirit, understood through fire and water, is: I feel tarnished and soiled; but God's Spirit comes into my spirit and makes me clean, makes me experience myself as changed and the world as new and fresh.

Fire also has the effect of burning away the rubble so that we can clearly see what is there and what is essential—that is, the *ruach* of fire is a judgment about justice (Is 4:4): it makes clear how things are and how they should be. Spirit as wind or moved-air also has a judgment function when the winnowing fan separates the desirable wheat from the undesirable chaff (Is 30:28). The empirical question is: What concrete experience do fire and winnowing fan capture about the effects of God as *ruach*? Perhaps this: whoever has received God's *ruach* is able to judge and discriminate accurately according to how things should go in God's desire for human history. However, when we put this fire/wind meaning together with heart as the "place within" where *ruach* transforms, we understand judgment and discrimination to be the instinctive response of affect rather than the careful analysis of some inexorable logic about events. It is the valuational structure of human affect that is corrected by the efficacious presence of God's *ruach*. Having been corrected, accurate judgment and discernment are more apt to guide historical decisions.

Water purifies; it also makes things grow and flourish. God's Spirit "pours" out from above and makes wasteland into forest (Is 32:15). "Justice" and "integrity" are a gloss upon what flourishing means (Is 32:16–17). Presumably, those who spoke of God's Spirit as "poured from above," that is, as rain, are saying that "where God's Spirit is at work, things happen that are right and good. What grows up out of God's raining Spirit is God's work. There are noticeable effects. Spirit has/gives power, to make things grow and thrive. Spirit makes things happen, and you can certainly tell the difference."

Oil is another important image that gets connected with Spirit. We have noted that the anointing of kings with oil is connected with the transformative gift of Spirit, that prophets too are anointed with the Spirit, especially the eschatological prophet. We have looked at these texts already. In its first literal meanings, oil is a penetrating liquid. It soaks in deep. Further, it lasts a long time—it does not evaporate like water. Because it "holds on" and holds on "deep," it is a good base solution for perfume. It holds fragrance, allowing it to penetrate. This latter is one of the principal religious uses of oil in the earlier scriptures. The recipe for chrism is given in Exodus 30:22–25. The literal experience of perfumed oil is that it makes whatever it touches exceedingly fragrant and pleasing, distinguished by aromatic loveliness. Holy places and holy vessels are anointed with chrism. Originally the high priest was anointed with oil: "Moses poured the chrism on Aaron's head, consecrating him by unction" (Lv 8:12; cf. also Lv 21:10). Later, all priests were consecrated. Consecrating oil sets someone or something apart for use for God. It makes them holy. Fragrance is diffusive: whatever is consecrated with oil is made holy and makes that which touches it share in its fragrance/holiness. "Messiah" and "Christ" literally mean "the one upon whom oil has been poured." Because this oil language is so important, let us look at the instructions given in the earlier scriptures:

> Yahweh spoke further to Moses and said, "Take the finest spices: five hundred shekels of fresh myrrh, half as much (two hundred and fifty shekels) of fragrant cinnamon, two hundred and fifty shekels of scented reed, five hundred shekels (reckoning by the sanctuary shekel) of cassia, and one hin of olive oil. You will make this into a holy anointing oil, such a blend as the perfumer might make; this will be a holy anointing oil. With it you will anoint the Tent of Meeting and the Ark of the Testimony, the table and all its accessories, the lamp stand and its accessories, the altar of incense, the altar of burnt offerings and all its accessories, and the basin with its stand, consecrating them so that they will be especially holy, and whatever touches them will become holy. You must also anoint Aaron and his sons and consecrate them to be priests in my service. Then you will speak to the Israelites and say, "This anointing will be holy for you for all your generations to come" (Ex 30:22–31).

The oil/anointing meanings in this passage just do not refer to God's Spirit. But they form some of the first meanings upon which oil as a Spirit metaphor is later constructed. Only with the first kings, and later with the prophets, do anointing and Spirit come together. The importance of the passage is that it discloses the original meaning base upon which further meanings are later erected. The meaning is that what is anointed is set aside—consecrated—for the work of God. It is to be a work of holiness. When anointing and Spirit are conjoined, what is named is the perception that God's Spirit is significantly at work in these two figures—king and prophet—who guide Israel's fidelity to God. The

behavior demanded of the Hebrew people toward their kings and prophets is that of respect and obedience, because God is at work in them.
They are anointed. They are God's. They are (to be) holy as the whole
people is to be holy.

Reprise

After this extended examination of events in which the efficacy of
God's *ruach* is invoked, we must begin to generalize (though some of this
has been done along the way). God's *ruach* is normally experienced as a
transforming presence. The change wrought by the Spirit is not so much a
change in plans directed to some specific action, but an inner transformation. It has consequenes, of course, in human behaviors. But it is a
transformation that is directed to the very center of personhood—
heart—where personality itself is constituted. It involves a reconstitution, a re-creation, of the very sources of selfhood. Montague stresses that
the inner effect of the transformation tends to be "steadfastness" (*nakon*
= steadfast).[12] The verb built upon the root means "to be set up, established, or fixed." The verb described how the earth is firm and not to be
moved, because established by God (Ps 93:1). Thus the prayer of Psalm
51 for a clean heart is also for "a steadfast spirit" (v 12). The prayer,
therefore, is for a transformation that amounts to being re-established, or
redefined, or rebuilt, or reconstituted, or remade. It is radical and vital; it
is enduring and steadfast. Thus, even in the midst of the most terrifying
circumstances, with enemies on all sides, "surrounded by lions" (Ps 57:4),
the psalmist is still ready to sing and praise, because the heart is "steadfast" (and note the importance of music again):

> My heart is steadfast, God,
>   my heart is steadfast.
>   I will sing and make music for you.
> Awake, my glory,
>   awake, lyre and harp,
>   that I may awake the dawn (Ps 57:7–8).

The Spirit of God "seizes" a person, "comes upon," "comes into,"
and changes a person within. The contemporary expression that comes
to mind is that of becoming "attuned." In whomever the Spirit is efficacious, there is a keen sense of the things of God. One who is attuned
knows "how it ought to go," because the oughts of history are derivative

from God's Spirit. Thus, among people of the Spirit there is a deep sense of what justice requires, or outrage when justice is violated.

Recall Joseph and the relation of Spirit to the non-rational, the interpretation of dreams. The same discernment powers that make it possible to interpret dreams give one the power to probe, as it were, the "unconscious" of history as well, that is, the "deeper movements" of history. Joseph is called to govern precisely because his interpreting of dreams makes clear that he is a man of the Spirit.

In sum, the mosaic goes like this: always in the interests of creative transformation, the Spirit of Yahweh is at work *within* the human spirit, the human *heart,* effecting change and conversion in the deepest reaches of interiority. The Spirit *cleans* and *remakes* the heart so that it is able *to judge,* that is, *to discern* what is *of God.* The superabundant efficacy of Spirit with the prophets emphasizes the importance of *living forward* in fidelity to how covenant unfolds. Spirit forms the human instinct in *wisdom* and *steadfastness.* We are conditioned by Spirit in the valuational structures of our own spirit, so that we are *attuned* to God, and feel accurately the things of God, the better to understand, to yearn for, and to cooperate with the effective power of God in the shaping of history. Most simply: God's Spirit is where God's deep story is. Our spirit is where our deep story is. Through the immanence of God's Spirit in the human spirit, the deep story that is intended for history is transmitted. God is in us, as Spirit, in that way.

Spirit Christology

Language about God as Spirit is invoked early and widely in the way Christian communities interpreted the Christological meaning of Jesus. To put the question theologically, given the meanings that Spirit had in the religious world of early communities, how was the Spirit efficacious in the life of Jesus in such wise as to be constitutive of Jesus' Christhood? The final volume in this three volume study will explore in detail how Spirit Christology might be reactivated. But as we leave this chapter, it might yet be fruitful to recall with phrases and sentences the Christological confessions from the synoptic gospel communities.

The opening of Mark's gospel says that Jesus contrasts with John in that Jesus baptizes not with water but with the Spirit (Mk 1:8). When Jesus himself is baptized, he sees the heavens open and the Spirit descending like a dove. The action of the Spirit is accompanied by the Word of God calling Jesus "Son" (Mk 1:10–11).

For Matthew, the Christological event begins not with baptism, but with conception. What is in Mary is there by the Holy Spirit (Mt 1:20). The efficacy of the Spirit in the conception of Jesus justifies the claim that "Immanuel" is an appropriate interpretation of Jesus, i.e. that Jesus is "God-with-us" (Mt 1:23–24).

In Luke, even before the moment of conception, an angel says that the Holy Spirit will come upon Mary, and that the power of the Most High will overshadow her. The effects are that the child will be holy, and will be called by others the Son of God (Lk 1:35). When Jesus is presented in the temple, we meet Simeon. The Holy Spirit rests on Simeon. The Spirit told him that he would see the Christ. The Spirit leads Simeon to the temple the day Jesus is presented, and Simeon recognizes the Christ (Lk 2:25–32). The Spirit is not only a Christologically constitutive presence in Jesus, but likewise in the Christological faith of the believer. This is consistent with Paul's conviction that only those in whom the Spirit is efficacious can know who Jesus is and can then in and through Jesus cry out "Abba" to God.

In Luke, the Spirit and Word are effective presence at the baptism of Jesus (Lk 3:21–22). The Dove descends and the voice speaks.

In Luke 4, the public life of Jesus commences as Jesus is filled with the Holy Spirit, is led by the Spirit into the desert, and led then by the power of the Spirit to return to Galilee. Jesus' first public words, citing Isaiah 61, are that the Spirit is upon him, and has anointed ("Christified") him to proclaim the good news (i.e. God's words) to the world, but especially to the underside of human history.

I will say now what I will lay out in more detail below. There is a right instinct at work among the many theologians whose faith prompts them to develop more fully a Spirit Christology. But a full-fledged Spirit Christology will have to be in tandem with a full blown *Dabhar*/Word Christology. I hope the reasons for that are clear by the end of this volume.

Notes

1. Here, as in my earlier discussion of heart, I follow H. Wheeler Robinson.
2. Robinson, 1958, p. 17.
3. Robinson, 1958, pp. 17–18.
4. George T. Montague, *The Holy Spirit: Growth of a Biblical Tradition* (New York: Paulist, 1976), pp. 22–23.

5. Montague, 1976, p. 45.

6. Montague, 1976, p. 68.

7. Lloyd Neve, *The Spirit of God in the Old Testament* (Tokyo: Seibunsha, 1972), p. 114.

8. Montague, 1976, p. 67.

9. John Spencer, "Meland's Alternative in Ethics," *Process Studies,* 6/3(1976), pp. 165–180.

10. Spencer, 1976, p. 167.

11. Paul Ricoeur, *Symbolism of Evil* (Boston: Beacon, 1967), p. 15.

12. Montague, 1976, p. 75.

5
The Narrative Structure
of Hebrew Experience
Part IV: God's *Dabhar*/Word

Introduction

When most Christians hear "the Word" used to interpret Jesus, it is John 1:14 that comes to mind: The Word was made flesh. But there slumbers in the materials of the Christian scriptures another "word" Christology, and it is one that awaits development. The one I ponder would be resourced in the Hebrew *Dabhar,* and not the Johannine *Logos.* The latter, which I will address in Chapters 7 and 8 of this volume, has deep resonances with the Wisdom Figure.

Prophets often say, "The *Dabhar* of Yahweh came to me," but no one says simply, "I am Yahweh's *Dabhar.*" Jesus did not say this either, but his earliest followers called him God's announcement, God's good word (gospel). It is but a short step from talking about the gospel/good news of Jesus Christ, to calling him the good news: to preach the gospel, for Paul, is to preach Christ.

The God metaphors of *Dabhar*/Word and *Ruach*/Spirit are current together. For reasons that I will be naming later, I believe these two metaphors must be understood tandemly or coordinately: they work together to mediate the experience of God. Each tells an accurate but incomplete story. Together they the recount the epic of Yahweh and the Israelites.

Let us proceed, then, to look at *Dabhar,* never forgetting that it is half a model for the efficacy of God.

A Word That Is a Deed

Both the word for "word" and its usage are far less complex than Spirit. It will be somewhat easier, therefore, to assess what kind of Ultimacy the word "word" alludes to in the immediacies of Hebrew history. The many uses of "word" also constellate rather easily and clearly. Yet there is still something about the Hebrew "word" that is for us westerners who are children of the Indo-European language system almost another world of perception.

The Hebrew word for "word" is *dabhar.* It means both word and deed. Sometimes it also means thing because of its kinship to deed. There is a meaning linkage between word and deed and thing of fact. That's where we begin to sense something quite different from the English word "word." The root "dbr" is also found in the verb "to speak," *dibber.* There is no clear common agreement on the root meaning of *dabhar.* Many scholars, including Thorlief Boman in his study of *Hebrew Thought Compared with Greek,* feel that "driving forward from behind" is the basic meaning.[1] However, W.H. Schmidt in his article on *dabhar* in TDOT does not favor this interpretation.[2] Given the many usages of the *dabhar* notion in both Hebrew and much Mideastern thought, the "driving forward from behind" meaning seems indeed plausible. Boman notes that all over the ancient world of the East, Assyria and Babylonia, and in Egypt as well, the Word of God was "a mighty and dynamic force," and never primarily an expression of thought, which is our fundamental sense of a word in English.[3] Two texts from the earlier scriptures will help make an initial statement about the word/deed sense of "word" and "speaking" in Hebrew.

Esau, Isaac's first-born son, should receive from his father the blessing that will give him charge over the inheritance. With his mother's help, Jacob tricks his blind father into believing for a few moments that he, Jacob, is Esau. During these moments Isaac pronounces over Jacob the blessing that is meant for Esau. The blessing now made the older brother subservient to the younger—a very "wrong" thing. But Isaac's words have been spoken and their effect is deed, and the deed is done, as simple as that:

> When Esau heard his father's words, he cried out loud and bitterly to his father, "Father, bless me too!" But he replied, "Your brother came by fraud and took your blessing." . . . Esau said to his father, "Was that your only blessing, father? Give me a blessing too." Isaac remained silent, and Esau burst into tears (Gn 27:34–35.38).

No court in the western world would uphold the binding power of Isaac's will, in view of the fraud involved. But for the ancient Hebrew, when it was said it was done. The saying made a deed, formed a thing, caused an objective fact.

"Word" and "deed" are thus not two different meanings of *dabhar,* but the "deed" is the consequence of the basic meaning inhering in *dabhar.* If the Israelites do not distinguish sharply between word and deed, they still know of very promising words which do not become deeds; the failure in such instances lies not in the fact that man produced only words and no deeds, but in the fact that he brought forth a counterfeit word, an empty word, or a lying word which did not possess the inner-strength and truth for accomplishment or accomplished something evil. An Israelite would not be able to burst out contemptuously like Hamlet, "Words, words, words!" for "word" is in itself not only sound and breath but a reality. Since the word is connected with its accomplishment, *dabhar* could be translated "effective word" (*Tatwort*).[4]

In biblical theology, there is rarely a discussion of "word" that does not cite Second Isaiah as a sort of *locus classicus* for *dabhar* as dynamic, effective *Tatwort:*

For, as the rain and the snow come down from the sky and do not return before having watered the earth, fertilizing it and making it germinate to provide seed for the sower and food to eat, so it is with the word that goes from my mouth: it will not return to me unfulfilled, or before having carried out my good pleasure and having achieved what it was sent to do (Is 55:10:11).

The *Dabhar* makes facts!

Not Like the English Word for "Word"

It will help to say what the primary meaning of word is *not.* A word is not a vocable which, through the help of convention, lets another person know what thought, desire or feeling the speaker wants to share. That is not contrary to *dabhar,* but is simply inadequate by much. "Word" is one of the Hebrew names for how a being has consequence beyond itself; in fact, where the reaches of word go, there are the reaches of the speaker of the word. When used of God, the meaning is not unlike the familiar situation exemplified with Isaac, Jacob and Esau, which is the literal first meaning upon which the second meaning is constructed. Who God is, who God is for us, what God says and what God does—these are of a piece.

Like and Unlike **Ruach**

It should be clear, already, that there is certainly some deep similarity between God's Spirit and God's Word. Both are self-communications of God whose "deed" payoff is experienced in the creative transformation of historical experience. Both Spirit and Word are human ways of experiencing and describing how God is with us. In the testimony of the earlier scriptures, there is not an absolutely clear distinction between the efficacy of Spirit and Word. Yet the fact that both of these words are used so frequently suggests that they are not merely interchangeable. If these meanings are not clearly demarcated, there is yet, I conclude, a constellated meaning for each that can be empirically discerned by examining the events in which each is used—there are "effects" of God, noted in events, that are objectively distinguishable. These objectively identifiable experiences of the "witness" of God are our best clues to the "otherness" of God.

The **Dabhar** *of Yahweh*

We encounter the *dbr* word root in several forms: we find "the Word of God/Yahweh" in the singular approximately 240 times, and "Words of God/Yahweh" in the plural only about 20 times. We also find the verb form that has God speaking. Overwhelmingly, these usages occur in the later prophets (sometimes a later editor introduces them into titles given the work of an earlier prophet, such as the opening verse in Hosea, Zephaniah and Joel).

Nearly half of the occurrences of the "Word of God" are the prophetic Word/event formula: "The word of God came to me," or, "I am telling you the Word of God that came to me." The call of Jeremiah is paradigmatic of the formula use:

The Word of Yahweh came to me, saying,
"Before I formed you in the womb I knew you;
before you came to birth I consecrated you;
I appointed you as prophet to the nations."
. . .
Then Yahweh stretched out his hand and touched my mouth, and
 Yahweh said to me:
"There! I have put my words into your mouth.
Look, today I set you
over the nations and kingdoms.

to uproot and knock down,
to destroy and overthrow
to build and to plant" (Jer 1:4–5.10).

Jeremiah also intersperses his preaching with frequent authentications:
"it is Yahweh who speaks." He names ways in which Israel has failed
against God (Jer 2), and he calls people to conversion in the present (Jer
3:1–13); but the call to conversion is in the light of the messianic age:
"When those days come, the House of Judah will join the House of
Israel; together they will come from the land of the North to the country
I gave your ancestors as their heritage" (Jer 3:18).

Let us look at Ezekiel's call to the prophetic vocation. For our
purposes, this is an important text because it details the collusion of
Spirit and Word:

> [The vision] said, "Son of Man, get to your feet: I will speak to you."
> As he said these words, the Spirit came into me and put me on my
> feet, and I heard him speaking to me. He said, "Son of man, I am
> sending you to the Israelites, to the rebels who have rebelled against
> me." . . . When I looked, there was a hand stretching out to me,
> holding a scroll. He unrolled it in front of me; it was written on back
> and front; on it was written, "Lamentations, dirges and cries of grief."
> He then said, "Son of man, eat what you see; eat this scroll, then go
> and speak to the House of Israel" (Ez 2:1–3.10; 3:1).

Recall Montague's suggestion that Ezekiel's theological hand can
be felt in the priestly tradition of the creation account in Genesis. There
is a parallel between the Spirit which disposes the chaos to hear the
Word in obedience at the moment of creation, and the Spirit which sets
Ezekiel on his feet to listen to the Word that is spoken to him at his
moment of creation into a prophet. The Word-event notion is made
clear in the eating of the scroll. A first literal experience of eating is that
the food we take in actually becomes a constitutive part of us—as the
German proverb goes: *Man ist was man isst* ("One is what one eats," a
pun that doesn't come out in translation). Ezekiel eats the scroll and
likes the taste which is "as sweet as honey" (Ez 3:3). Because the
prophet speaks what he has heard and eaten, there is a near identification between Yahweh and prophet:

> The House of Israel will not listen to you because it will not listen to
> me (Ez 3:7).

Notice too that the prophetic pattern in Ezekiel is like that of Jeremiah: he tells Israel what it has done wrong, and how it should be living now in view of the new covenant, the age to come that is promised.

Haggai is the prophet who promotes the reconstruction of the temple. The Word-event formula begins the text: ". . . the word of Yahweh was addressed through the prophet Haggai to Zerubbabel . . ." (Hg 1:1). He recalls the rotten experiences people have been having: poor crops, terrible weather. He indicates that what must be done now is to rebuild the temple. This is a prelude to a new age which Haggai prophesies: there will be grain and fruit (Hg 1:19b); he will shake the heavens and the earth, and in the new age he will make Zerubbabel like a signet ring, for he is Yahweh's chosen (Hg 1:21–23). The word says what must be done now in view of what is to come.

Zechariah too is a prophet because the Word of Yahweh was addressed to him (Zec 1:1). After recounting his visions, Zechariah tells the people of the North that they must leave and return home. For Zechariah too the things that must be done are to be done in view of the new age that Yahweh promises.

> Yahweh Sabaoth says this.
> Aged men and women will once again sit
> in the squares of Jerusalem;
> each with a stick to lean on
> because of their great age.
> And the squares of the city will be full
> of boys and girls
> playing there.
>   . . .
> Yahweh Sabaoth says this.
> In those days
> ten men from nations
> of every language
> will take a Jew by the sleeve
> and say,
> "We want to go with you
> since we have learnt
> that God is with you" (Zec 8:4–5.23).

In Zechariah we see again a now familiar prophetic pattern. The Word of God comes to a person and makes that person a prophet. The prophet in turn discloses the Word received. The prophet, under the power of the Word, names ways of living that must be changed. The prophet announces the particular behaviors that are required right now as a response to a new age that is promised. And the new age is proclaimed in fantasized images of considerable particularity.

Speaking: **Dabhar's** *Verb Form*

Thus far we have focused especially upon the noun form of Word, *dabhar.* The intimate connection between word and deed can be sensed in translation difficulties with the verb form of "speaking." To catch the power of the Hebrew usage, often an English word other than simply "speaking" must be used, because the historical context conjures up the "deed" character of what God is saying[5]—for example:

> 1. Abraham went as Yahweh "said" = as Yahweh "commanded" (Gn 12:4).

> 2. If you listen carefully to his voice and do all I "say" = and do what I "command" (Ex 23:22).

> 3. Yahweh relented and did not bring on his people the disaster he had "spoken" about = the disaster he had "threatened."

> 4. Yahweh will carry out for Abraham what he has "said" to him = what he had "promised" him.

Yahweh's "speaking" is sometimes, in fact, Yahweh's "ordering," "commanding," "threatening," "promising," etc. Yahweh's saying and doing are the same.

Dabhar *and Law*

In addition to the preponderantly prophetic use of Word of God, God's Word or speaking occurs in the context of the law. A clear example is found in Moses' words to the people: "Yahweh revealed his covenant to you and commanded [said] you to observe it, the ten sayings which he inscribed on two tablets of stone. . . . He let you hear his voice out of heaven for your instruction; on earth he let you see his great fire, and from the heart of the fire you heard his word" (Dt 4:13.36). "Words" of Yahweh can also mean the entire Mosaic law. Moses addresses Israel: "Listen, Israel: Yahweh our God is the one Yahweh. You shall love Yahweh your God with all your heart, with all your soul, with all your strength. Let these words (the whole law) I urge on you today be written on you heart" (Dt 6:4–6). We also notice here that Word, as well as Spirit, is to work on the heart.

Reprise

It is time now to generalize. I want to suggest two generalizations about the "Word of God" as a way of experiencing and recounting how Ultimacy traffics with Hebrew immediacy. Schmidt observes that "aside from the construct expressions, *dabhar* [word] or *debharim* [words] refers to God more than 300 times. Approximately three-fourths of these passages relate to the prophetic word of revelation, and approximately one-fifth to the legal words of God."[6] *Dabhar* and its cognates occur, as Yahweh's Word of speech, almost entirely in the context of prophecy and law. About three-fourths of these uses (240 times) are simply "Word of God," almost all in respect to prophecy. More than 110 of these are the Word-event formula: "The Word of Yahweh came to me," or the like. Some 60 or so usages are in respect to the decalogue, or the law more generally, or to specific legal proclamations. While these law usages are certainly not negligible, what we find is that God's Word seems to favor the prophetic function. Like Spirit, Word emphasizes the messianic age to come, and how one must live now because of that promise. The Word of God, then, like the Spirit of God, seems particularly in the service of history's "living forward."

A second generalization, and it is this that I want to stress, is that the Word has a kind of historical particularity that does not so much characterize Spirit. God's Word tends to promote the historical transformation of a people by "shaping them up" in quite particular ways. If Yahweh's Spirit is valuationally and non-rationally transformative in the interior depths of the human heart or spirit, Yahweh's Word is a more pragmatic and programmatic effective presence of God. It tends to be *specific address* to *specific people* in respect to *the particularities of particular historical occasions.* The Word, in both prophet and law, specifies the shape which Israel's history is to take.

The constelled meaning that I feel a phenomenological generalization yields is that the Word of God is *occasion-specific.* The Word of God takes people where they are in their own lives, their own times, and their own histories. It then summons them on those grounds to the creative transformation that covenant offers. The occasion-specific Word is efficacious and dynamic. It has consequences, and thus its name is "Deed" as well. The Word of God accosts actual historical circumstances with concrete proposals about how lives need to move in order for covenant to unfold and usher in a new age. It is not as specific as: "Blow your nose" or "Cook stew today." It does say, however: "Move from way up north back to the south," or "Get going on building the temple," or "These (decalogue) are the behaviors you must do while those are the ones to avoid."

The Joint Efficacy of Ruach and Dabhar

Although some differences between Spirit and Word have been noted, as well as similarities, I want to press the question: Why Spirit *and* Word? To do this, I am going to suggest two interpretive schemas. The first will make use of the structuralist categories of deep story and particular story. The second will be based upon a belief that self-transcendence is always an option for human experience. The call to conversion presupposes the possibility of self-transcendence. The use of interpretive schemas to explore the interrelational between Spirit and Word involves an imaginative use of generalizations taken from other areas of experience and made to play upon the early Hebrew experience of God. At this point we have moved methodologically from the first empirical moment to the moment of reasoning with the help of generalized descriptions imaginatively and rationally applied.

Spirit AND Word / Deep Story AND Particular Story

Recall Crites' distinction, based upon structural anthropology, between the religious story (the deep story) and the mundane story (the particular historical shape the deep story takes). Every culture has a deep story, as it were, in its arms and legs and bellies. The deep story shapes all consciousness, but can never itself become, without remainder, a clear object of consciousness. We do not create our deep story; we awaken to it. But the deep story is not concretely actual. To be concretely real, it must be actually lived out in some historical setting, some place, some time. It must be instanced somehow. No one can sit down and decide to alter a deep story. Yet in gradual, organic ways it can undergo change over time. World views (not unlike deep stories) are born and die. A culture is under requirement to see to it that all its particular historical events are faithful to its deep story (a nation's Constitution is one of its attempts to symbolize its deep story; its holiday choices ritualize its deep story in celebration). Sufficient infidelities to a cultural deep story make a nation sick.

Analogously, individual persons have a deep story that is at the core of identity. We reflect our experience of an individual deep story when the particular actions of someone we know well make us observe: "Isn't that so like her?" or "He's not himself today; he never does that sort of thing!"

I want to suggest that God's own Spirit is close to what we mean by someone's deep story. We are talking about the very "who" of who someone is, in this case, who God is. The early Hebrews use the strongest "who" language that their experience has put at their disposal to talk about God's "who": the *Ruach* metaphor.

The very who of God communicates itself to human hearts (which is where they experience the seat of their own identity to be located). A people's deep story, then, takes shape in response to God's communication out of God's own deep story. The motif the Hebrews use to experience and describe their sense of who Yahweh is to them and who they are before Yahweh is covenant, with justice as its primal character. I am suggesting that the transformation of a people's interior sensibilities in keeping with God's deep story is what the earlier scriptures attribute to the immanence of Yahweh's Spirit.

Still the deep story must be lived out in particular ways. The Hebrew experience is that Yahweh gives them help here too. Based upon God's experience of God's people's actual history, the Word of God proposes scenarios for particular stories that are faithful to the deep story. These scenarios are not exact scripts ("blow your nose," "cook stew"). Their story possibilities are partly shaped and partly open. While some direction is given, a people must yet use its own ingenuity to implement.

The fullness of God's immanence and formative presence in covenant history are often experienced and described as Spirit and Word. *These are not two parallel models. Together they are one model. Apart, each is half a model.* Some—perhaps most—of western Christianity's awkwardness with the Spirit is that Spirit is half a model that goes with *dabhar*/word as its other half. Spirit hasn't been able to find its right place in respect to *logos*/word, for that's a model from a culture with a significantly contrasting narrative structure of experience.

Spirit AND Word / The Two Parts of Conversion

Now I want to suggest another analogy for Spirit *AND* Word. Most people believe that at any given moment life is open to improvement, that history can go better. It doesn't always happen, but at least there is usually a belief that creative transformation is always possible. We are open always to some forms of self-transcendence. If self-transcendence, for individuals and groups and all of history, is always a possibility, then this open-endedness is actually part of the world's deep story.

Tomorrow can be better than today. The possibility of self-transcendence presupposes two factors. The first factor is that there are genuine alternatives for tomorrow. There are stories that might be told that contrast with the story now being told. The second factor is that there are also some clear valuational implications. There is some referent structure that helps make a judgment that a particular alternative for tomorrow is in fact better than what we have today.

Self-transcendence presupposes that from the multiple stories that might be told, some of them would truly represent growth and qualitative increment. Otherwise there might be random increment, but that is different than believing that life regularly, not randomly, is open to self-transcendence. Therefore, when poised before a whole array of possibilities, a person needs a "nose" for sniffing out those possibilities which are indeed likely to result in something better. A person needs as well some drive for adventure in order to be willing to take the risks always involved in pursuing an often probable but not certain "better." This is especially true when the present situation is not a wretched one contrasting with a possibly better one, but a truly good one contrasting with a possibly better one. It's hard to give up an experienced good for a merely possible better. The good is often the enemy of the better!

These two factors are natural components of creative transformation: the presence of genuine alternatives and a felt valuational structure that makes possible the discernment about which of those alternatives is/are truly better. If God is experienced as fully involved in the world's creative transformation, then God must be involved in both of those ways. I am suggesting that God, trafficking with history as Word, has something to do with proposing particular alternatives for history to consider, as God did with successive transformations of covenant and with the instructions from law and prophets about how to live faithfully. And I am suggesting that God, trafficking with history as Spirit, makes available to the human spirit those powers of discernment that help us recognize the goods that are offered, urging us through the lure of qualitative increment, to go in pursuit. Given the natural dynamics of self-transcendence, one who believes deity to be at work within them would be likely to locate God's efficacy in this double momentum. It is not any less God's work because it is the "natural" way to go! It is God meeting us as we are!

Another Reprise: Imaginative Historicist Generalization

The ancient scriptures do not, of course, say that *Ruach* and *Dabhar* are metaphors. Clearly they are, and are so integral to the experience of Yahweh that it is more than fair to suppose that they belong to the nascent moment of experiencing God, and not simply to the afterword. These are metaphors that structure the experience before they structure the articulation.

Nor do the ancient texts offer any systematic treatises on *Ruach* and *Dabhar.* We only catch them as present in historical events and present in Israel's historical praise. I have attempted to see what kinds of events the metaphors *Ruach* and *Dabhar* mediate, and then to generalize based upon the historical events in which they are found. In Whiteheadian terms, I feel I have offered an "imaginative generalization" based upon observation of historical events. I stress the "free construction" at work in the imaginative generalization. There always is. There is no act of interpretation without some free construction.

The two analogies I suggested for relating the efficacy of Yahweh as *Ruach* and Yahweh as *Dabhar* are perhaps instances of a mega-story. It is clear to me that these generalizations are rooted in a task I thought I would undertake a dozen years ago (in a metaphysical fervor, I must admit): a process theology of Trinity. But my interests got redirected toward the Jewishness of Jesus, partly through an empiricist concern for what *Ruach* and *Dabhar* originally meant experientially, and before the development of a Stoic interpretation.

When I tried to force a fit between Spirit and Word and the primordial and consequent aspects of God in process natural theology, I saw some interesting parallels, even if not a fit. Those resemblances, however, play themselves out in the generalizations that I offered above.

After the end of Volume 3 in an epilogue, therefore, I will sketch out some parallels between the Hebrew metaphors of *Ruach* and *Dabhar* and Whitehead's immensely fertile natural theology. At the risk of introducing a "logos" that post-modernist leanings suggest shunning,

I will, I suppose, suggest a modest megaphysics around these two stunning metaphors for God.

Ruach/Dabhar *and Christology*

Ruach and *Dabhar* are metaphors that interpret (and thus mediate) God's effective presence. God makes the world through them, and redeems history through them. They are not hypostases of Yahweh; they are not even personifications. They are metaphors that speak of the modes of God's presence, sometimes with exceptional vividness.

We are called to be holy as Yahweh is holy. As Spirit, Yahweh remakes us at the depths of "who" we are. That "who" must be lived out in our relational daily world, i.e. in occasion-specific ways. As *Dabhar* Yahweh is present in our specific histories, guiding us in those occasion-specific ways. The "covenant" metaphor specifies the most general plot in the mega-story, and justice is the first face of history's holiness.

The Christological question is this: When Yahweh is known, experienced and interpreted through *Ruach* and *Dabhar,* how do we use these metaphors to interpret Jesus as Yahweh's anointed? That is the major task of the final volume.

In the chapters that follow, we will be looking at the *Sophia*/Wisdom metaphor and the *Logos*/Word metaphor. We will look at similarities and differences between them and *Ruach* and *Dabhar.* We will see how both of those metaphors of God have mediated our experience of God, and of Jesus as the Anointed, the Christ of God. Each shift in metaphor for God is a shift in what God means for us, and each God-shift is also a shift in what Jesus means for us—for, as Paul said, Christian faith recognizes God at work in Jesus, reconciling the whole world.

Notes

1. Boman, 1960, p. 68.
2. W.H. Schmidt, *"Dabhar," Theological Dictionary of the Old Testament,* Vol. III, Johannes Botterweck & Hilmer Ringgren, eds. (Grand Rapids: Wm. B. Eerdmans, 1990), pp. 94–95.
3. Boman, 1960, p. 58.
4. Boman, 1960, pp. 65–66.
5. Schmidt, *TDOT,* p. 97.
6. Schmidt, *TDOT,* p. 115.

6
Sophia Wisdom: Metaphor and Megastory

A Metaphorical Move

The metaphors, symbols and rituals of a living religion help adherents make religious sense out of everyday life. As Clifford Geertz has put it, religion is socially powerful precisely when it is able to help people to place their proximate acts in ultimate contexts.[1] We have already seen what the metaphors *Ruach* and *Dabhar* do: they correlate a people's daily life with their relationship with Yahweh. That is also what *Sophia*/Wisdom does in a different cultural context.

The practical wisdom of daily life was placed by these several Near Eastern cultures in an ultimate, religious context by relating the order of practical wisdom to a sacral order: *Sophia* exists in and comes from God. She orders life. And in many of the Near Eastern religious traditions, *Sophia* is finally hypostatized as deity herself.

People eavesdropping on Israel's conversation about God in the sixth century B.C.E. would surely have heard much about *Ruach* and *Dabhar*. But had we eavesdropped in the third, second or first century B.C.E., as we intend to do, we would have heard a new metaphor for God's active presence among God's people: *Sophia*/Wisdom. *Sophia* is often, in this setting, a feminine figure who mediates God among us. This would have been especially true among Jews in the diaspora. The conversation that we might have overheard is important to Christians because the *Sophia*/Wisdom about which they would have been talking was used to interpret the meaning of Jesus in very early communities. In fact, once this tradition got going and then facilitated a major move to a *Logos* understanding of Jesus, a fuller development of *Ruach/Dabhar* was precluded.

Ruach and *Dabhar* are metaphors for God whose literal meanings are grounded in human breathing and human speaking. Like all metaphors, they are richly polyvalent. The surplusage of meaning in metaphorical polyvalence does honor to the surplusage of meaning that tumbles out of any religious experience. And, of course, God is only "sort of" like those literal meanings. God is also "sort of" not like them as well. God is both sort of like and sort of not like *Sophia,* and *Logos*. In each case, the meaning of God undergoes significant change and so do human religious behaviors in response to this God-meaning or that God-meaning. The changes in metaphors for God happen because of cultural changes.

A culture's root metaphor changes in the same way that culture itself changes. No one plans an epistemic shift. New root metaphors well up out of new experience, new relationships, new challenges, new frustrations. The welling up is extra-rational. No one strategizes an epistemic shift; people do it without intending to by naming their experience in new ways, with enough cultural resonances that the naming sticks.

Those who forge religious metaphors don't leave records of the spiritual odyssey that led, in some "nascent moment," to that naming. The naming is not recorded, because religious root metaphors are co-primeval with the knowing they mediate. The knowing and the metaphor arise together. My sense of *Sophia*'s extra-biblical origins is that the foundational religious intuition which underpins her is bound with the experience of order. When *Sophia* begins to interpret Jewish religious experience in a central way, she/it is related to the narrative order of that great story. Christians press *Sophia* into service to interpret Jesus. I do not mean that with wily reason they choose her. But when *Sophia* is a natural part of religious consciousness, she wells up in the very experience of Jesus as God's ordering and saving presence.

In the several centuries before Jesus, *Sophia* is fashioned out of multiple impulses for multiple reasons. Some of her essential impulses are in the proverb tradition of common sense experience and sound human judgment. Other of her impulses are in the court schools of the Near East. Still other important impulses are from goddess traditions, such as Astarte, Ishtar, Ma'at, and especially Isis. The Hebrews borrow from these sources, but they reinterpret and adapt what they find to their own master story.

When *Sophia* replaces *Ruach/Dabhar* at center stage, it is not without reference to its predecessors. New symbolic meanings are constructed upon, presupposed, and need many of the earlier layers of meaning. But you cannot change your center stage metaphor for God and leave the rest of your drama intact. The master story is itself re-created in a shift of significant metaphor. There is continuity in the new story, but there is also novelty.

If the change of metaphor for God re-creates the Hebrew story, so too does the Christian story get re-created when there is a shift in metaphors for God, whose Christ Jesus is. In the re-creation there are continuities and novelties. If there are three and a half Christs in the early stages of Christian origination, then there are also three and a half Christianities, linked by their respective continuities and distinguished by their respective novelties. There cannot be a Christological pluralism without a Christian pluralism. For some that may be a disaster (and it can be that, too). But it can also be a necessary expression of an event of massive surplusage forging indigenous expressions in sharply contrasting cultural deep stories, stories which in their own turn spring from different root metaphors.

What is clear is that in the very early period of Christian origination, *Sophia*/Wisdom was used to interpret the meaning of Jesus and to create a community story among his committed followers. My long range interest is in seeing *Ruach* and *Dabhar* pressed further for Christological faith in a contemporary setting. It will be useful, however, to examine how *Sophia*/Wisdom and *Logos*/Word expressed early faith, what continuities web the diverse Christological traditions into a single faith, and what discontinuities mark the pluralism of faith. Hereafter in this and the following chapter I will regularly use the Greek words for Wisdom and Word, *Sophia* and *Logos,* to help signal their difference with popular English meanings for wisdom and word.

The literature on both *Sophia* and *Logos* is immense, as are the controversies. I hope in both cases to summarize some of the mainstream positions. My concern will be less with the philosophical intricacies, though philosophy can't be avoided, and more with their metaphorical epistemic functions.

I will first name some of the "places" in which *Sophia* is resourced, in the common sense traditions and in the goddess traditions. I will then reflect upon the metaphorical appropriation of *Sophia* by Jewish interpretation, naming some of the continuities and discontinuities with non-Hebraic resources. I will be distinguishing between the widespread wisdom tradition, and the narrower but important tradition of the *Sophia* personified figure. The latter is particularly relevant to *Sophia* Christology. Within Jewish tradition itself, I will point out continuities and discontinuities between *Sophia,* and *Ruach/Dabhar,* since these have formidable Christological implications. I shall be following a similar procedure with *Logos* in the following chapter.

The **Sophia/*Wisdom* Resources**

When we talk about the Wisdom tradition, wisdom is not really a technical term with a clearly defined range of meaning. It is, rather, a convenient way of grouping together some materials that share some characteristics. Wisdom, for example, includes the books of Proverbs, Job, and Ecclesiastes/Qoholeth, which Christian and Jews both include in the canon of scripture. The Catholic tradition, but not the Jewish tradition, also includes Ecclesiasticus/Sirach and the Wisdom of Solomon. But there are wisdom influences elsewhere as well, such as in the Psalms and in Esther.

Some of the wisdom materials are profoundly empirical. They transmit the common sense experience of daily living, and imply that right ordering in human life, discovered by experience, derives from God's ordering acts. Let us begin with these.

Many of the wisdom sayings are pithy statements that suggest the truth of long experience. The truth of relationships: "Iron is sharpened by iron, one person is sharpened by contact with another person" (Prov 27:17). For students and/or children: "Whoever loves discipline, loves knowledge; stupid are those who hate correction" (Prov 12:1). To a leader: "For want of leadership a people perishes, safety lies in many advisors" (Prov 11:14). The instruction in these kinds of sayings covers family life as well as the conduct of business among nations. And here the origins of the sayings are evoked. Many of these proverbial sayings appear to be, on the one hand, the kind of experience a family teaches its children, and, on the other hand, the kind of advice provided in court schools where younger people are being prepared for the service of the palace, or even, perhaps, where princes are schooled to become kings or pharaohs.

Indeed, not all the pithy little sayings that anyone utters get recorded in literary history. Before a saying gets the status of a proverb it must have been given a certain amount of currency among the people. These sayings that emerge initially out of a people's concrete lived experience must be "striking enough," in Roland Murphy's words, "to be taken into the patrimony of a people."[2] With the wisdom tradition of proverbs, then, we are really talking about embodiments of a tribal ethos. This wisdom tradition reflects how life is experienced, and instructs others how to get along in life, since this is the way it is. Wisdom, as von Rad points out, is really a whole world view. It names a way of understanding the really real.[3] Wisdom is a way of being in the world.

In the court or palace school, the didactic function of passing along tribal wisdom is widespread in the nations around Israel: Sumer, Akkad, Canaan, Egypt and Greece. Sumer has a wisdom tradition with many genres. We are familiar with these traditions because they are well preserved on clay tablets. The wisdom tradition in Sumer is associated with schools that functioned close to the temple and to the palace. There is speculation about whether Israel had such schools, since there is no clear testimony to that effect. Given the influence especially of Egypt, which had such schools, it would be quite plausible that Israel had them too, and that some of her wisdom comes from this point of origin.

There are some marked similarities between the Egyptian and Israelite wisdom traditions in the proverb genre. The influence from Egypt to Israel must have been large. Egypt gathered proverbs together under the names of various teachers. About a dozen of these collections have been preserved. One such is the collection of Amenemope, whose influence upon chapters 22 and 23 of Proverbs is obvious.

In Egypt there is a move from a didactic wisdom tradition to the hypostasis of wisdom in a divine figure. The central notion in the wisdom tradition of Egypt is *ma'at,* which is usually translated as justice and order—or an ordering based upon justice. *Ma'at* also becomes a deity for the Egyptians. There are temples to *Ma'at* and priests for *Ma'at.* With the goddess Ma'at we make the move from a wisdom tradition of sayings and schoolings to a *Sophia* figure. There are analogous goddess figures in other traditions, such as the Canaanite Astarte, and the Mesopotamian Ishtar.

It was probably the Egyptian cult of the goddess Isis more than anything else that finally prompted the Hebrew tradition to develop the feminine *Sophia* figure. Temple inscriptions and coins with her likeness show that worship of Isis was widespread in the Hellenized Mediterranean world in the final centuries B.C.E. Isis creates the world, and orders human civilization, with special attention to human love. This cult was attractive to Jews as it was to so much of the Mediterranean world.

There is a widespread agreement among scholars that *Sophia* came to prominence in Jewish religious consciousness as a response to the immense attraction of a mother goddess tradition. Jewish *Sophia* is praised in many of the same ways that the goddess is praised. Many of the traits of Isis became traits of the Jewish *Sophia,* and even textually, some first person speeches of the Jewish *Sophia* remarkably resemble those of Isis. The Egyptian goddess proclaims, "I am Isis, sole ruler forever, and I oversee the ends of the sea and the earth. I have authority, and though I am but one, I oversee them" (Cyrene 4).[4] *Sophia* "strongly reaches from one end of the world to the other, and she governs the whole world for its good" (Wis 8:1).

Christians will recognize quickly how much of this *Sophia* language becomes also Jesus language, including the soteriological element of being saved from sin through *Sophia's* instruction. It is my understanding that making the metaphoric connection between *Sophia* and Jesus is primarily an epistemic event and not a literary event—not a contrived embellishment, but an immediate religious knowing. It's the way people know when their assumptive world is a wisdom world. Let us look more closely at the Jewish *Sophia*.

Sophia *in the Jewish Experience*

During the two centuries before the birth of Jesus, *Sophia* rivals and in some places replaces *Ruach* and *Dabhar* as the major metaphor of God's creating, ordering and saving presence in the world. Because of *Sophia's* functions in the world and her unique relationship with God, it is no surprise that followers of Jesus quickly turn to her to understand Jesus: Does Jesus teach in the *Sophia* tradition? Is Jesus *Sophia's* child? Or is he the very incarnation of *Sophia?*

As I have already indicated, there is a very large wisdom tradition in Near Eastern culture. It has to do with wise teachings, with sage advice, with some of the psalms, etc. However, in the remainder of this discussion I will be primarily concerned with personified *Sophia,* or what I shall call the *Sophia* figure.

The wisdom literature that does not involve a personification of *Sophia* is larger than that which does. The *Sophia* figure functions principally in three places. She has a large presence in the first nine chapters of the book of Proverbs. Those nine chapters are the youngest part of the book; they serve to introduce the various collections of older sayings which follow. *Sophia* also speaks marvelously in the twenty-fourth chapter of Sirach. And some of her most vivid portrayals are to be found in the Wisdom of Solomon, composed a bare fifty years before the birth of Jesus.

Let us look in turn at some of the characteristics of *Sophia*. First, *Sophia* is a feminine personification of aspects and functions of deity. Second, a pre-existence is attributed to *Sophia*. Third, to her are attributed the acts of God: she creates at the beginning, she orders the world on-goingly, she saves and makes holy. Fourth, there is an insistent ambiguity about her equality (sometimes almost equivalence) with and her subordination to God.

Sophia *and Divine Feminine Personification*

Let us begin with the fact that *Sophia* is a feminine personification. To introduce the woman *Sophia* into a religious culture's language about God is no small thing when previously that language moved around "king," "male warrior," and (less often) "father." As I indicated in earlier chapters, there are small openings (especially in Isaiah) to feminine characteristics of God, and the male tenderness of God is sometimes affirmed in the prophets. Yet there is no development of divine femininity. *Ruach* is grammatically feminine, but never becomes a personalized feature of God's Spirit.

Sophia has the traditional feminine characteristics of nurturing and of sweetness. The foods she provides are like herself: sweeter than honey.

> Approach me, you who desire me,
>   and take your fill of my fruits,
> for memories of me are sweeter than honey,
>   inheriting me is sweeter than the honeycomb.
> They who eat me will hunger for more,
>   and they who drink me will thirst for more.
> No one who obeys me will ever have to blush,
>   no one who acts as I dictate will ever sin (Sir 24:19–22).

These descriptions are appropriated for Jesus in early Christian interpretation.

The addition of the feminine into the Jewish understanding of God's presence is a considerable move from the *Ruach/Dabhar* understanding of Yahweh. *Sophia* is even called the Consort of God who sits on the throne of God (Wis 9:4). That is the place for a goddess, alongside the god; yet the goddess notion is never entertained realistically. *Sophia* is only a personification. As vivid as *Sophia's* personification is, she is never hypostacized. There is no monotheistic space for a second divine subjectivity. There are no temples for *Sophia,* no priests, no holy days. Her status as a personification would never have been questioned.

It is also interesting to note that over the long term, Judaism does not finally mainstream the *Sophia* figure. Sirach and the book of Wisdom are not in the Jewish canon. In the rabbinic tradition, it is *Shekinah's* presence rather than *Sophia's* that titillates the religious imagination. For different reasons, Christianity never finally mainstreams its

Sophia Christology. But for a time, and in some places, *Sophia* is a serious and profound metaphor for God's presence in the world, and serves as well as a Christological metaphor.

Sophia's *Pre-Existence*

A second characteristic of *Sophia* is her "pre-existence" (which has become a familiar Christian category because of the Johannine *Logos* Christology). What does she pre-exist? Did she also have a beginning, and therefore post-exist something else? We will respond propositionally: *Sophia* exists before the world and after God. More important than the philosophical propositions is the poetry of the texts themselves, where we encounter the first language of religious experience, the metaphors of the nascent moment. Let us be reminded that the "stuff" for these metaphors was ready at hand from exposure to the larger religious and cultural currents around Judaism.

> Yahweh created me, first fruits of his fashioning,
>   before the oldest of his works.
> From everlasting, I was firmly set,
>   from the beginning, before the earth came into being.
> The deep was not when I was born,
>   nor were the springs with their abounding waters.
> Before the mountains were settled,
>   before the hills, I came to birth;
> before he had made the earth, the countryside,
>   and the first elements of the world.
> When he fixed the heavens firm, I was there,
>   when he drew a circle on the surface of the deep,
> when he thickened the clouds above,
>   when the sources of the deep began to swell,
> when he assigned the sea its boundaries
>   —and the waters will not encroach on the shore—
> when he traced the foundations of the earth (Prov 8:22–29).

Sophia, then, clearly has the personified status of a creature, albeit the first fruits of God's creating activity. She exists before the world exists, and that is what pre-existence names in her regard. Sirach makes the same affirmation: "Wisdom was created before everything. . . . It was he who created her" (Sir 1:4.9). Let us never forget, however, that the mode of her pre-existence is that of personification. A personified pre-existence differs, as we shall see, with both ideal and real pre-existence.

Sophia: *God's Presence in the World*

The next characteristic of *Sophia* to which I want to call attention is that she mediates God in the world. In earlier times Yahweh's manifestations are interpreted to be more direct. Yahweh talks with Adam, with Abraham, with Moses. And *Ruach* and *Dabhar* are neither personifications nor hypostases, but simply ways of interpreting the different modes of God's real presence in history. For the most part, *Ruach* and *Dabhar* are modes of God's activity in human history. But in the *Sophia* world of meaning, God tends to remain behind the scene, and *Sophia is* God's presence in the world. She and Yahweh understand each other perfectly. "She shares the secrets of God's knowledge" and she alone knows the works of God (Wis 8:4; 9:9). And if she has privileged knowledge of God, the reverse is also true: "God alone understands her path and where she is to be found" (Job 28:23). *Sophia,* therefore, can teach human beings about God because of how she is with God, both before the world and in the present moment.

Sophia is so totally configured to God that the experience of her is tantamount to the experience of God. "She is a reflection of the eternal light, untarnished mirror of God's active power, and image of his goodness" (Wis 7:26). The phenomenality of *Sophia is* the phenomenality of God. It is no wonder that Christian believers, familiar with *Sophia,* and convinced that their experience of Jesus is also their experience of God, use *Sophia* as a metaphor for Jesus as well.

How near to Yahweh is *Sophia?* I already named the image of *Sophia* as Yahweh's consort or queen. There is also a remarkable tent image for *Sophia's* privileged nearness to God in Sirach, an image not lost to those who live in the Negev desert today. Many of the bedouins who tend sheep or camels still live in tents. The tents are large pieces of canvas stretched over the tops of poles, but without sides all the way around. Some of the tents, in fact, still use stitched-together camel hides instead of canvas (they shed water even better, in the unlikely event of rain). When you pitch your tent with others, therefore, you live quite an exposed life with those other people. "Pitching your tent" is the equivalent of "living" or "dwelling" someplace. However it carries a meaning that "dwelling" cannot convey in English. That important meaning is the sense of exposed closeness. Pitching one's tent is a different metaphor than moving into a house.

> I came forth from the mouth of the Most High
> and I covered the earth like mist.
> I had my tent in the heights,
> and my throne was a pillar of cloud. . . .
> Then the creator of all things instructed me
> and he who created me fixed a place for my tent.
> He said, "Pitch your tent in Jacob,
> make Israel your inheritance."
> From eternity, in the beginning, he created me
> and for eternity I shall remain. . . .
> In the beloved city he has given me rest,
> and in Jerusalem I wield my authority.
> I have taken root in a privileged people,
> in the Lord's property, in his inheritance (Sir 24:3–4,8–9,11–12).

Especially since *Sophia* is spoken of as coming forth from God's mouth, the nearness of this statement to *Logos*/Word is easy to understand. Once Christians express their faith in the language of a *Sophia*/Jesus, the appearance of the tent/dwelling imagery for Jesus is also easy to understand. And that is exactly what we find in John 1:14: The Word was made flesh and pitched its tent among us. The fuller context is also similar to that of *Sophia:* created from eternity in the beginning, being sent from there (from the mouth of God) to here, and being here as a presence of God that saves the world.

Sophia *and the Divine Functions*

Yahweh created the world and with continuing providence, orders and guides the world. Covenant is the privileged form of ordering with Yahweh's chosen people. All salvation comes from Yahweh. *Ruach* and *Dabhar* were implicated in these divine operations, but as modes of God's activity. But *Sophia* seems to have a personality and an agency different from *Ruach* and *Dabhar,* albeit a personified agency.

Sophia comes from God before the creation of the world, and at creation she is there as a master craftsperson (Prov 8:30). It was in her that Yahweh laid the earth's foundations (Prov 3:19). Whatever has been created, all of it, has been created through her.

Secondly, like God—and, as it were, in place of God—*Sophia* guides human life. In Proverbs she is a street preacher, sharing her message in the public squares (Prov 1:20). Her guidance keeps people safe (Prov 4:6) and makes them honest (Prov 4:11). Wisdom brings up her own children and takes good care of them (Sir 4:12). In fact, wherever good guiding or even ruling is done, it is through the power of *Sophia* that monarchs, princes, nobles, and all human authorities are able to know and decree what is right (Prov 8:14–16).

Sophia is a saving presence. She renews the world generation after generation and turns people into God's friends; against *Sophia* evil is unable to prevail (Wis 7:27,30). Those who listen to her teaching come to understand God (Prov 2:5), for she is with him forever (Sir 1:1). Whoever finds her obtains Yahweh's favor (Prov 8:35)

Chapter 10 of Wisdom is perhaps the strongest statement of *Sophia's* saving activity, for to her is attributed simply and without qualification what Yahweh has done. There is a near identification of *Sophia* with God. She rescues Adam from the fall. *Sophia* saves the world from the flood by intervening through Noah. *Sophia* delivers the Hebrews from Egypt, takes them across the Red Sea, guides them through the desert by day and by night, etc. *Sophia's* activities in guiding and saving history are precisely Yahweh's activities. I insist again that for Jews *Sophia* remains, however vivid, always and only a personification and not an hypostasis. Or, to put it differently, she is a metaphor of God, facilitating a new cultural experience of Yahweh, adopted and adapted from goddess worship.

I have roamed rather randomly through Wisdom texts that reflect how *Sophia* does what God does. Each of the Wisdom texts has its own character, and it is not fully fair to their disparate character to roam randomly there. Yet there is in all of them a strong, direct sense that *Sophia* is doing God's work, and that while "from God" she is so close to God as to be nearly identified with God—but never beyond the limits of metaphorically mediated religious experience.

Sophia *and Her Ambiguities*

There are two different kinds of ambiguities in *Sophia's* religious world. The first concerns her derivation from Yahweh from before the world, and yet her near equivalence to Yahweh. The second concerns her relationship with the metaphors that dominated religious experience before her emergence, namely, *Ruach* and *Dabhar*.

Proverbs 8:22–31 is a key passage. *Sophia* is created by Yahweh before the world is made, and she is the first thing created (the first fruits of God's fashioning). Clearly she is *from* Yahweh, and not an equal. Yet how far back her derivation goes does not even seem to be a temporal question that is raised. She is there from the beginning. Sirach says that she is with him all the time (Sir 1:1).

It is important not to expect philosophical logic from metaphors that are polyvalent and contain elusive "is not likes." Metaphors contain no internal footnotes clarifying what is like or not like.

Sophia is like the other goddesses in the kinds of divine things she does. Goddesses and gods are from forever, and that temporal (or non-temporal!) sense hangs around the Jewish *Sophia*. The book of Wisdom is a Jewish book, even though not in the Jewish canon. Jewish monotheism, however, is satisfied by the derived status of *Sophia* as being *from* God. Still there is (were one to literalize the language) an equivalence with Yahweh when all of Yahweh's saving acts in history are accredited to *Sophia*. Yet she is never for Jews a divine hypostasis. In Jewish religious experience, *Sophia* is always and only a personification. The power of metaphor is precisely all the room it leaves for surplusage of meaning by steadfastly refusing to be specified without remainder, all the while telling a great truth. One of the great truths of *Sophia* is bringing the feminine into play as an essential metaphor for God.

The second ambiguity has to do with *Sophia's* relationship to *Ruach* and *Dabhar*. A new metaphor does not come forward and simply replace what went before. There are correlations with *Ruach* and *Dabhar* that *Sophia* must entertain. The new metaphor absorbs some of the old metaphor meanings so that continuity is signaled, though this does not seem to be done explicitly or consciously.

Let me give my conclusion ahead of time. *Sophia* performs both of the functions attributed to God through *Ruach* and *Dabhar*. Like *Ruach*, she attunes us to the deep story of God's intentions. Like *Dabhar*, she is concerned to direct us in historically specific ways. She is, though, more like *Ruach* than like *Dabhar*. Like *Ruach* she tends to speak from the heart to the heart. Less like *Ruach*, *Sophia* has more concern for intelligence and understanding than for affective knowing, especially in the book of Wisdom where the Hellenistic influence is more marked. In a word, *Sophia* takes on a more rational agenda than *Ruach*, orienting her activity to mind as well as to heart. And there are more descriptions of her that either relate her to Spirit, or attribute *Ruach* functions to her rather than *Dabhar* functions.

Here are a few typical examples. *Sophia* is a spirit that is friendly to people (Wis 1:6), and she is directly called the Lord's spirit who holds all things together (Wis 1:7). She asks that you keep her principles in your heart (Prov 3:1), and that you treasure her instruction in your heart (Prov 4:4). She is the "spirit of *Sophia*" (Wis 7:7) and the "holy spirit of instruction" (Wis 1:5).

On the other hand, *Sophia,* like a word, issues from Yahweh's mouth (Prov 2:6). She seems to be equated with the word through which Yahweh created (Wis 1:1–4). She makes clear exactly what Yahweh wants (Wis 9:16). Like *Dabhar,* she gives occasion-specific directions for historical work in history. To her is also attributed the Torah.

Little wonder then that this ambiguity is reflected in the early Christian tradition as well. *Sophia* is correlated with Spirit for Theophilus (Ad Autol. 2.15) and Irenaeus (Adv. Haer. IV.20.1). But for Justin Martyr (Dial. 129.3) and for Tertullian (Adv. Prax. 6) *Sophia* is correlated with Word. All this occurs in the larger context of interpreting the Christological meaning of Jesus

Because of their respective Christological implications, let us look at the contrast between *Ruach/Dabhar* and *Sophia* as metaphors of ultimacy.

The Key Figure(s)

Ruach & Dabhar: two correlated figures do two tasks	*Sophia* as one figure does both duties
Ruach: the deep ordering from God that orders the instincts of the world	*Sophia* is also the source of deep ordering
Dabhar: the historically specific ways in which God guides history	*Sophia* like *Dabhar* also gives specific guidance to history

Where They Operate

Ruach normally changes the hearts of people	*Sophia* is syncretistic; sometimes like *Ruach* she addresses the hearts of people; other times her work is more rational and mind-directed

What Kind of Existence?

Ruach and *Dabhar* are functionally modes of God's active presence	*Sophia* is a personification of God's presence

We will broaden this comparison in the next chapter by adding *Logos* to the chart.

Sophia *and Jesus*

I want to insist still again that, at least as I understand it, making the metaphoric connection between *Sophia* and Jesus is primarily an epistemic event and not a literary event—not a contrived embellishment, but an immediate religious knowing. It's the way particular people in a particular time and place ransack their culture in the very coming-to-know of Jesus, people in whose assumptive world *Sophia* is powerful and ready at hand. It is local knowledge of Jesus (which is the only kind there is!).

The meanings that both *Sophia* and Jesus have before the metaphoric connection is made are altered in the process. Womanhood is gone from the *Sophia*/Jesus, though gentleness and mildness remain. Personified pre-existence, absent from the synoptics except for a possible reference in Matthew, now is spoken of Jesus in John and in the letters. The two terms of the metaphor are not identical. The connection is based on the experience that in some ways one is like the other—even *very much like* the other, enough like the other to bend into a powerful metaphor.

Let us keep remembering that there is always a secret "is not like." The "is not like" is basically ignored so that the "is like" can do its work. As a result, we are seldom even vaguely aware of the distortions that occur in the making of the metaphor. Yet out of these two "distortions," new thinking territory is sculpted. Once the metaphoric connection is forced and gains currency, no one can think of Jesus again "in the same old way." Nor can those who have made this connection ever know *Sophia* again "in the same old way."

Sophia/Jesus is still primary religious language. It belongs to a nascent moment of knowing what Jesus means. We turn now to the Christian scriptures.

The Sophia *Jesus in Pauline Writings*

One of the difficult pieces of interpretation is allowing another voice to speak from its own horizon. Whether it's more difficult to hear a voice on a vastly different horizon or one that's barely different is a toss up. If the difference "seems" slight (but it is not thereby less crucial), we easily miss the strategic differences because we are beguiled by the resemblances. The strain in fathoming a very different world view is formidable for a different reason: we have to think the unthinkable, or at least until the moment of encounter, the unthought horizon.

When Paul speaks of the *Sophia*/Jesus to Greeks already seeking Wisdom, he must make clear how Jesus is a vitally different *Sophia* than their current pursuit, even though their own love/*philo*- for wisdom/ *sophia* provides a connecting link with the more Jewish love for the *Sophia* we were discussing above. In fact *philo-sophia*, or love of wisdom as a systematic, rational pursuit, is a Greek invention and probably Greece's most formative contribution to western culture. *Sophia* was a current enough daily word, at least for the educated, that being clear about a new *Sophia*/Jesus took a lot of Pauline work, as we see in Paul's correspondence, especially with the Corinthians.

But for us, the interpretative task is fiercely difficult because we do not live in daily ways in either a Greek or a Jewish *Sophia* construction of reality. Wisdom has a widespread popular meaning for us, something akin to good sense in older people who have profited from long experience. That meaning is not entirely wrong if developed in ways that Egyptians, Hebrews and Greeks developed it. Yet our normal connotation for wisdom is far too thin to work a good Christological metaphor.

For Christians reared in the western tradition, there is another, more serious obstacle to the original voice of Jesus/*Sophia*. Our doctrinal tradition has been so deeply shaped by later philosophical reflection upon Johannine materials that the real, personal pre-existence of later reflection tends to replace the personification that was *Sophia's* kind of pre-existence in her original context. There is not room to recount research already done, so I am simply indicating my basic agreement with the conclusions of James Dunn, that we must let *Sophia* mean to Paul, to Q, and to Matthew and Luke, what it meant in the world they inhabited.[5]

She, created by God before all ages, was the one through whom God in turn created all that is, and through whom God continually orders and saves human history. Paul follows this sense when he reminds the Corinthians that there is only one God from whom and for whom all things are—and while they are from and for God, they exist only and always through Jesus (1 Cor 8:6).

The phenomenality of the *Sophia* figure is the phenomenality of

God, and that is the claim that *Sophia* Christology makes for Jesus. One of the aphorisms of historical biblical criticism is that Jesus had all his followers stand with him and face the Father, whereas the tradition soon has his followers face him. I must admit my suspicion that the later tradition would have shocked the "Galileanly" Jewish Jesus. As a motif it does catch the immediacy of Jesus' experience of God and the incredible nearness of God to those who experience Jesus in faith. But the distortions that occur in the metaphor have disappeared from view, that is, the "is not like" does not hang around anyplace to instigate a critical balancing act of meaning. This is our problem more than Paul's.

Corinth is probably as tough an urban environment as one can find in the Mediterranean world for the rooting of Christian community. It has all the vices of a thriving port; in fact, Corinth has an international reputation for its moral disarray. It has the unwieldy complexity of immense religious pluralism, for it is a city that had opened itself to the cults and sects of its many merchants. And it has all the interest and advantages of being a very intellectually alive cosmopolitan city.[6] Paul finds himself having to deal with an intellectual elitism among the more philosophically minded, and with the gnostics who, for somewhat different reasons, also look for salvation in knowledge. There are deep disagreements and virulent arguments among the Corinthian house churches themselves.

Profound cultural appropriation is an integral process to the Christological transplanting of a Galilean Jew and his God into a major Greek city like Corinth. Paul is uniquely suited to the task because he himself was a child of both worlds. James D.G. Dunn paraphrases Paul's words to Jew and Greek:

> "What you understand by divine Wisdom, the divine image, etc., all those deep and profound insights into the reality of the cosmos and into the relationships between the divine and human which you express by those concepts, we see and proclaim to have been most fully expressed and finally realized in Jesus our Lord." And if this is the case [Dunn adds], then in the final analysis to speak of Jesus as Wisdom and in the role of divine wisdom is just another way of saying, "God was in Christ reconciling the world to himself" (2 Cor 5:19), "God in all his fullness was pleased to dwell in him" (Col 1:19).[7]

Paul, then, ransacks in *sophia* the partly similar and partly dissimilar traditions of Greek and Jew to force a connection.

But Paul must remind the Corinthians, of course, that the *Sophia* with which he identifies Jesus is not simply the equivalent of their *sophia,* not that of the Stoics and not that of the Gnostics. Paul stands on their heads both of those *Sophia* meanings by juxtaposing folly and the cross:

> After all, Christ sent me . . . to preach the gospel; and not by means of the *Sophia* of word(s) [*logos*] lest the cross of Christ be emptied of meaning. . . . As scripture says, "I am going to destroy the *Sophia* of the wise and bring to nothing the understanding of any who understand. Where are your philosophers? Where are your experts?" And where are the debaters of this age? Do you not see how God has shown up human *sophia* as folly? Since in the *Sophia* of God the world was unable to recognize God through [your] *Sophia,* it was God's own pleasure to save believers through the folly of the gospel. While the Jews demand miracles and the Greeks look for *sophia,* we are preaching a crucified Christ . . . a Christ who is both the power of God and the *Sophia* of God. God's folly is wiser than human *sophia* (1 Cor 1:17–25, passim).

Paul first locates Jesus' life within the *Sophia* of God, and then makes a direct Christological identification of Jesus with God's *Sophia.*

I want to cite also a passage from Paul's letter to the Romans in which *Sophia* is not mentioned by name, even though she provides the most likely context for the statement Paul makes:

> But the saving justice of faith says this, "Do not think in your heart, *Who will go up to heaven?*—that is, to bring Christ down; or *Who will go down to the depths?*—that is, to bring Christ back from the dead?" What does it say then? "The word is very near to you; it is in your mouth and in your heart," that is, the word of faith, the faith we preach (Rom 6:6–8)

Deuteronomy uses the same language for the Torah:

> For this Law which I am laying down for you today is neither obscure nor beyond your reach. It is not in heaven so that you need to wonder, "Who will go up to heaven for us and bring it down to us, so that we can hear and practice it?" Nor is it beyond the seas so that you need to wonder, "Who will cross the seas and bring it back to us, so that we can hear and practice it?" No, the word is very near to you, it is in your mouth and in your heart for you to put into practice (Dt 30:11–14).

The dependency of Paul's language on the Deuteronomy language is obvious. But we must recall that in Sirach the instruction which Wisdom gives is equated with the Torah, a theme which the rabbinic tradition also develops. In a Wisdom passage in Baruch the same pattern is found. Where is *Sophia?* Neither those who have risen above nor those who have gone below to Sheol have found her (Bar 30:15–23, esp. 19–20). The passage from Romans, then, is quite likely a *Sophia/Torah* interpretation of Jesus.

It is worthwhile noting that when the *Sophia* tradition develops, the fact that she gives instruction from God and that the *Torah* is also instruction from God makes the connection an easy one. In the world of *Ruach* and *Dabhar,* Torah is attributed to *Dabhar,* that is, to God's specific directives for human life. That task slips from *Dabhar* over to *Sophia.* But the larger thing happening is the slippage from one root metaphor to another, with a critical crossing over of attribution from *Dabhar* to *Sophia.* This is also a critical crossing over from a more indigenous Jewish *mentalité* to a more syncretistic Greek *mentalité.* And that is, of course, exactly what Paul is up to! By playing upon *Torah/ Sophia* and Jesus, the Galilean and his God play their way into Corinth and Athens. I would still want to claim that in Paul's presentation, this is more of an epistemic event than a literary predilection. Jesus/*Sophia* is how he is *first* known and *then* articulated. Paul, I think, is not winking at philosophy, but is speaking the primal language of his own bi-culturally mediated faith experience.

Whether Colossians is Pauline or deutero-Pauline is not settled by the scholars. But in either case, the cosmic Christology of the hymn in the first chapter can and should be heard as a *Sophia* hymn, and not as an expression of Johannine pre-existence:

> He is the image of the unseen god [so is *Sophia*]
> the first-born of all creation, [so is *Sophia*]
> for in him were created all things
> in heaven and on earth: [so too through *Sophia*]
> everything visible and invisible,
> thrones, ruling forces, sovereignties, powers—
> all things were created through him [and through *Sophia*]
> and for him [and for *Sophia*]
> He exists before all things [so does *Sophia*]
> and in him all things hold together [in *Sophia* too] . . . (Col 1:15–
>   17a).

That all these statements made about Christ can also be made of *Sophia* is clear from the *Sophia* figure literature we have purveyed.

After making these *Sophia* parallels in the Colossians hymn, the letter then weaves a soteriology upon the hymn. It makes attributions to Jesus that are not made to *Sophia*—that in the "holding all things together" function, for example, Jesus is the head of the body, the community (1:18), and that Jesus reconciles and makes peace through the cross (1:19–20). The *Sophia* metaphor is granted but then rebuilt as well. And with Colossians' reconstructed language is built a new house of being, a new way of interpreting and being in the world. And it is a different way of seeing and being in the world than would have been daily fare for a Galilean Jew in Jesus' day or for a Greek in Paul's day. It is a new creation.

The **Sophia** *Jesus in Q, Matthew and Luke*

Did Paul create the *Sophia* Jesus? Or did *Sophia* come from Jesus' own sense of himself, the memory of which is in Paul? The fact that *Sophia* interprets Jesus already in Matthew and Luke raises the question about whether we are hearing Jesus' own voice seeping through the Pauline reflections. The presence of *Sophia* in Q might bolster the case, since Q is so very early, and may even come from Galilee itself, or at least western Syria.[8] After careful historical critical analysis, W.D. Davies concludes that "the evidence does not warrant the view that Jesus himself had entertained a Wisdom Christology."[9] Dunn likewise concludes that "there is no evidence in the earliest traditions of Jesus' ministry that he understood himself as Wisdom, or as the incarnation of (pre-existent) Wisdom. . . . [And] the Synoptic tradition strongly suggests that there was a time when there was no Wisdom christology."[10]

In the three source theory,[11] the Q collection of Jesus' sayings which Matthew and Luke used is at least as early as Paul, and may well have been initiated soon after Jesus' death. Like other oral traditions that are later written down, Q itself would have undergone development, with some of the layers disclosing themselves to biblical criticism. I would argue that it is in Q that the *Sophia* interpretation of Jesus gets underway, and that *Sophia* is a development in Q. Let us get a glance at the evolution of this tradition.

Jesus complains that John the Baptist is rejected because he is too abstemious, and Jesus because he is not abstemious at all. In Luke's gospel, Jesus concludes that "*Sophia* is justified by all her children" (Lk 7:35), while Matthew has Jesus say that "*Sophia* is justified by her deeds" (Mt 11:19). It is likely that under Luke and Matthew is the Q saying that Wisdom is justified by John and Jesus who, despite the differences in their life style (abstemious and non-abstemious), are both *Sophia's* children. Matthew changes the text to the "deeds of *Sophia*" probably because he began the passage with reference to the deeds of Christ (Mt 11:2). This Q saying may represent the earliest *Sophia* interpretation of Jesus, i.e. as *Sophia's* child.[12]

Luke, probably close to Q, has Jesus attack the Pharisees/lawyers because of their treatment of holy people. Jesus reminds them that the *Sophia* of God says, "I will send them prophets and apostles; some they will slaughter and persecute . . ." (Lk 11:49). In a stunning move— stunning for then, perhaps not for us who read it now—Matthew's Jesus does not quote the *Sophia* of God, but rather *with his own voice* says, "Look, I am sending you prophets and wise men and scribes; some you will slaughter and crucify . . ." (Mt 23:34). Jesus, the child of *Sophia* or the doer of the works of *Sophia,* is now presumed to be *Sophia.* In Q Jesus is interpreted in relation to *Sophia,* but is still distinguished from her. In the passage just cited from Matthew the metaphorical knowing of Jesus has evolved in the faith community—the "she" and "her" are gone, and Jesus is *Sophia!*

Above I cited texts which indicate that only God truly knows *Sophia,* and only *Sophia* truly knows God. but because she does, she can instruct others so that they then truly know God from her. And by that knowledge they are saved. In a passage that, with its Johannine ring, seems strangely out of place in Matthew, Jesus says, "No one knows the Son except the Father, just as no one knows the Father except the Son and those to whom the Son chooses to reveal him" (Mt 11:27). Although Dunn suggests that this passage may be better understood as an expression of treaty/covenant, I am inclined to see here a *Sophia* metaphor since in the surrounding text *Sophia* is so manifestly invoked. The behaviors that belong to *Sophia* belong to Jesus, with the intimation, of course, that Jesus is *Sophia.* Metaphorically, the relationship of Jesus to God and God to Jesus is experienced as *Sophia* and God.

Reprise

The case I am making is this. It is unlikely that Jesus' self-understanding includes an essential reference to *Sophia.* But very early in Christian faith *Sophia* begins to mediate a community's experience of Jesus, their understanding of Jesus' relationship to God, and their interpretations of the presence of God to history in and through Jesus. It is a captivating, engaging and insistent way of experiencing the Christ-event which reaches easily into both Jewish and Greek social constructions of reality and makes a new house of being (Christological being) with telltale architecture from Alexandria, Athens, Jerusalem, Syria, etc. However, to let this early Christological faith speak authentically, it is important to let it speak with its own original voice, and not through the optique of a later *Logos* Christology.

The *Sophia*/Jesus has not evolved into a full-blown Christological trajectory in Christian tradition, and even less so a developed *Ruach/Dabhar* Christology. It may be that the feminist critique will recall *Sophia* to retrieve and develop the femininity of God through Jesus. Some fine theological reflection is moving in that direction.[13]

We turn now to the difficult territory of *Logos,* its meanings, and its metaphorical, epistemic function in the Christian experience of Jesus. The *Logos* of Stoic thought, and especially in Philo's development of it, has stunning likenesses to *Sophia.*

Notes

1. Clifford Geertz, *Interpretation of Cultures* (New York: Harper, 1973), p. 122.

2. Roland E. Murphy, *Wisdom Literature* (Grand Rapids: Eerdmans, 1981), p. 4.

3. Murphy, 1981, p. 3.

4. Cited by Elizabeth Johnson, "Jesus the Wisdom of God: A Biblical Basis for Non-Androcentric Christology," *Ephemerides Theologicae Lovaniensis, LXI (4), Dec. 1985, p. 270.*

5. James D.G. Dunn, *Christology in the Making* (Philadelphia: Westminster, 1980), pp. 163–212.

6. Gerd Theissen, *The Social Setting of Pauline Christianity: Essays on Corinth* (Philadelphia: Westminster, 1982).

7. Dunn, 1980, p. 196.

8. Ivan Havener, *Q: The Sayings of Jesus* (Wilmington: Glazier, 1987), p. 43.

9. W.D. Davies, *Paul and Rabbinic Judaism* (Philadelphia: Fortress, 1980), p. 158.

10. Dunn, 1980, 210.

11. Havener, 1987, pp. 19–29.

12. Havener, 1987, pp. 78–83.

13. E.g. Elisabeth Schüssler Fiorenza, *In Memory of Her* (New York: Cross-road, 1983), pp. 188–192; and Susan Cady, Marian Ronan and Hal Taussig, *Sophia: The Future of Feminist Spirituality* (San Francisco: Harper & Row, 1986).

7
A *Logos* Faith in Jesus as Christ

Get used to taking any word for your name, as God does. It is the only
way to take words on fully. (Edmond Jabes[1])

Introduction

The Johannine *Logos* wells up out of the immediacy of a community's faith experience and its finest cultural instincts. No verses anywhere in scripture have had the impact upon the evolution of western
Christian faith that the Johannine Prologue has. In the words of Jabes,
the Christian tradition has taken these words on fully, above all verses 1
and 14:

> In the beginning was *Logos*.
> And the *Logos* was with God.
> And the *Logos* was God. . . .
> And the *Logos* was made [real human] flesh,
> And pitched its tent among us (Jn 1:1.14).

The faith that promoted *Logos* displays a remarkable instinct for
supple metaphor. To begin with, *Logos* can reach into the *Dabhar*/Word
of earlier, more indigenously Hebrew metaphors. It is really rather different, but has enough in common to allow a felt connection. Secondly,
it allows Hellenized Jewish Christians who are already attaching *Sophia*/
Wisdom meanings to Jesus to bond readily with a *Logos* faith in Jesus.
James D.G. Dunn says that *Sophia* provides the bridge between the
exalted Christ of the earliest tradition and the pre-existent *Logos*
Christ.[2] And lastly, and very importantly for the spread of Christian
faith, it could speak to literate Greeks and Romans of that time who had
Platonic and Stoic *Logos* meanings running around in their heads and
hearts.

These Graeco-Roman Christians may not have been philosophically educated, they need only have been culturally attuned. Catholics
who may not have studied either scholasticism or Trent still had those
faith perspectives inside their religious sensibilities because they were
embedded in popular Catholic culture (e.g. the catechisms). And that is
what I am suggesting about Graeco-Roman culture. *Logos* was espe-

cially effective because it had resonances not only with the Stoic presence in Graeco-Roman culture, but because as a metaphor it has resonant first literal meanings in two other traditions: the more ancient *Dabhar* and the more recent *Sophia*.

All symbols are polyvalent. That makes them supple and arresting. *Logos* is a good example of very rich symbolic polyvalence. Polyvalence is also a matter of ambiguity since because of it metaphors are never univocal. The blessed ambiguity of metaphors is exactly what allows for so many layers of meanings. Metaphors are *graciously* polyvalent. Yet the polyvalence and ambiguity are not without limit because metaphors stay grounded in their first literal meanings. In the case of *Logos,* the referentiality is threefold: *Dabhar, Sophia,* and the Platonic/Stoic *Logos*.

No one knows for sure how much of the Johannine *Logos* is just John, how much is *Sophia,* how much is *Dabhar,* and how much is Greek philosophy. In an earlier era, scholars were more inclined to see a strong Greek influence. Scholars today tend to emphasize the Jewishness of John (without denying some Platonic/Stoic influence), and affirm a stronger *Sophia* influence.

What is apparent, however, is that *Logos* is a different metaphor of God than we have encountered in the synoptics or in Paul. With *Logos* there come new Christ meanings for Jesus. We have lived in a rich and long doctrinal tradition so deeply shaped by the *Logos* Christology that it is, in fact, very difficult to read the synoptics without importing meanings from the Johannine *Logos* Christology.

James D.G. Dunn's *Christology in the Making* has been a significant influence upon my reading of the Christologies of the Christian scriptures. He holds that incarnational theology makes its first appearance in the Johannine texts, and that other texts that have been read incarnationally are probably better read as an Adam Christology (e.g. the hymn of Philippians 2, or the *Sophia* Christology in Colossians 1).

This chapter is unavoidably the most philosophical of the chapters in this volume. Some of the *Logos* metaphor's literal first meanings are found in Stoic philosophy. Since so many of the issues that both promote and haunt the evolution of Christian doctrine are couched in those terms, we must hear these first and second century voices.

I will move chronologically in this chapter, beginning with Philo of Alexandria, a near contemporary of Jesus. We will move then to John's prologue. We will note a direct Philonic or a Philo-like influence upon early Christological exploration. Finally, I will speak to what I feel is religious damage done to any primal religious metaphor when it is ontologized, and what "the overcoming of metaphysics" (Joseph O'Leary's expression[3]) might have to say to the retrieval of primal experience.

I count *Logos* as one and a half metaphors because the word/ metaphor appears to originate more than one Christological meaning (maybe it should be two or three or four metaphors). John's meaning, of course, is not simply identical with Stoic philosophy. I think it is primal metaphor. It is highly "local" and original in its mediation of experience, even if influenced by Hellenistic voices. However, Stoic philosophy had a great hermeneutical presence to early Christian interpreters of John, and accounts for enough divergence to count them as at least one and a half metaphors.

Philo of Alexandria

Philo was born in the splendid Egyptian city of Alexandria about 25 B.C.E. and died about 50 C.E. He was a contemporary of the great rabbis, Hillel and Shammai, and of Paul, and of course of Jesus.

That Philo was *of Alexandria* is of no small consequence. The city was founded by Alexander the Great about three centuries earlier on the northern coast of Egypt. In the time of Philo, Alexandria was second only to Rome and had surpassed even Athens as an intellectual center. From early on, there was a large Jewish population in the city. In the early first century there may have been as many Jews in the city of Alexandria as in all of Judea.

The city is important because of the kind of meeting that occurred there between the Jewish way and the Greek way. In the first volume of this study, *The Galilean Jewishness of Jesus,* I gave my reasons for concluding that while Palestinian Judaism had indeed been Hellenized, the Greek way never penetrated into the innards of the Jewish soul, most notably in Galilee. But in Alexandria it was different and Philo is the finest witness we have to the difference.

Philo provides more than a passing glimpse into the syncretism of Greek and Hebrew that quickly characterized early Christian Christological faith before the Greekness effectively subsumed the Jewishness. With Alexandrian Philo in mind, it is easier to understand both the "why" and the "what" of the triumph of Alexandria over Antioch in the later battle for Christianhood. It was that Alexandrian victory that set the boundaries for orthodoxy and heterodoxy.

Alfred North Whitehead remarks that Alexandrian Greek thought in the early centuries of the common era is a different mode of thought than that of the great Athenian era.[4] Somewhat with tongue in cheek, he says that speculation and delight are the marks of Athens while the great Alexandrians were either right or wrong. Plato could never be converted into a respectable professor, Whitehead observes; but not so the Alexandrian scholars. There is, I believe some truth in this. One does not find in either the Alexandrian (or Antiochene, for that matter) theologians much sheer delight on speculating about the wonder of Jesus Christ. Polemic is the mood.

Philo's use of Stoic thought involves some development as well as reuse, yet his motives are apologetic and not primarily speculative. He is not, however, as argumentative as the later Christian theologians who interpret out of a similar philosophical system.

As I have indicated earlier in this volume, the great distance between Christianity and Judaism is not, therefore, between Athens and Jerusalem, but between Alexandria and Usha. It is in those cities of Egypt and Galilee respectively that the formative documents of Origen, Cyril, Athanasius, etc., on the one hand are part of a Christian catechetical school in Alexandria while, during the same period, the great sages are composing the Mishnah in Galilee.

Translation of the Hebrew scriptures into Greek, the *Septuagint,* was done in Alexandria by Jewish scholars thoroughly educated in Greek philosophy and rhetoric. But in Galilee the prophets and the law were read in Hebrew and commented upon in Aramaic. It was also in Alexandria, barely a generation before Philo, that the book of Wisdom was written, which insinuates into the *Sophia* tradition a marked influence of Stoic philosophy. Wisdom was admitted into the Christian canon but not into the Jewish canon. Judaism did not ingest Philo's experiment. It stuck with Hebrew and Aramaic. The rabbinic texts self-consciously reject Greek. But Christianity, embarking upon its own Philonic experiment, uttered a resounding yes, and left Hebrew and Aramaic, its mother speech, behind. There is not a right and a wrong here, but a deep cultural cleft.

Philo deserves some specific attention.

Logos *as Metaphor in Philo's Thought*

It is sometimes remarked that Philo is a religious Jew, but that all the reasons for his Jewish commitments are Greek reasons. His roots are in Plato, Aristotle and Pythagoras, but above all in Stoic thought. My brief discussion of Philo is very selective, in that I am focusing on *Logos* in his work. This is not unfair since *Logos* is indeed at the very core of his philosophical/religious belief system, even though it is a partial approach (neglecting, for example, his development of allegorical interpretation).

Philo is not just an appropriator of Stoic thought. As he uses it in his interpretation of the Jewish tradition of religious experience, it undergoes Philonic development. And no less, of course, does the interpretation of Jewish religious experience undergo Philonic development. Metaphor transforms meaning in both directions: the first literal meaning and the phenomenon interpreted. Thus, when the Stoic *Logos* becomes a religious metaphor, its own first meaning is itself transformed. The first meaning, to use the Gerhart/Russell image, inevitably undergoes some "distortion" (= change) when it is force-folded over the second experience to create a new meaning. And both the first meaning and the experience being interpreted are modified by the metaphoric fold.

This sort of language from the Gerhart/Russell book may seem somewhat convoluted, but it does name a truth that we see exemplified in Philo, that his way of using *Logos* changes both Stoic thought and Jewish experience. The Christian appropriation of *Logos* in a later Alexandrian interpretation does the same thing: it remakes the Alexandrian intellectual landscape as it revamps the terrain of Christological faith in Jesus.

When Christians first encounter Philo, especially Philo's descriptions of *Logos,* they are immediately struck by "how much that sounds like Jesus." That, I suggest, is testimony to how easily Philonic-like meanings folded over upon Christian faith in the tradition that quickly and assertively became normative.

The Ontological Otherness of God

The worshipfulness of God, no matter how it is interpreted, is central to religion. To deserve our worship, deity cannot just be "one of us." There is some greatness and power in God that is beyond (transcends) ours. Contrasting earlier Hebrew convictions about the worshipfulness of God with those of Philo will help us understand Philo.

That Yahweh was greater than all other gods, and the only one deserving of Hebrew worship, was a mark of Israel's henotheistic faith. This developed into an enduring, uncompromising monotheistic faith that there is no God but Yahweh alone. This one God is the Lord of Hebrew history, and is worthy of worship on the basis how God is disclosed in Hebrew history.

That Yahweh was interactively present with and in human history was clear to the ancient Hebrew experience. Being there in history seemed but utterly natural to the Lord of history. There was no puzzling over why or how one as great as Yahweh took history seriously—no surprise even, only profound gratitude and praise.

Part of being worshipful, then, is that Yahweh is not "just like" one of us. Yet neither is Yahweh totally unlike us. The feelings of anger, love, jealousy, compassion that interpret the Hebrew experience of Yahweh are analogous to ours. Without diminishing the fear of God, those like-us qualities of Yahweh kept God approachable.

For Philo God is radically other and radically inaccessible. He names God with the Greek, *to On,* Being Itself. And to make the same point vociferously, he adds a modifier, *to ontos On:* that Being which *existingly* exists! Created being is always made by another, so it does not existingly exist, it just exists. Because God is uncreated, only God is truly *to On.* For Philo, this radical difference makes God inaccessible to even the purest created intellect (*Legum Allegoriarum,* I 36; *De Posteritate Caini,* 15, 168F). There is an ontological divide between Being itself and derived being, between created and uncreated being.

The religious problem, and it is that, is how such a God can ever be experienced by created beings, given the metaphysical divide between them. That is an issue to which the *Logos* interpretation of divine reality is able to respond. The utter inaccessibility of God to creation requires a mediator. We need to look at the role *Logos* played in daily Greek discourse to understand how Greek philosophy made it a metaphor for divine presence. No one has demonstrated better than Bernard Cooke the effects of this distancing of God upon Christian piety.[5]

In Homeric Greek, *Logos* was not the common word for "word"— it was *rhema.* With the rise of democracy in Greece, rhetoric and logic (from *logos*) become very important disciplines. In a democracy, that political solution is chosen which is most convincing to those who decide. Rhetoric embellishes truth to make it attractive. And logic displays the reasonableness of the choice, based upon how things should go. Logic implies order.

In this cultural milieu, *logos* becomes a very common Greek word, with an increasingly important role in philosophical anthropology. In these meanings are rooted, I believe, the first meanings that underpin the evolution of *logos* as a metaphor that discloses the nature of reality. Reality is ordered and the order can be rationally discovered. Ultimate reality is ultimately ordered, and ultimately *logos* in the world is related to it. *Logos* names ultimate ordering. The world's ordering, if it is truly ultimate, cannot but be derived from the orderer of all. A word from political discourse is ransacked as a metaphor for God. Thus, even in Stoic thought, there is a credible case for the metaphoric nature of *logos,* and a second metaphoric evolution occurs through Philo's further use of it in Jewish religious thought.

The Logos / *Stage One*

The first-level metaphor that Philo invokes for the nature of God is mind, *nous,* and he plays this out with inexorable logic. What a mind does is think. What a mind thinks is thoughts. In the case of God, the mind thinks all thoughts that are thinkable, all ideas that are entertainable. The thought of God is the *Logos* of God. This is the most primal existence of *Logos,* the thought of God's mind.

There is a strange situation here whose analogue will haunt *Logos* Christology. Logically, mind comes before thoughts; therefore God/ *nous* comes before *Logos.* But chronologically, since to be a mind is to be thinking thoughts, mind and thought are as old as each other. *Logos,* even though it is *from* the divine mind, is nonetheless co-eternal with the divine mind. While there seems to be a causal priority, there is no temporal priority. *Logos* has the double character of being derived which no true God is, yet of having always been, which no true creature can claim.

The root of *logos* is *leg-,* which means "to gather," and not simply to gather in random ways, but rather to order or arrange as one gathers. This meaning carries over into the way God is interpreted. The *Logos* is not just a random collection of all ideas, but an ordered collection—or, better yet, a thoroughly, rationally ordered collection. Deity and order are inextricably bound together in Philo's thought.

Now when we ask about *Logos'* kind of existence in Philo, we must say it is ideal existence, in the Platonic sense. This notion is difficult for twentieth century western minds to interpret. In the popular meanings most of us share in this culture, ideal is opposed to real. Who wouldn't take a real five dollars over an ideal hundred dollars? In Platonic thought, however, ideal being has a perfection that no individual existing item ever replicates, even though every existing thing is somehow patterned after the ideal, and dependent upon there having been an idea(l) after which it could be patterned. For a Stoic like Philo, ideal, as a mode of being, is not the vacuous sort of existence it would seem to us "realists." In Philo's thought, the kind of existence which *logos* has is ideal existence. The first stage of this *Logos* is the ordered holding of all ideas in the mind of God, and its kind of existence is ideal existence.

The Logos / *Stage Two*

According to Philo, God doesn't just know all of the ordered thoughts in the same way all the time. God knows some of the ideas together, the way an architect might be imagined to think about some of the possible buildings that could be made from some of the possible materials. Yet no real city in the world can simultaneously instance all possible cities, nor can any building instance all possible buildings. No building can be all wood and all brick. One must choose one form or another, i.e. some specific, limited combination. So the architect *thinks* one buildable prospect from among the many buildable prospects. And that "thought building" is the seed of the real building that will emerge. It is along these lines that Philo sees God as analogous to an architect:

> [As the architect] begins to build the city of stones and timber, keep-ing his eye upon his pattern (i.e., in his mind) and making the visible and tangible objects correspond in each case to the incorporeal ideas, just such must be our thoughts about God. We must suppose that when he was minded to found one great city, he conceived beforehand the model of its parts, and that out of these he constituted and brought to completion a world discernible [first] only to the mind, and then, with that for a pattern, the world which the senses can perceive (*De Opificio Mundi,* 18).

The second stage of *Logos* is the selective thought of God that is the pattern for the world that God actually creates, like the blueprint of the architect. This is the *Logos* of God readied for expression in a created universe. This is still, however, only a divine, incorporeal thought world, and cannot be directly experienced by us creatures. It is only the physi-cal, corporeal world that finally is available to human experience through the senses. And that world will always be less perfect than the ideal, i.e. than the *Logos* itself, the incorporeal actual thought world, upon which the existence of the corporeal world depends. Even though the created world is less perfect than the Logos through which it was created, it nonetheless participates, through its ordered reality, in the *Logos.*

The two stages of the *Logos*/Word are characterized by Philo as the Word which remains internal to God, the unuttered Word, the *Logos endiathetos;* and the *Logos* which is manifested in creation, the uttered or spoken Word, the *Logos prophorikos.* The *Logos Endiathetos* is a pre-existent word, there from the beginning. The *Logos Prophorikos* is the creative word through which the created world comes into being. In the formative period of Christian doctrine, some writers make use of this twofold distinction to interpret Jesus as God's incarnate Word, a kind of *Logos Prophorikos.*

Logos/*God and* Nous/*God in Philo*

Philo's religious language for *Logos* will sound strangely familiar, even though it preceded Christological reflection by two generations.

Philo calls the *Logos*/Word the son of God, and sometimes God's first-born son (*De Confusione Linguarum, 146*). Through the *Logos* all creation is framed (*De Cherubim,* 37, 127). And "that same *Logos*/Word by which he made the universe is that by which he draws the perfect person from things earthly to himself" (*De Sacrificiis Abelis et Caini, 8*).

The *Logos* is a strange sort of hybrid. Since mind is always thinking thoughts, there never was a time when there was no *Logos.* The *Logos* shares existence from always with God. Yet the *Logos* is causally dependent upon mind, and as such is unlike true God. *Logos* is from God, while God is from nothing. God just IS!

Based upon the "like-God" character of *Logos,* Philo calls the *Logos* a second god. But based upon the "not-like God" character of the *Logos,* Philo uses a peculiarity of Greek grammar to protect the only One who is literally and truly God.

If one were to write that "That One is God, truly God," in Greek the article "the" would be used before the word "God" (in Greek, *Ho Theos*). It would sound clumsy in English to say "that One is 'The God.'" But it makes a clear statement in Greek. On the other hand, in order to say that someone is very much like God yet not exactly in all ways like the one true God, that one is called "God," but without a "the" before it (in Greek, just *theos*). In our idiom, we might attempt the distinction by writing God and god, but there would be no telltale when the word is spoken. This may seem picky, but the grammatical distinction is an important meaning distinction: a predicate noun with an article tends to say, "This is the real thing (the person)." But a predicate noun without an article makes more of an adjectival statement, "This is so like the real thing that I'll give it the real thing's name, but without the 'the' in front of it!"

Using this distinction, Philo calls the *Logos* god, but without the article, meaning so God-like that it is right to use the word. In Philo's understanding, the *Logos* is the only access human beings have to *Ho Theos,* so something true is named by calling *Logos* with the *Theos* name, for *Logos* is the human experience of God.

Philo's *Logos* stands on the border between God and the world, one foot in heaven, the other on earth. *Logos* is without beginning, and that is to have a foot in deity. *Logos* is derived, though, and has another foot in creation. And this border existence of *Logos* is the fulcrum of religious experience in Philo. Let us look then at the character of religious experience.

Logos *and the Spiritual Life*

Spirituality is the perspective from which a religious faith is lived. It will be shaped above all by how God is interpreted and how human meaning is construed. There is, then, a Philonic *Logos* spirituality.

The religious problem, as I noted before, is how a radically other God can be experienced by creatures. In Philo's thought, it is the *Logos* that gives God accessibility—*Logos,* that "borderline," mediating figure.

Logos, unlike *Ho Theos,* but like us, is *from* something or someone other than itself. Yet *Logos* is not merely a creature like us. Philo does not suggest that God created the *Logos* in the same way he created us. So *from* on the *Logos* side is quite different from *from* on our side. Different as it is in each case, *from* gives us a common meeting ground, for a shared *from* status means that *Logos,* while very other than us, is not totally other than us, as is *Ho Theos.*

Further, and equally significant as a basis for religious experience, there is the radical connection between *Logos* and *Ho Theos* from whom *Logos* comes. And there is a radical connection between us and *Logos* through whom we are created. Thus, *Logos* has a radical connection in God's direction and in ours. We have something truly in common with *Logos,* but nothing with God/*Nous.* God, as *to On,* remains outside our ken.

In Stoic anthropology, there is both a lower mind and a higher mind. The lower mind is the faculty of knowing that depends upon sense experience. It's the way we know particular created things.

The lower mind experiences individual things and events. Higher mind can then ponder over lower mind's data, coming as it does from immediate experience of individual things and events: "What is its nature?" or "What kind of order holds it together and relates it to other things?" or "What would this be like if I could imagine it as perfect, which no created thing ever really is?" This is the higher mind; it is our rationality at work. The higher mind considers data from the lower mind, but then abstracts from it nature and order. It lets go of the sense world to contemplate the order and nature of the world. When the order is reached in contemplation, a person makes true contact with *Logos*. When the perfect idea is reached by higher mind, even though imperfectly embodied in the created thing that initiated the pondering, then too a person makes true contact with *Logos*.

> . . . the world discerned by the intellect is nothing else than the *Logos* of God when God was already engaged in the act of creation. For (to revert to our illustration), the city discernible by the intellect alone is nothing else than the reasoning faculty of the architect in the act of founding a city (*De Opificio Mundi, 24*).

Thus Philo recommends that religious people should live according to true reason, *orthos Logos* (*De Opificio Mundi, 143*). We must not get entangled in created things in their concrete particularity. We must cut loose from them and rise above them, and in so doing connect with *Logos,* God's Child [Son]. What these interpretations do is desensualize holiness, disconnect us from body values, and also disconnect us from historical commitment.

If the *Logos* itself is called God's Son, then all people in the world who live patterned after *Logos*/reason are also God's sons (*De Confusione Linguarum,* 145–147). Notice that this too is what *Sophia* does. Those who follow her become God's children [sons]. That too is what Paul's tells us that *Ruach* does. It makes us call out Abba! and we become God's children [sons].

What kind of religious experience, then, is the human experience of *Logos?* A person

> . . . does not actually reach him who is the very essence of God (*ton kata to einai theou*), but sees him from afar; or rather, not even from a distance is he capable of contemplating him; all he sees is the bare fact that God is far away from all creation, and that the apprehension of him is removed to a very great distance from all human power of

thought. . . . The "place" on which a human being "lights" [however]
is . . . the *Logos* of God (*De Somniis I 65, 68*).

So the *Logos* becomes the great mediating figure who presences God in
the world through Reason, only through reason, yet truly through reason.

To his *Logos* . . . the Father of all has given to stand on the border
and separate the creature from the Creator. This same *Logos* both
pleads with the immortal as suppliant for afflicted mortality and acts
as ambassador of the ruler to the subject (*Quis Rerum Divinarum
Heres Sit*, 2–5).

The mediating function of *Logos* that Philo just described resembles the religious function of priest in Judaism. I recalled in *The Galilean
Jewishness of Jesus* that Jesus is a lay Jew. He is not a Jewish priest (he is
not from a priestly family, but from a kingly family). But it is not difficult
to see how the category of priest becomes a powerful metaphor for
interpreting a Christological faith in Jesus.

Stoic thought would have been part of the intellectual life of profoundly Hellenized people wherever there were great centers of learning
in the last century B.C.E. and the first century C.E. It should come as
no surprise that these Stoic ways of describing God's redemptive presence in human experience would be ransacked by followers of Jesus
Christ. Philo's thought would have been especially useful since he had
already put Stoic philosophy to work hermeneutically in interpreting
Jewish experience. Ceslaus Spicq, O.P., my New Testament professor at
the University of Fribourg, a great scholar of the letter to the Hebrews,
was convinced at one point that the author of Hebrews could only have
been a student of Philo.

Logos *as Philonic Metaphor*

We must recall now that *Logos,* or ordered reason, was a statement
about ultimacy, i.e. what ultimately should characterize the good human
life. What ultimately seems to count in Greek anthropology is used to
interpret God in religious experience. Jewish and Christian scholars both
tend to agree that Philo did not violate Jewish monotheism, and that
Logos is a vivid personification, though certainly a *very* vivid one.

It is the character of metaphor to be both like and unlike what it
mediates. *Logos* is enough like God to deserve sometimes to be called

with God's name, and enough unlike God to call for dropping the article before the noun to moderate the meaning. *Logos* is enough like us to require the *from-* word to describe its being, but enough unlike us to forbid the name creature.

There are manifold similarities between *Logos* and *Sophia,* but it is my perception that the radical connection with God in one direction and with us in the other deepens with the *Logos* metaphor in Philo.

Reprise

James Dunn's characterization of *Logos* is helpful and to the point:

> The *Logos is what is knowable of God, the Logos* is God insofar as he may be apprehended and experienced. . . . In the end of the day the *Logos* seems to be nothing more for Philo than God himself in his approach to man, God himself insofar as he may be known by man. . . . The importance of Philo at this point is that he demonstrates the sort of cosmological speculation which must have been present at least in certain circles of his day, and also that he shows how far a monotheistic Jew could go in using such speculation without, at least in his own eyes, compromising his monotheism.[6]

Philo, of course, had no person in mind as an incarnation of the *Logos.* And Philo is so patently committed to monotheism that it is also clear that he is engaging in vivid personification when he speaks of the *Logos* as the first-born Son of God. And it is a personification of ideal being, not concrete, personal being.

These concepts, and many like them, are ready to hand when Christians who have experienced God in the Christ-event go ransacking for metaphor in the sort of intellectual world in which Philo lived. The Philonic-like *Logos* interpretation of deity folds soon and effectively in metaphor upon the Christ experience.

Logos *and* Dabhar/Ruach

It is useful to recall some comparison and contrast between the Stoic *Logos* and *Dabhar.* Both can and do name the fact of an uttered word. Both can and do name the effective power of God in the world.

But the fuller anthropological contexts for these words contrast so deeply that the words finally carry profoundly different cargo. *Logos* is set in a culture in which rational functions are the defining characteristic of human nature. Reason is put to work as metaphor in religious experience. Then, in turn, the total rationality of God becomes a formidable "sacred canopy" under which this anthropology is legitimated, as the nature of a *Logos* spirituality makes clear. Being holy occurs through being rational.

That rational accoutrement, however, is not to be found in *Dabhar*'s cargo hold. *Dabhar* is a specific word of address to specific occasions, and thus trafficks intimately with the particulars of history. As something to do, *Dabhar* does not sidestep concrete particulars nor take leave of them. *Logos* too touches each concrete occasion, but in contrast one must take leave of concrete, historical particulars, and move to the abstract (the ideal) to meet *Logos*. *Dabhar* is a practical word, first and foremost. *Logos* is a rational word, first and foremost. *Dabhar* is preoccupied with concrete historical event, while *Logos,* as first mind, pulls away—abstracts—from the particularities of the world which second mind apprehends.

Ruach rather than *Dabhar* is the larger, more sweeping impress of divine order on history, an order fundamentally affective in character. Heart is its locus. Philo's *Logos* subsumes *Ruach*'s ordering presence, casting it much more rationally than affectively. Mind finds *Logos* while heart finds *Ruach.*

Dabhar and *Ruach* are modal in the character of their existence, while the Philonic *Logos* is pre-existent ideal being, highly personified. *Logos* is much more like *Sophia* than *Ruach/Dabhar. Logos* and *Sophia,* each as a single figure, tend to do double duty for the two complementary functions of *Ruach* and *Dabhar.* Dunn holds that *Logos* and *Sophia* are virtually interchangeable in Philo.

I think we must not underestimate the theological import of this very point, that *Logos* and *Sophia* are single "figures" for the work of God which the complementary metaphors, *Dabhar* and *Ruach,* are interpreted to carry on together. It is that which has made it difficult to find a truly comfortable place for pneumatology within a *Logos* Christology.

Logos *and* Sophia

Sophia like *Logos* is pre-existent, i.e. pre- the existence of the created world. Each originates *from* God, and each is also from God from the beginning, before all ages. Through each does creation take place. *Sophia,* unlike Philo's *Logos,* never assumes God language for herself. That feels like a clear religious intuitional choice, since the goddess language for Wisdom is so near to hand in Israel's proximate world, but is not taken up.

It is not unimportant that *Sophia* is feminine, grammatically and in its personification. *Logos* is grammatically masculine, and also carries the rational stereotype of the masculine. While both figures absorb the double functions of *Dabhar* and *Ruach, Sophia* tilts in a *Ruach* direction while *Logos* tilts a little more than *Sophia* in a *Dabhar* direction. Here I am naming tendencies, not equations.

The Johannine Logos

About the Johannine *Logos* there is not much to say and there is too much. There is not much to say because after the prologue, there is no further explicit *Logos* Christology. There is too much to say because the impact of the prologue has been so overwhelming not only upon later doctrinal development, but upon how the earlier gospels have been heard ever since (because of the doctrinal trajectory).

It is sometimes observed that the nineteenth century quest for the historical Jesus had the effect of breaking the hold of later doctrinal development over the interpretation of biblical texts. To understand these originative sacred texts, we must, as best we can, strive "to let the NT writers speak for themselves, to understand their words as they would have intended, to hear them as their first readers would have heard them, and thus to let their own understanding(s) of Christ emerge."[7] If later doctrinal development had made that difficult, so too has biblical understanding itself sometimes encroached upon other biblical understandings, e.g. the influence of *Logos* Christology upon the hymn of Philippians 2.

To repeat the leitmotif of most of this book: hearing those early and ancient voices adequately is never easy because stepping out of a present context is also never easy. As Max Weber once observed, we are suspended in webs of significance that we ourselves have spun. To continue the image, an Ethiopian metaphor says that when spider webs unite, they can stop a tiger. The western web of Christological significance, spun of *Logos* webs, has stopped the *Ruach/Dabhar* and *Sophia* metaphors from spinning their own webs of significance, at least from spinning enough in which Christian life might be suspended in significance.

It is next to impossible for most of us to hear the Christological significance of Mark or Luke or Matthew without *Logos* voices penetrating our inner ears. Some impact of a later world upon our interpretation of an earlier world is simply unavoidable. It does matter, however, that we listen with learned attention to the otherness of the other. And that's part of what this chapter is about.

This is a loaded task. The continual quickening of Christian life would not be served by a biblicism that leapt over two thousand years of experience and stayed where it landed, as if the interim had not been valid faith. However, the recovery of some early surprises, such as the Jewishness of Jesus, must enter into critical conversation with the accumulated and accumulating faith of Christian communities.

The prologue of John is unique. It is the only text in the entire New Testament that speaks of an incarnation of the *Logos*. I find convincing the evidence of James D.G. Dunn and others that this late text is the first New Testament text that refers to the incarnation of the *Logos,* and then speaks in terms of a real pre-existence. As I have indicated before, other texts are susceptible to this interpretation, e.g. the hymn in Philippians 2, or Hebrews 1:1–2, or Matthew 11:27. The first I take to be an Adam Christology, as a more adequate Pauline reading; the second I take to show a Philonic/Stoic influence; and the last is generally understood today in terms of Wisdom influence.

The dissimilarities between the gospel of John and the synoptics is a reflection of the pluralism of faith interpretations in the early churches. Given their different cultural moorings, the pluralism is not assimilable into some meta-structure. For example: the "kingdom of God" dominates the teaching of Jesus in the synoptics and is virtually absent from John. Another example: the Father metaphor for the God Jesus faces takes on a larger and larger life in the evolution of the gospels. In Mark's gospel, Jesus speaks of God as "Father" or "the Father" four times (and the retention of the Aramaic *Abba* makes Jesus' historical use of it highly probable). Matthew has Jesus speak of God in those terms 32 times. This language is in Jesus' mouth 173 times in John's gospel.[8] We are surely witnessing evolution in the faith articulation of the early communities. Phenomena like these alert us to the need to hear each gospel independently of the others to catch its own vocalizations of faith.

In the synoptics, Jesus focuses upon God and God's reign, with himself as its proclaimer and initiator. The disciples with Jesus face God. They are together *ad patrem.* In John's gospel Jesus often places himself at the center of his discourses, yet this does not mean that Jesus simply replaces the Father. Rather, the relationship between the Father and Jesus, his Son, is such that to see the Son is to see the Father. As awkward as the phraseology is, Jesus and the Father are there present in each other, a kind of mutual insertion of persons: I am in the Father and the Father is in me (Jn 10:38). Seeing Jesus is seeing the Father—that is patently clear to the faith of the Johannine community.

If one stands way back from the Johannine texts and asks what is the shape of the faith of the Johannine community (or better, as Raymond Brown points out, of the multiple Johannine communities), Joseph O'Leary attempts this generalization:

> The phenomenality of Jesus Christ, as apprehended in faith, is one with the phenomenality of God. . . . The phenomenality of Jesus is a divine phenomenality; it cannot be named in lesser terms.[9]

It is treacherous to try to catch any book of the Bible (or any book anywhere!) in a phrase. O'Leary's summary is as partial as any summary. But it effectively names a faith community's religious experience of Jesus in a way that explains why *Logos* had such power in mediating its experience. The metaphor, in the incarnation context, may have been articulated ever so briefly in but a single verse of the opening Johannine hymn. But that articulation was so perfect for the faith of that place and that time that it quickly seized the imaginal powers of the Christian mind and the incipient doctrinal development.

The Prologue

How Greek and/or how Hebrew is the Johannine material has long been a debated question. A major subset of the questions is: How Greek and/or Hebrew are voices that speak through the Johannine words? How indebted is John's *Logos* to *Sophia?* The presence of Stoic thought in Hellenized regions of Asia Minor, North Africa, and of course Europe—all areas of early Christian development—leads me to suspect that the prologue faith can at least not be oblivious to Philonic-like interpretations of *Logos.* Equally, it seems to me improbable that *Sophia* meanings are not hovering around the Johannine *Logos,* especially with the "tent pitching" that both *Sophia* (Sir 24) and *Logos* do. And given the example of Philo's conversion of *Dabhar* into *Logos,* I conclude that we must also presume that *Dabhar* is there in John's *Logos* too as perhaps a faint echo. Until we reach the incarnation verse, there is little said of *Logos* that is not sayable of *Sophia,* or of Philo's *Logos.*

Let us look at the first verse:

In the beginning was the *Logos* (true of *Sophia* and Philo's *Logos*)
and the *Logos* was with God [pros ton theon] (also *Sophia* and
  Philo's *Logos*)
and the *Logos* was God/divine [*theos*] (Philo, not *Sophia*)

The final part of the verse is perhaps crucial (though ambiguous). When
the *Logos* is with God, the article is there: *the* God, clearly God in the
most proper sense one can name God. But when the text says that the
Logos is God/god/divine, the article is not there with the God/god word.
In a Philonic sense this would suggest that *theos* does not apply to *Logos*
in the same identical way that it applies to the Father.

I called the usage ambiguous, however, because predicate nouns
sometimes omit the article, i.e. they are anarthrous.[10] So we do not
know whether the omission of the article reflects Philo's sense that this
means divine but not in the same sense as God's own godhood, or
whether the omission is simply grammatical. I suspect the Philonic-like
influence because of the ambiguous assertion of divinity on the one hand
and the subordination of Jesus to the Father that is consistently sounded
in John's gospel (and is consistent with Philo's *Logos* but less so with
later developments in western Christian thought).

The **Logos** *as Divine*

It is Yahweh who says simply "I am!" While that English is not an
adequate translation of the words of Yahweh to Moses, to hearers at that
time, it—with high probability—sounded clearly the note of divinity.
When John's Jesus says "Before Abraham was, *I am*" (Jn 9:58), the
implication is unmistakable.

This claim is implied further when Jesus authenticates his message
about God because "I am from him" [*hoti par'autou eimi*] (Jn 7:2, and
other places). While there is a sense in which this is true for any creature,
Jesus names it as that which distinguishes him, and as the basis of his
unique knowledge of God to which no mere creature can have access. He
is saying that his being is like the being of God rather than like the being of
creatures. Creatures are for the first time when they are created in the
world's creation. Jesus is the only human being who can speak of the glory
he had with God before there was any world (Jn 17:5).

The clearest expression of faith in the divinity of Jesus is in the
mouth of the most articulate doubter of them all. Thomas, who de-

manded empirical sense evidence of the resurrection, with an almost Petrine impetuosity says to Jesus: "My Lord and my God!" (Jn 20:28). In this case, the article is clearly with the God word, *ho Theos mou,* "the God of me," or "my God." This is the only instance in the Christian scriptures in which *ho Theos* is explicitly said of Jesus.

A *Possible* Sophia *Presence in the Prologue*

As we have seen already in Sirach, *Sophia* comes from God into the world and offers salvation to those who heed her. In Sirach 24 *Sophia* tells us that her tent has been in heaven (in the clouds), but that at one point Yahweh, who had fixed her tenting place with him, now tells her to pitch her tent on earth, in Israel. "Tenting" is exactly John's word in the prologue: The Word became flesh and tented among us. *Skene* is the Greek word for "tent." John uses the verb form, *eskenosen,* i.e. "pitched its tent."

One can't prove that John either did or did not have the Sirach text in mind. But given the similarities of John's *Logos* to *Sophia,* it's at least tenable. Certainly the tenting image was there in the Hellenized Jewish world of the Johannine community. It was at hand when profound religious experience was ransacked for religious metaphor.

The Logos *as Subordinate*

While the Johannine Jesus names the unique way that he is from the Father, there is also a clear affirmation of subordination. While the Son like the Father has life in himself, the life of the Son is granted by the Father (Jn 5:26), and does not reside primordially in the Son. Jesus does not speak from his own impulse, but says what the Father commands him to say (Jn 12:49–50). By himself, Jesus says he can do nothing (Jn 5:30).

The subordinationist texts are abundant. I simply want to point to the fact that they stand there along with divinity texts that do not elicit a subordinationist interpretation. This is not bothersome as long as one does not treat the Johannine texts as a systematic theological treatise and expect scholastic coherence, but rather as a record of faith expressed in a variety of metaphors that were there at faith's emerging [the epistemological function of metaphor]. The order is more that of a mosaic, many separate pieces that together do the portraying.

Two Interpretations Are Possible

The subordinationist texts are sometimes understood as statements which Jesus makes as a human being, i.e. how divinity comports itself in its human incarnation, conditioned thus (freely, albeit) by the very nature of human creaturehood. It is not likely, however, that this kind of distinction was explicit in the faith of the Johannine community. The two-nature conceptual model is forged through several centuries of Christological faith, and seems likely to require some Aristotelian presuppositions for its formulation.

There is yet another way to interpret these strange differences in John's Jesus, where Jesus is sometimes just like God and sometimes quite subordinate. The "like-deity" and "not-like-deity" texts perhaps reflect every metaphor's ambiguous condition as both "like" and "not like." If there is some Philo-like coloration to the *Logos,* which I am suggesting is both plausible and probable, we may be seeing the implications of metaphor.

The Stoic *Logos* itself is ambiguous. It is both exactly like God in that it existed from all time, and it is also exactly not-like God, because it originates from another. It has a "from" character which true deity cannot have. It is derived rather than primordial, and therefore is not like "the" God. I find it easy to imagine that the *Logos* Christological interpretation of Jesus simply and understandably bears the remarkable character of metaphor as it mediates a community's knowing of the Christ event.

These reflections are about metaphor. They do not and are not meant to be a metaphysical discussion of the nature of divinity and/or humanity. I presume that *Logos,* like *Sophia,* and like *Ruach,* and like *Dabhar,* are metaphors. When *Logos* is "folded over" on Jesus, the folding adds distortion to both the received meaning of *Logos* and to Jesus as folded upon and newly interpreted. The distortion is not a fault or failure, but a condition of disclosure which also tenders the gift of revelation. The revelation is what it means for Jesus to be the Christ of God when God is *Logos*/God. Further, it is that kind of revelation to a community of faith whose religious experience is that the phenomenality of Jesus is the phenomenality of God.

I said above that the Christological appropriation of *Logos* alters [distorts] the received meaning of *Logos* in the same act whereby it interprets Jesus. As I see it, there is a formidable distinction between Philo's *Logos* and John's *Logos.* The kind of pre-existence that characterizes Philo's *Logos* is personified and ideal (as in Platonic idealism) while for John the pre-existence of the *Logos* is personal rather than personified, and real rather than ideal. While there are many similarities between the two *Logos* traditions, it is because of the important differences that I have counted *Logos* as one and a half rather than as a single metaphor, as two considerably different constructions of meaning. Nonetheless, a Johannine *Logos* experience would probably not have been there in that community's knowing of Jesus had it not been culturally available in some form or another to ransack and reshape.

A Nod to a Philonic Presence in John

I concur with much of the contemporary recovery of strong Jewish elements in John and in the Johannine community. The issue, however, is not just Jewish or Greek, but "Jewish" whose root metaphors have been deeply touched by Greek root metaphors, and "Jewish" whose Hellenization has left the Jewish soul relatively intact at the level of root metaphor. I see the Johannine tradition more in the first of these two, not that the Jewish soul has been replaced by the Greek, but that a new sort of Jewishness emerges from the syncresis. Further, when I speak of a nod to a Philonic presence, I am not implying a direct, self-conscious appropriation of Philo, but of the influence of religious resources that are culturally at hand.

Jew and Greek alike have a concern with signs. "Were Jesus not from God, how could he do such good things for people?" is good Hebrew logic. From a different culture the saying that "the proof of the pudding is in the eating" is also a good Hebrew instinct: "A sound tree produces good fruit but a rotten tree bad fruit. . . . You will be able to tell good people by their fruits" (Mt 7:17.20). One son says "yes" to what his father asks, and then does not comply. Another son says "no," but finally goes about doing it. The proof is not in what one confesses but what one finally does (Mt 21:28–31). The judgment scene in Matthew 25 places primary emphasis upon having done the right things, regardless of any explicit reference to Jesus.

In John there is of course Jewish concern for the good things Jesus does, and their sign value. But there is also a more formal concern for signs, i.e. that the form of Jesus discloses the form of the Father, that one can see the Father in Jesus. There is further in John the sense that seeing this and confessing it frees us from condemnation. The experience of Jesus must be formally in our minds and formally in our words.

As Raymond Brown has pointed out, there is so much pointing by Jesus away from this world to the other world, that the Johannine letters have to be formulated to offer a corrective focus upon this world and this history and the redemptive possibilities for our behaviors here and now.[11]

Another characteristic of John's gospel that I judge to be a function of Greek roots is an explicit passion for truth, and for its conceptualization (seeing) and articulation. The Greek word for truth, *aletheia,* means removing (*a-*) from hiddenness (*lethe*), bringing out into the light, making visible. It is the antithesis of darkness. In the synoptics Jesus tends to be a discloser of the breaking in of God's reign, in terms of how we are supposed to be together with each other, and how together we are with God. All of this is, of course, because of who God is. In John's gospel, Jesus is a sign of God and calls attention to himself as that sign; he signs the truth about God. And the call is to the individual believer in God and in Jesus whom he sent.

I want to track a little further with differences between John and the synoptics, and formulate a possible conclusion favoring a nod toward a Philonic presence.

Mark's Jesus speaks of the kingdom of God 18 times, Luke's Jesus 37 times, and Matthew's Jesus 47 times. In contrast John's Jesus uses kingdom of God language only 5 times.[12] Contrast this with the fact that there are but 9 self-references from Mark's Jesus, but 118 from John's Jesus. Further, Mark's Jesus refers to God as his Father 4 times (but this includes the very important Aramaic *Abba* text), while John's Jesus calls God his Father 173 times.[13] These numbers signal a major change in how Jesus is interpreted, and I am guessing that the setting of the Johannine community's cultural narrative is not of passing significance.

The Father/Son relation between Jesus and God is there from early on, and the retention of the Aramaic *Abba* in Mark surely recommends "Father" as authentically and centrally interpretive of Jesus' sense of his own reality. In the synoptics, however, what Jesus seems to know most from that relationship is what the kingdom of God requires of us, and that the requirements are immediate because the kingdom of God is at hand. The parables are not so much inclined to say specifically that their point is to disclose who God is, but rather to say what the kingdom of god is like and what it requires of us (which, of course, also says much about God). The contrast between these traditions is marked: one tends to point us into history, the other out of it. One dwells upon the nearness of God, the other upon the distance (which Jesus breaches for us).

Further, in the synoptics Jesus does not focus principally upon each individual's relationship with God as much as upon how God's people are to be together with each other in this world because of the reality of the kingdom. Gerhard Lohfink says that while Jesus, of course, has immense compassion for those to whom he brings healing, the healing results not from the compassion but from the kingdom of God that is already breaking transformatively into our history, the kingdom that Jesus is ushering in.[14] Healing is what happens when God's reign is in place. Jeremiah told the Jews in exile to get on with living creatively even as exiles in Babylon and to make sense of life there as best they can because their own welfare (*Shalom*) can only be found in the welfare (*Shalom*) of the city itself. This is a kindred sensibility to Jesus' sense of God's reign. Welfare happens to individuals when it happens to the community in which they live. There are political implications to synoptic discipleship.

In John's gospel, salvific grace operates above all in and through one's personal relationship with Jesus and with the Father who is in Jesus and whom Jesus discloses. These sensibilities evoke the mystical encounter with God.

I think it vital that we not choose between the mystical and the political.

Three and a Half Metaphors

If there is no uninterpreted fact, then there is equally no uninterpreted experience of God. The metaphors that mediate the experience also interpret the experience and help create the experience. In so doing they contribute something of their own to the experience, but it is not detectable as such. We are hard pressed always to identify the free construction. We always hanker to get the uninterpreted "historical Jesus," unlacquered by any free construction.

The terra firma that western culture has sought in foundations loses its firmness under the post-modern critique, under the hermeneutical intuition, under the spell of historical consciousness. If we find our balance, it is a new kind, less like secure footholds on the land, and more like sea legs that learn to be secure upon a surface that rolls and waves and is always there. We even become aware that "foundations" is itself an architectural metaphor in need of critical reappraisal, because the "is not likes" become more apparent.

After these long chapters on three and a half metaphors, I want to compare and contrast them, illustrating what I think are the continuities and discontinuities (free constructions differing from other free constructions). I have tried to make the generalizations that follow respond to what experience has indicated, based upon the witness to experience in texts.

Kind of Functions

Ruach and *Dabhar* are not the only ways in which God's presence in the world is experienced, but they surely dominate religious discourse in much of the earlier scriptures. *Ruach*/Spirit/Breath/Wind names the deeper kind of ordering that Yahweh's does, when the who of Yahweh impacts profoundly upon the who of individual persons, and upon the who of a people called Israel. *Ruach* touches individual persons, but they are communal individuals and the touch through them is for the people.

Grammatically, *Ruach* is feminine. But *Ruach* is not developed as a feminine figure.

Dabhar is more specific in character. It doesn't convert personhood at its depths (like *Ruach*) as much as it addresses quite specific things that are to be done or not done in historical circumstances. The *Torah,* the way, is the speech of *Dabhar. Dabhar* gets specific things done according to God's intentions, which are best clarified under the rubric of justice. It is not surprising therefore that the prophets are the most frequent place where both *Ruach* and *Dabhar* are experienced, and that their essential passion is the righteousness or justice of God.

Ruach and *Dabhar* together are close to the total presence of God in Hebrew history. Their functions are coordinate and complementary as they enlist human collaboration with God in the redemption, or even co-redemption, of human history. Co-redemption is not an exaggeration, since human agency is a genuinely redemptive agency when it lives out its "yes" to *Ruach* and *Dabhar.*

Sophia does as a single figure what *Ruach* and *Dabhar* do coordinately. A first contrast is that *Sophia* is quite specifically a woman, a feminine figure marking the presence of God. She is once called the consort of the king, seated at the king's throne. *Sophia* is with God from the beginning. Through her the world is created.

It cannot but be a different kind of adventure with God that *Sophia* names, a different kind of religious narrative that unfolds from a *Sophia* root metaphor. What that might be has yet to be explored. Neither in

Judaism nor in Christianity did *Sophia* become a significant mainstream religious trajectory. *Shekinah* dominates the rabbinic description of God, as *Logos* dominates the evolution of the Christian doctrinal tradition. *Sophia* Christology, though very early, is sublated into *Logos,* and easily so because of metaphorical analogies between them. *Sophia* is largely a Judeo-Christian drama still in search of an author.

Sophia not only grounds the general ordering of the world; she, like *Dabhar,* helps order historical specifics, and is also sometimes correlated specifically with Word. To her as to *Dabhar* is attributed the fashioning of *Torah.*

In the biblical texts that deal with *Sophia,* she is more often described in ways that elicit *Ruach* than *Dabhar,* though both are there. In sum, *Sophia* as a single figure addresses the religious experience of God that *Ruach* and *Dabhar* present in their double functions.

Logos in both the Johannine and Philonic meaning also does double duty. The general order of the world is in and from the *Logos* of God. John's *Logos,* using *Sophia* imagery from Sirach, pitches its tent in the world, and like *Dabhar* guides the specifics of human history according to the divine plan. Sometimes *Logos* is like *Dabhar* in being at the root of particular instruction, but it is more like teaching than like the strategic planning that *Dabhar* sometimes seems to instigate.

Generally speaking, *Logos* like *Sophia* does double duty for both *Ruach* and *Dabhar.* Because some of *Ruach*'s function is absorbed by *Logos,* the Spirit has a difficult time in the tradition getting clarified, as I think the Nicene-Constantinopolitan Creed illustrates.

Kind of Order

Heart is the place where *Ruach* often leaves its mark, precisely because heart is the seat of Hebrew personhood. The ordering of *Ruach,* therefore, is rather affective in character. In ancient Hebrew anthropology, heart is not exactly in contrast with the rational, for "rational" is not an ancient Hebrew concept. Yet heart is not just a substitute metaphor for head to name the rational. As I indicated earlier, usage itself seems to indicate that heart/affectional names a different social construction of human reality than does head/rational.

Sophia, like *Ruach,* is the source of the deep ordering of the world. Biblical texts sometimes associate her with Spirit when that function is described. She, too, often addresses the heart. But also, in other biblical texts, and unlike *Ruach,* we begin to hear more rational attributes for

Sophia. Her intelligence and her clarity are celebrated. *Sophia,* syncretistic metaphor that she is, straddles two anthropologies.

Logos, while it does indeed have very much in common with *Sophia,* is not a heart-tending metaphor. *Logos* in the Stoic and Philonic traditions is profoundly rational and ideational. The bent of *Logos* in John for light, clarity and truth is consistent with the metaphorical cargo that comes from Greek anthropology.

The kind of order that *Ruach/Dabhar* requires tends to be under the rubrics of justice and mercy. The kind of order that *Logos* requires is that of reason. The latter is the great ally of those in power, the former the ally of those who live on history's underside. There is no politically innocent interpretation of God. I do not mean that there are always deliberate, consciously selected ideologies—only that the social location of one's interpreting always has a tilt. Our Christologies are no different.

Kind of Existence

The three and a half metaphors that mediate the experience of God differ with each other vis-à-vis the kind of existence implied for them. This may seem like a very esoteric exercise, but in fact these metaphors have the power to function as root metaphors, that is, they are large enough and splendid enough to create narrative structures for the lives of Christians.

Ruach and *Dabhar* are modes of God's active presence in the world. This modal presence is occasionally so vivid that it borders on the language of hypostasis, but it is more likely to be a personification. Most activity of *Ruach* and *Dabhar,* however, is not personified, but is simply a mode of God's active, historical presence.

While the Wisdom tradition is far broader than the feminine figure *Sophia,* I have dwelt upon this figure because of its appropriation in the Christological interpretation of Jesus. And very simply, *Sophia* is a personification of the cosmic and historical presence of a very other God brought near to human experience by her.

The *Logos* of Philo is indebted to Platonic thought. Its existence is that of ideal being. Ideal being is more perfect than real, concrete being, which is always a flawed instance of the ideal. Further, the ideal *Logos* is regularly personified by Philo.

The *Logos* of the Johannine tradition is presented as both real and personal, a significant contrast with ideal and personified.

The chart following this chapter summarizes the comparisons and contrasts among these three and a half metaphors of God.

So What?

Since the very earliest decades, the social location of the Catholic tradition has been largely Eurocentric, sometimes tribally so. It has been especially responsive to the *Logos* tradition, and singularly non-responsive to a *Dabhar* tradition, e.g. the Ebionite attempt to give the category of prophet a Christological centrality. As Karl Rahner has pointed out, for the first time since perhaps the apostolic period, the church is called to let go of its familiar Eurocentric identity, and open itself to broader cultural instantiation. One of the very fruitful ways of working at that is through the hermeneutical retrieval of the Jewishness of Jesus and of Christian origins. These, as Johannes Metz likes to say, are dangerous memories because they illuminate the historically conditioned character of faith and its forms. If at first blush there is the pain of having one's world view called into question, at second blush it is the suppleness and mystery of the Christian fact that are celebrated, and the release that comes—the permission, perhaps—to have as many alternative futures as we have alternative pasts. For all memories, Metz says, have future content.

The future content of the memory of *Dabhar* and *Ruach* Christology is the theme of Volume 3.

Notes

1. Edmond Jabes, *Book of Resemblances* (Hanover: Wesleyan Press, 1990), p. 103.

2. James D.G. Dunn, *Christology in the Making* (Philadelphia: Westminster, 1980), p. 162.

3. Joseph S. O'Leary, *Questioning Back: The Overcoming of Metaphysics in the Christian Tradition* (Minneapolis: Winston, 1985).

4. Alfred North Whitehead, *Adventures of Ideas* (New York: Mentor, n.d.), chapter 7, esp. p. 111.

5. Bernard J. Cooke, *The Distancing of God* (Minneapolis: Fortress, 1990).

6. Dunn, 1980, pp. 226–29 passim.

7. Dunn, 1980, p. 9.

172   Jesus and the Metaphors of God

8. James D.G. Dunn, *The Evidence for Jesus* (Philadelphia: Westminster, 1985), p. 44.

9. O'Leary, 1985, p. 221.

10. F. Blass, A. Debrunner, *A Greek Grammar of the New Testament and Other Christian Literature* (Chicago: Univ. of Chicago, 1961), p. 143.

11. Raymond E. Brown, *The Community of the Beloved Disciple* (New York: Paulist, 1979), pp. 103–109.

12. Dunn, 1985, pp. 34–35.

13. Dunn, 1985, pp. 43–45.

14. Gerhard Lohfink, *Jesus and Community* (Philadelphia: Fortress, 1984), pp. 12–14.

	RUACH & DABHAR	SOPHIA	PHILONIC LOGOS	JOHANNINE LOGOS
METAPHOR'S HISTORICAL FIELD OF MEANING	*RUACH*: Moved air, breath, wind; metaphor for the WHO of a person *DABHAR*: Speech that does deeds, utterance that makes be	*SOPHIA*: Insight accumulated from experience, pointing to order and right	*LOGOS*: Like *Sophia*, concerned with order, human and divine / clear stress on rational order / clarity / light	*LOGOS*: Affinity with Philo and contact with *Sophia* / hard to say how much of which / order disclosure, light, clarity
PLACE OF DIVINE ACTIVITY	*RUACH* addresses the affective core, the heart / remakes us at deepest levels *DABHAR* addresses the actor in human history in occasion specific ways	*SOPHIA* as a single figure does the two activities of *Ruach* and *Dabhar*—but tilts in the *Ruach* direction *SOPHIA* addresses the heart, but rational intelligence is likewise her concern / but more toward heart	*LOGOS*: Like *Ruach*, belongs to the inner life of God (*endiathetos*) / mind-*nous* But like *Dabhar*, *Logos* is also spoken to create the world (*prophorikos*)	*LOGOS* tends to do the same double duty as *Sophia* for the activities of *Ruach* and *Dabhar* / not easy to locate the Spirit philosophically/in addition preoccupation with relationship of Word to Father
KIND OF DIVINE ACTIVITY	*RUACH*: The WHO of God transforming the Who of people / remaking person at the core *DABHAR*: The world-making speech of God that addresses particular historical situations in particular ways	*SOPHIA*: The order as made by Yahweh and given to the world The world is made through *Sophia*	*LOGOS* helps creation bridge a relationship with the totally other. Is eternal like *Ho Theos*, but unlike *Ho Theos* is derived and is *theos* / the soteriological function has much to do with right ordering	*LOGOS*: the story it helps generate has a larger concern with orthodoxy than with orthopraxy (because of the rational centrality) / -praxy should follow -doxy
KIND OF EXISTENCE	These are strong personifications of Yahweh's experienced activity (two kinds of it) in Hebrew history.	Personified as a Woman / pre-existence, as a vivid personification, but not an hypostasis	*LOGOS* in Philo has an ideal (Platonic) pre-existence, and behaves in many ways like *Sophia*	*LOGOS* in John has a real, personal pre-existence / but there is a subordination in John that does not enter into mainstream *Logos* Christology

8
The Remarkable Career of *Logos*

Introduction

From early on, western Christian theology has had metaphysics as its primary mediating partner in its reflection upon faith. Its role has been manifold, but principally it has sought to make the experience of faith more plausible and more intelligible. In this final chapter, however, I will be suggesting that metaphysics is injurious to the metaphoric process. It pins exactitude on metaphors whose special disclosive powers shimmer with polyvalence.

Again, Metaphysics to Megaphysics

To call metaphysics "injurious" in this way is, of course, a critique that comes from two modern—or post-modern—directions, neither of which is blame-laying in character. Both of these have been addressed all along the way in this book, and bear summarizing. The one is concerned with historical consciousness, the other with the epistemological character of metaphor.

The historically conditioned and limited perspectival character of all thought and articulation could not have been perceived and acknowledged until the rise of historical consciousness. But with it, we recognize that no system of thought can fully transcend the social location of its origins. No system of thought is translatable without remainder into another system (another language, for example, or another culture). Large narrative accounts make sense: mega-stories or mega-accounts of nature [mega-physics]; but metaphysics as metahistorical is the -physics that needs to be overcome.

Further, there is no innocent system of thought. Every system has biases, and has a dark side as well as immense powers of illumination. All lights cast shadows. The Greek philosophical traditions that funded formative Christian thought could not have been aware of its historical and cultural limitations. It felt itself to be perennial. Today a "once and for all" claim to truth validity for any articulation is already a dark and deep shadow. To call the western Christian tradition Eurocentric is simply to acknowledge the social location of its origins, and its limitations.

The tension of a tradition is keenly felt in the Vatican II document on the liturgy, *Sacrum Concilium.* Paragraph 37 strongly encourages cultural adaptation: the church respects the gifts of different races and peoples, and those things not indissolubly bound up with superstition are responded to sympathetically, and sometimes admitted into the liturgy itself, "as long as they harmonize with its true and authentic spirit." This is a very sweeping invitation. The very next paragraph, however, requires that the substantial unity of the Roman rite must be maintained. A particular cultural expression is set as a meta-cultural norm. The serious problem/challenge of liturgy is analogous to that of Christian doctrine.

In the late twentieth century, the invitation to become a world church challenges a Eurocentric church to let new incarnations occur. "It belongs to the goodness of the world," writes Alfred North Whitehead, "that its settled order should deal tenderly with the faint discordant light of the dawn of another age. . . . How shallow, puny, and imperfect are efforts to sound the depths in the nature of things. In philosophical discussion, the merest hint of dogmatic certainty as to the finality of statement is an exhibition of folly."[1] No one doubts that norming must occur, but "how" it shall occur is at the front of the agenda for the third millennium. The old "how" is a "no how" in the age of historical consciousness.

Every system of thought sooner or later reaches the limits of its internal logic and its powers to elucidate. The fullness of being retains mystery at the outer edges of any thought system that broaches it. I shall be trying to hint that Nicea and Chalcedon both show tattered limits on the edges of their great confessions of faith.

I believe that there is probably no better way of "practicing" to become a world church than by addressing seriously the Jewishness of Jesus and, therefore, of our Christian origins. These are dangerous memories that call into question the present order and widen the road ahead—they are memories as Metz reminds us—with a future content. By "world church," I do not mean a Christianity or a particular historical version that has absorbed all other faiths, but rather a faith that has learned to adapt to multiple cultures.

Metaphors and Epistemology

When Aristotle discusses metaphor, he is concerned with its poetic functions of embellishment. That is a valid concern, but incomplete. He did not perceive, as does Paul Ricoeur, that thought arises in the first place from symbol[2] and metaphor,[3] that symbol and metaphor mediate knowledge in the very act of knowing, and therefore give knowledge itself a metaphoric hue. The implications of this for classical metaphysics' self-understanding are considerable.

The polyvalence of symbol belongs to the richness of interpretation. One thing is like another in several ways, and whichever of those several becomes centrally interpretive has the most to say, but the other possible meanings do not disappear. They are there on call. For example, *Ruach* means both breath and wind. As breath it stands for the depths of personhood, the "who" of a person. When used of God, it means, then, the depths of God's personhood as well. In 1 Corinthians 2:10–16, Paul uses Spirit to refer to personhood at its depths. Because *Ruach* is polyvalent, it also means wind, and can mediate our experience of God in another way. This meaning is on call for John. Some of the mystery of God, the otherness of God, is responsible for the unpredictability of God, and the unpredictable God is the *Ruach*/wind: you don't know where it came from and you don't know where it's going. Polyvalence at the very root of knowing enhances our sense of mystery, but also takes some of the starch out of knowledge's sails. They are not unflappable. For its own historical and cultural reasons, classical metaphysics would not have been aware of its metaphorical incubation, and therefore could not have had the modesty to acknowledge its ambiguity.

The second implication of metaphor for metaphysics is that every metaphor, including those from which metaphysical speculation takes rise, works for two reasons: that one thing "is like" another, and that the same thing is simultaneously "not like" the same other. In commitment of metaphysics to describe being as being, the "not like" does not consciously condition the system of thought. The "is not like" also participates in the metaphoric disclosure of what we know, but it is such a secret that classical metaphysics heard not its whisper.

As a root metaphor in the Greek social construction of reality, the first literal meaning of *logos* is founded in the values of rationality and clarity. But as a philosophical system, there is no attention to the "secret" ways in which reality is not all reason and all clarity. That remains a secret. And when *Logos,* because of its immense philosophical prowess, mediates a community's Christological experience of Jesus, the community gets caught in huge problems, many of which have to do with the never-owned ways in which the Christ-event "is not like" the *logos* metaphor that mediates the community's faith experience.

These then are some of the issues I wish to address here at the end of this study.

The Greek Presence

The very early presence of Greek philosophy to Christian theological reflection has been so well documented that there is no need to repeat.[4] Platonic and Stoic philosophy are especially influential in these early centuries. Aristotle is not absent, but his impact comes especially in the high middle ages, and most especially through Thomas Aquinas (through his metaphysics, at that time; but earlier through his logic and his rhetoric).

The preoccupation of this early period is with the relationship between Jesus as Son and God as Father, with some awkwardness about how the Spirit fits in. In the synoptics, the Spirit is Christologically active at the beginning of the story of Jesus, which is Jesus' baptism in Mark and his conception in Matthew and Luke. However, in the 18 verses of John's prologue there is no mention of the Spirit. In the concluding verse, John says that "No one has ever seen God; it is only the Son, who is close to the Father's heart, who has made him known." Here is expressed the distance of God which only one simultaneously close to God and close to us can bridge.

In the *Ruach/Dabhar* era, it is clear that both Word and Spirit make God known. But there is a certain dailyness to this presence. Even Moses saw at least God's backside through the slit in the rock.

The apologists of the post-apostolic times are primarily concerned with the Father-Son relationship, and pay scant attention to the Holy Spirit's relationship to them. Before the logic of *Logos* becomes clearer, some theologians equate *Logos* with Word (the majority), but some with Spirit. The Shepherd of Hermas considers that the Spirit is the Son of God become incarnate (Sem. IX, 1,1). For him, the Spirit is pre-existent, earlier in birth than all creation, and created the world—all Stoic attributes of *Logos,* and also attributes of *Sophia.*

Theophilus and Irenaeus make a correlation between Spirit and Wisdom. Justin Martyr also equates *Logos* with Wisdom: "As a beginning before all creation, God begot from himself a certain rational [*logiken*] power who is called . . . *Logos.* . . . He whom Solomon calls Wisdom was begotten as a beginning before all creation and as an offspring of God" (Dial. 61, 62). Tertullian also connects *Logos* with Wisdom. James Dunn concludes that throughout this early tradition, *Logos/ Word* is the principal category, and Wisdom is little more than a variant.[5]

While there are indeed many variations among the patristic writers, *Logos* is the controlling motif. The following sentences from Tertullian are not untypical of the larger conceptual framework: "Before all things, God was alone. But even then God was not without reason or *Logos*. . . . But he [God] has not always been the Father and judge, merely on the ground of his having always been God. He could not have been Father before there was a Son, nor judge before there was sin. He became Father by the Son and judge by sin" (Adv. Prax., 5, 6, and Adv. Hermog. 3). I think it clear that the Stoic *Logos* is metaphorically being "folded over" upon the Johannine *Logos* in ways that alter both experiences, Philonic and Christian.

Recall Philo's distinction between the *Logos endiathetos* which is *internal* to God, and the *Logos prophorikos,* which is *uttered* by God in the act of creation. That very language is appropriated by Theophilus of Antioch:

> God then having his own *internal Logos* within his own bowels, begot him, emitting him along with his own *Sophia* before all things (Ad Autol. II, 10). When God wished to make all that he had determined on, he begot the *Logos, uttered* the firstborn of all creation (Ad Autol. II, 22).

There is no such thing as uninterpreted fact, because our hermeneutical equipment always sneaks unnoticed into the inside of all our "facts," and then appears there as fact. I am anxious to indicate how deeply and rapidly the Greek mind got into the inside of the Christian fact. That will be true in every age. I do not doubt for a nano-second that someone other than me and probably later than me will point out how a particular theory of hermeneutics itself penetrates the "facts" to which I have been attending.

By glancing briefly at the two Councils of Nicea and Chalcedon I want to show that much of the problematic (heterodoxy) is owed to the systems of thought guiding interpretation.

Arius and Nicea

Commentators on Philo are generally agreed that Philo did not violate Jewish monotheism. But given the vividness of his development of the *Logos,* commentators have felt the need to affirm his monotheistic faith. The gray area in Philo's use of Stoic thought to elucidate Hebrew religious experience is perhaps some of the reason that Philo's was not the way the rabbinic tradition developed. No small part of the issue is the use of language that can simultaneously be interpreted in the framework of a Platonic/Stoic idealism, or an insistent realism. Using paradigms that traffic with idealism to interpret an experience of God for which the experiencers claim realism is a problem that plagued the formative period of western Christian thought.

The distance of God in the Stoic framework is foreign to the nearness of God which the synoptics show to be part of Jesus' profound awareness of "our Father." The need for a breacher of the distance is felt in John's gospel, and perhaps in the Wisdom Christology in the eleventh chapter of Matthew, but does not represent, I would hold, the interpretation of a fully Jewish Jesus.

It is my belief that Arius does not simply make a serious mistake, but shows the limits of a particular system of thought when used to interpret the Christ-event. If the *Logos* is created by God, or is the first-born of God, or is simply derived from God the way thought comes from a mind, then Arius feels compelled to say that "there was a time when he was not." For Arius, this can only mean that *Logos* is a creature, even if he is the first and the only perfect one of them.

In defense of Philonic Stoicism, a mind is a thinking reality and can only be a mind by dint of thinking thoughts. There is a causal priority of mind over thought, but not a chronological priority. Therefore *Logos* could be derived without there having ever been a time when *Logos* was not. But in the crossover from idealism to realism, the difference between causal and chronological priority becomes insurmountable. The issue is how to talk about the incarnate *Logos* as derived but without a beginning. Replacing creation language with that of begetting and processing satisfied the tradition but does not, of course, satisfy Arius. Recall the language of Nicea:

> And [we believe] in one Lord Jesus Christ, the Son of God, begotten from the Father, only-begotten, that is, of the essence of the Father, God from God, light from light, true God from true God, begotten, not created, one in substance with the Father.

Two things are to be noted: first, the preoccupation with interpreting Jesus in the language of Greek philosophy, and the awkwardness in finding language that still admits derivation (God *from* God), but doesn't imply a chronological beginning; and, second, the absence of the efficacy of the Holy Spirit from the innards of the *Logos* Christological interpretation of Jesus. As the formulation is further nuanced we confess that Jesus proceeds from the Father and the Spirit; but the nature of the Spirit's efficacy is not indicated. Uncertain how to integrate the Spirit philosophically into the internal structure of Christology, but knowing that trinitarian faith is incomplete without Spirit, the council opts for a liturgical solution: the Spirit, like the Father and the Son, is worshiped and glorified. As I have been indicating, no small part of the problem is that the efficacy of *Logos* has assimilated much of the efficacy of Spirit that is evident in the *Ruach/Dabhar* framework.

I want continually to make clear that I am not commenting upon the nature of Christian deity but upon the metaphoric processes that are involved in whatever and all we know about God from our experience of God.

What Arius did was make clear the limits of an interpretive framework. That is, of course, a greatly incomplete assessment of Arius, but, I believe, an accurate one. The recent study, *Early Arianism: A View of Salvation,*[6] makes a convincing case for the soteriological concerns of Arius in which way the debate comes out. I find their case especially interesting since there is little explicit soteriology in most of the Christological debates of the early centuries.

The Poetics of New Testament Christology

The New Testament, with its multiple metaphors of God, does not and cannot yield a single coherent systematic Christology. It is more a poem of faith than a treatise. Instead of Elizabeth Barrett Browning's "How do I love thee, let me count the ways . . ." we have a New Testament counting of the way: "How art thou the Christ, let me count the ways: thou art Son of God, thou art Son of Man, thou art Son of David, thou art Lord, thou art Master/Teacher, thou art the Alpha and the Omega," etc.

I am trying to say in this book that there is another poem that counts the ways in metaphor: "How art thou the Christ, let me count the ways. Thou are the Christ of *Ruach* God, thou art the Christ of *Dabhar* God, thou art the Christ of *Sophia* God, thou art one and a half times the Christ of *Logos* God." This is a very important sonnet today.

Ontologizing the images of a poem disempowers and makes brittle the metaphors through which the poem expresses meaning.

Chalcedon, Leontius of Byzantium, Piet Schoonenberg, Martin Heidegger

I have suggested that Nicea/Constantinople are responses to problems inherent in the philosophical model that interprets *Logos* Christology, namely, having to account for some form of derivation that does not imply creation. Procession and generation become the chosen terms. The non-use of creation was felt to keep divinity from being compromised. The derivation, however, is also maintained in the formula. The Son is not simply true God, but God-*from*-God; not simply pure Light, but Light-*from*-Light. Arius saw the philosophical problems as clearly as anyone, but was unable to pull back from ontology to let a mediating metaphor clarify experience the way that a metaphor can and ontology cannot. Spirit remained on the philosophical periphery of this discussion, and therefore on the theological sidelines as well.

The issues around Chalcedon have similar roots in a philosophical system and its limits. Alexandrian Christians, long practiced in having Stoic and neo-Platonic thought help express its *Logos* Christological faith, were committed to have nothing compromise the divinity of Christ. The Antiochenes were closer to those very regions where the Ebionites, whom orthodoxy found wanting, were trying to make "prophet" do major Christological function, to abide within Judaism which tended to interpret *Logos* Christology as incompatible with monotheism (also forgetting the difference between metaphor and ontology).

I think John McIntyre is correct in seeing Aristotelian categories brought into play in the Christological formula of Chalcedon[7] (but mingling Aristotelian realism with issues earlier set up in terms of Stoic and Platonic idealism). I want to lay out the terms to see once again the issues raised when philosophy moves further and further away from the metaphor-originated experience.

I will not be addressing the political dimensions of the Council of Chalcedon, but at least want to indicate that serious note of this council must attend to the electric socio-political energies between the power figures in Alexandria and those in Antioch, and the pitched alliances with pope and emperor. My concern is more limited to philosophical interpretation, but the social location of the arguments is important for other reasons.

The Greek word used for nature in positing the reality of both a human and a divine nature is *phusis* [also transliterated as *physis*].[8] The Greek word that is usually translated as person is *prosopon*. *Prosopon* means a concrete, particular instance of a nature. What Chalcedon affirms—and it is a minimal affirmation—is that one must affirm two natures, but only one person (to affirm two persons would destroy the personal unity of Jesus).

In Aristotle's work, *Categories,* we find a close parallel. Every individually, concretely existing thing is called a *first substance,* in Greek, *prote ousia.* Every *prote ousia* has a nature, is an instance of a nature. The nature is the *second substance,* in Greek, *deutera ousia.*

As a realist, Aristotle insists that there's no such thing as a nature that doesn't exist *in* things. Natures are only in things, unlike the Platonic system where natures (ideas for things) exist *before* the things that instance them. There is no nature of anything except insofar as there is a thing that has the nature. The *second substance* or *nature* word is also the word used in the Chalcedonian formula, i.e. *phusis.*

For Aristotle, an alternative word for Chalcedon's *prosopon* is *hypostasis.* You can't have a *phusis* that isn't instanced in an *hypostasis,* that is, in a concrete act of being.

This is the philosophical world that picks up issues which the Chalcedonian formula didn't. There is a philosophical problem inherent in the formula: if nature only exists really when instanced in a particular act of being, how do two natures get instanced when there is only one act of being, i.e. only one *hypostasis.* When the dust settles down, the position that holds the day is articulated by Leontius of Byzantium: the *hypostasis* belongs first to the divine nature, and later the human nature instances itself in the same *hypostasis.* This creates a unique reading for the human nature: it doesn't have its own original act of being, but "borrows" another's.

Therefore, following Leontius, the statement that Jesus' nature is divine is consistent with any other nature/instance statement, a nature with its own act of being. But then the statement that Jesus is human is unlike all other claims about anyone else being human. In all our instances, our humanhood is instanced in our personal act of being, but the humanhood of Jesus is instanced in an act of being that belongs properly to another nature. Take the sentences:

"Jesus *is* divine."
"Jesus *is* human."

The word *is* functions differently in the two sentences. In the first sentence (in Leontius' sense), the *is* is like any other *is* when we say, Abraham or Sarah *is* human, or the object in my front yard *is* an oak tree. There is a fullness in the divinity claim that Jesus *is* divine because the divine *phusis* has a proper *hypostasis*.

But the *is* in the second sentence is not like any other *is* since the human nature lacks its very own original act of being to instance it. So the "*is* human" does not not function in the case of Jesus as it does in the case of every other human being. There is not an exact parallel in "true God and true man" because the *is* predicates differently in the two sentences.

Most of the faithful have never grappled with these philosophical intricacies, but we have all been heirs to a way of interpreting Jesus as Christ that has made it difficult to believe he really was fully a human being. For many centuries we have been asking about the Christ the questions that Watergate made famous: "What did he [Jesus] know, and when did he know it?" The docetist heresy holds that Jesus is truly divine, but then also has some of the appearances of being human, but they are merely appearances. The tradition of Christian piety has largely been docetist in hue.

What the Dutch Jesuit theologian, Piet Schoonenberg, suggested in his book *The Christ* is that since we are historically certain of the humanity of Jesus, could we not reverse the interpretation of Leontius and posit that the *hypostasis* of the person Jesus is a properly human *hypostasis,* and that the divinity assumes the human *hypostasis,* just the reversal of Leontius.[9] The Chalcedonian formula itself does not take a position on this. In this case, the "Jesus *is* human" sentence would predicate of Jesus the same kind of humanity as every other human being, but would not make the *is* in "Jesus *is* divine" the same kind of *is* as the *is* in the sentence "God the Father *is* divine," for in the latter sentence, the divine nature has its own *hypostasis*.

Although Schoonenberg has added many qualifications and has strongly affirmed *perichoresis,* the mutual compenetration of natures in the one *hypostasis,* he has not been allowed to publish in all these intervening years. His proposal seemed to call into question that Jesus is truly divine. I believe that if Schoonenberg's proposal has that effect, then we must acknowledge that by the very same logic, the long held interpretation of Leontius calls into question that Jesus is truly human.

My concern is not to debate possible interpretations of Chalcedon, but to suggest that all systems of thought sooner or later exhaust the ability to illuminate experience. Some of the Chalcedonian "problems" are, in fact, the exhausted borders of a system of thought brushing shoulders with the mystery of being. Modern science calls into question many of the interpretative categories of Aristotle, e.g. the distinction between substance and accidents, the stability of natures, etc. Edward Schillebeeckx pointed some of these challenges to classical metaphysics in his book *The Eucharist*.[10]

Secondly, when the Stoic philosophical system is folded upon the Christ-event to interpret it, there is some distortion in both directions. The philosophical system is forced to describe an experience that was not among the experiences from which the system was deduced by philosophical intuition. The distortion in the philosophical direction is in having to posit two natures, one of which lacks *its own hypostasis*. The distortion in the direction of the Christ-event is in a preoccupation with a *Logos* Christology that does not account adequately for the subordinationist passages in John, does not in that context find a coherent pneumatology, and certainly does not philosophically integrate the kingdom of God soteriology of the synoptics.

These are not, perhaps, primarily faith issues at this point, but an acknowledgment, forced by the problems named, that all philosophical systems are limited in what they can account for, and, further, that the validity of classical metaphysics for our time is radically called into question.

Having said that, I want to name a tantalizing suggestion that comes from Martin Heidegger. In his opus magnum, *Being and Time,* as well as in multiple other places, Heidegger is eager to develop a new ontology by allowing being to speak for itself in the ways that it makes its appearances to us, there where it is when we meet it. He calls us to remember that the noun for nature, *phusis,* is etymologically related to the verb *phuo* and the noun *phos*. The verb *phuo* means to bring something out into the light (*phos* means light), to disclose something, to let something be seen, to make an appearance, to break through concealment, to let be known.

The root Greek sense of *phusis,* Heidegger feels, is precisely the way we name something based upon how it has made itself known to us, how it has come out into the light for us, what kind of a phenomenon it shows itself to be. The Latin word *natura* translates the Greek word *phusis*. But *natura* is derived from the Latin word for birth. And "with this Latin translation the original meaning of the Greek word *phusis* is thrust aside, the actual philosophical force of the Greek word is destroyed."[11]

I think that Heidegger overdraws the point, for Aristotle does sometimes equate *phusis* with birth.[12] But birth as well can be read in two ways. It can carry the weight of the "stable nature" that one is born with, the more Latin sense. Or it can also indicate what it is at birth that comes out into the light of day—almost a sense "that what you see is what you get." The second reading is more congenial to the Greek notion of truth. *Lethe* means hiddenness and concealment. To put the alpha negative in front of concealment, *a-lethe,* or unconcealment, is to get the root for the Greek word for truth, *aletheia.* In John's gospel from which *Logos* Christology takes rise, the Greek notion of truth has a large and haunting presence. What was in darkness Jesus brings into the light. Jesus is truth and Jesus is light. Jesus is disclosure. Jesus is the unconcealing of the concealed God.

However, it is the more Latinized sense of nature, as stable identity rather than disclosure, that has significantly conditioned our Christological tradition. We pinned the meaning down to that which is stable and enduring in itself, and lost the more phenomenological Greek sense that we are responding to being's self disclosing.

When Joseph O'Leary interprets the faith of the Johannine *Logos* as the experience of the community that the phenomenality of Jesus is the phenomenality of God, I think the original Greek meaning of *phusis* is very powerful: what God means for us is fully disclosed in Jesus and what human means for us is fully disclosed in Jesus, and the two meanings are not confused. Thomas can truly say, "My Lord and my God!" If Heidegger is not correct in his assessment of the original instinct (though I think he is), then Heidegger's own interpretation of *phusis* can be used heuristically instead, and we come to the same tantalizing possibility.

In any case, what I have tried to do is indicate how the problems of early western Christianity have been in great measure problems of heuristic equipment reaching its limits. They perhaps reach their limits even sooner because they are thoroughly Greek interpretations of a quite Jewish event. The Jewishness of that event must henceforth make clearer "appearances" in faith's reflection upon its experience of Jesus. For that to happen, we also need a fuller Jewish horizon upon which to locate that event. A lot of contemporary scholarship is addressing that very issue, but in so doing places great regions of the great tradition under great suspicion.

Spirit Christology

There has been an interest in recent decades in Spirit Christology. I believe there's a theological intuition that *Logos* Christology needs the complement, or even supplement, of a Spirit Christology. One of the most recent formulations is a Spirit Christology in dialogue with the *Shekinah* motif.[13] What I have tried to demonstrate in this volume is that *Dabhar*/Word and *Ruach*/Spirit are metaphors that together mediate the Jewish experience of God during one long and important period of Jewish history. When *Sophia* gains metaphorical prominence, she, as a single figure, largely does what was attributed to both *Dabhar* and *Ruach*. The texts we have suggest analogical connections sometimes (more often) with *Ruach*, and other times with *Dabhar*. But there is no secure sense that *Sophia* is a presence of God clearly distinguishable from *Ruach*. Therefore a Spirit Christology around a *Sophia* strains with an awkwardness built into the metaphoric structure of contrasting, even while similar, religious experiences of God.

Similar reflections pertain to the *Logos* metaphor-mediated experience of God. As I have indicated, *Logos*, like *Sophia*, absorbs the double functions of *Ruach* and *Dabhar*. But unlike *Sophia*, *Logos* tilts a little more in the *Dabhar* direction. Yet there is no secure sense that *Logos* is a presence of God clearly distinguishable from either *Ruach* or *Dabhar*, nor is it simply indistinguishable either. I would surmise that the non-appearance of Spirit in the Johannine prologue signals the issue. Spirit is not needed to make the Christological claim of the *Logos*. The relegation of Spirit to the final moments of the Nicea/Constantinople Creed (even then a liturgical and not a theological affirmation) signals the same issue. Therefore, a Spirit Christology around *Logos* strains with an awkwardness built into the metaphoric process of contrasting, even while similar, religious experiences of God.

I think that a Spirit Christology must be in tandem with a fully developed *Dabhar*/Word Christology to do the Christological work it needs to do. That is a task at which I shall work in the third and final volume of this Christology. This is not a judgment about the nature of God, but about the metaphors of God that mediate our experience of God, and the integrity of the metaphors.

Overcoming Metaphysics

At the end I return to some of the methodological concerns named at the beginning.

The rise of historical consciousness is concomitant with the demise of metaphysics. One can—and probably should—formulate mega-interpretations that operate within a language, a culture, and a specific temporal location. And mega-interpretations should be in dialogue across their boundaries, a conversation that is transformative in both directions. But we can no longer claim any meta-system validity across cultures and across ages.

I do not question the good will and intelligence of a long western theological tradition with metaphysics as its mediating science. It could not have been any other way, and it was immensely effective in the western appropriation of Christian faith. But at a time when we could not have recognized the culturally conditioned nature of a formidable doctrinal tradition, we canonized our articulations, and restrained faith in a Eurocentric thought-net.

Joseph O'Leary has stated the case for overcoming metaphysics as clearly as anyone I know, and in the short reflections that follow I am indebted to his book, *Questioning Back:*

> In practice the overcoming of metaphysics is closely associated with this *new exposure of Christianity to its Jewish matrix.* . . . This step back can be nothing less than a remembrance of the Jewish matrix of Christian faith and of the historical decisions which found a separate Christian identity. To focus Christian identity it is not enough to think *back* from the horizons of the contemporary Christian denominations, all of them shaped by Western metaphysics and culture; one must think *forward* from Judaism. . . . This dialogue with Judaism can be fruitfully pursued only in the context of a search for truth which transcends both Judaism and Christianity as *historically constituted* and in partnership with other participants in the search.[14]

What is at stake is not Christian or Jewish identity simply, but these identities as they have been "historically constituted." Historically constituted identity is always finite. The three and a half metaphors of God are testimony to the plurality of historical constructions in Christian scriptures themselves.

O'Leary notes, of course, that the classical texts are never totally alienated from the originating religious experience.[15] There is always some truth to be had. But there is some distortion to be had too—from the limits of language when one interpretation is folded upon another. Over and over, the mediating metaphors of the originative religious experience must adjudicate later utterances, in the spirit of an art critic

even more than as a philosopher. Even those first metaphors are historically constituted. The post-modern era is congenial to apophatic instincts, for, in the words of Meister Eckhart, God is beyond God. God is
beyond the metaphors, beyond the philosophies, beyond the theologies,
beyond the doctrines, beyond the liturgies—even while truly there too.
O'Leary says that metaphysics colonizes religious experience—give
metaphysics an inch and it takes a mile.[16] The Beyond of God, perhaps
like the Behind of God which was all that Moses glimpsed, is palpable in
the deconstructions which post-modernism exacts.

The Last Word

The human experience of God is always mediated by metaphors.
Metaphors are always historically situated in how they mean. The more
deeply they are respected for working the way metaphors work, the
better do they in turn respect the surplusage of meaning attending all
experience, all the more so the surplusage of meaning that attends our
experience of God.

I have spoken of the metaphors *of* God. I mean both forms of the
genitive case: an objective genitive, the metaphors that mediate our
knowing of God; and the possessive genitive, for God makes the metaphors God's metaphors in meeting us through them on their grounds.

Christian faith interprets Jesus as the Christ of God. If the meaning
of God changes, so then does the Christological meaning of Jesus
change. I have shown that there are three and a half principal metaphors
that mediated the experience and meaning of God in the New Testament
texts: *Ruach/Dabhar, Sophia,* and *Logos* (which I count as one and a
half because of its Johannine and Philonic variations). That means in
effect that there are three and a half Christs, not disparate but clearly
not interchangeable.

The one and a half metaphors very quickly took charge with the
able assistance of Greek philosophy (Stoic, Platonic, and later Aristotelian). This developmental trajectory enabled Christian faith to grow and
to flourish in the Eurocentric setting of Greco-Roman culture. It is
clearer now that what helped our faith flourish has also had the effect of
a virtual imprisonment, felt more keenly as we struggle backward to
retrieve all that can be recovered of our Jewish beginnings, and forward
to become a world church.

It is my supposition that *Ruach* and *Dabhar* would have certainly
belonged to the religious world of Jesus and would have mediated his

own sense of God meanings, that *Sophia* meanings probably were not part of his religious consciousness (i.e. specifically the *Sophia* woman figure), and that *Logos* almost certainly was not.

It is my contention that working for a new development of a *Ruach/Dabhar* Christology would help us formulate the Christological meaning of Jesus in ways that are not supersessionist and do not belie his Jewishness. This would also help free us from metaphysics. And trodding the road less traveled might perhaps uncover some new paths on the road to world church.

Each "Christ" originates its own form of discipleship. Why this task has seemed so important to me is my intuition that a *Ruach/Dabhar* recovery of the Jewishness of Jesus and of our Christian beginnings will originate a way of discipleship that can make an important new gift of Jesus Christ to human history today. At least, that is the exploration that constitutes the final volume of this work.

> Words owe their strength less to the certainty of their articulation than to the lack, to the Abyss, the inventive uncertainty in what they say. . . . Perhaps we write only to save a few words from the fire smoldering inside us. . . . Whenever I address myself to God I am afraid of jarring His sensibility because I am so clumsy with words. But if I did not talk to Him, He might infer that he has hurt me (Edmond Jabes[17]).

Notes

1. Alfred North Whitehead, *Process and Reality,* corrected edition (New York: Macmillan Free Press, 1978), pp. 379, xiv.

2. Paul Ricoeur, *The Symbolism of Evil* (Boston: Beacon, 1967), pp. 347–357.

3. Paul Ricoeur in the Preface to Mary Gerhart and Allan Russell: *Metaphoric Process: The Creation of Scientific and Religious Understanding* (Fort Worth: Texas Christian Univ., 1984), p. xii.

4. E.g. Aloys Grillmeier, *Christ in Christian Tradition, Vol. 1* (Atlanta: John Knox Press, 1975); J.N.D. Kelly, *Early Christian Doctrines* (San Francisco: Harper & Row, 1978); and Harry Austryn Wolfson, *The Philosophy of the Church Fathers* (Cambridge: Harvard Univ. Press, 1990).

5. James D.G. Dunn, *Christology in the Making* (Philadelphia: Westminster, 1980), p. 214.

6. Robert C. Gregg and Dennis E. Groh, *Early Arianism: A View of Salvation* (Philadelphia: Fortress, 1981).

7. John McIntyre, *The Shape of Christology* (Philadelphia: Westminster, 1966), pp. 82–113.

8. I choose the *phusis* transliteration because it displays the etymological connection with *phuo* and *phos*.

9. Piet Schoonenberg, *The Christ* (New York: Herder and Herder, 1970), p. 87.

10. Edward Schillebeeckx, *The Eucharist* (London: Sheed & Ward, 1968).

11. Martin Heidegger, *Introduction to Metaphysics* (Garden City: Anchor Doubleday, 1961), p. 11.

12. E.g. *he phusis he legomene hos genesis hodos estin eis phusin, Physics,* 193b 12.

13. Michael E. Lodahl, *Shekhinah/Spirit. Divine Presence in Jewish and Christian Religion* (New York/Mahwah: Paulist Press, A Stimulus Book, 1992), esp. Chapter 5, "Toward a Shekhinah Christology," pp. 151–195.

14. Joseph O'Leary, *Questioning Back: The Overcoming of Metaphysics in the Christian Tradition* (Minneapolis: Winston, 1985), pp. 209–210 passim, italics added.

15. O'Leary, 1985, p. 136.

16. O'Leary, 1985, pp. 147, 16.

17. Edmond Jabes, *The Book of Dialogue* (Middletown: Wesleyan Univ. Press, 1987), pp. 27, 15, 11.

AFTERWORD

Resemblances

Each in its own way, *Ruach/Dabhar, Sophia,* and *Logos,* knows that God is indeed "more than" a mathematical one-more-entity among all the entities that are reality. While granting that, the Hebrew resemblances for God in *Ruach* and *Dabhar* mutualize God and the world at the highest pitch, and without prejudice to the "more than" of God.

In all of our relationships, the resemblances to one another which constitute our knowing of each other set the paradigms for our relationships. Whether the resemblances are good or weak, they still weave our relational web. So then I guess God has little choice but to ape the resemblances of God that we have fashioned, within the scope of their truth and before their limits set in. And God resembles us:

> It is comforting
> that God
> resembles us.
> Recognizing ourselves
> in God
> gives us
> solidarity with
> one another.[2]

So here at the end I return to the mood of the opening reflections. All our knowing resembles what we know, but it always does so fallibly. Fallibility is inevitable, not because of untruth, but because of limits in how our knowledge resembles. The limits escape detection, always at least somewhat. Yet still we speak and write because slippery resemblances do yet honor how great is God, and each other, and all our world. "Words owe their strength less to the certainty of their articulation than to the lack, the abyss, the inventive uncertainty in what they say."[3] I remember a plaintive William James saying that perhaps every sentence should just end with the word "and . . ."

191

If then there are three and a half resemblances of God, then the Christ of God that Jesus is, is three and a half Christs. Like God, Jesus as these Christs apes Christs for the benefit of humankind. If Karl Rahner is right that for the first time the Catholic Church is open to becoming and under requirement to become a world church (or else the word "catholic" doesn't mean anything), then the resemblances of God will multiply, and more Christs of God will tell God to the world in Jesus.

As resemblances multiply, so too do questions. "Every question is tied to becoming. Yesterday interrogates tomorrow just as tomorrow interrogates yesterday in the name of an always open future."[4] Jesus the Jew interrogates tomorrow in no lesser way than what is coming interrogates what has been, including that Jew. For his divinity resembled the resemblances of God as only a first century C.E. Galilean Son of God could have done it. "You resemble what resembles you for the time of resembling. No image is eternal. God's eternity is the absence of image."[5]

While no image is eternal, I have been suggesting for reasons many times iterated that *Ruach* and *Dabhar* are important to the questions that Jesus' Jewish past poses far today. *Sophia* is a different past, *Logos* still another. It is helpful to note their linkages and similarities, but finally to let each have its own entitativeness. The "is not like" that frames disclosure forbids collapsing multiple Christologies into a single coherent meta-Christology, The "is like" is compelling and the "is not like" is inexhaustible.

Does the time of resembling create a relativity from which there is no escape? Of course, there is a yes and a no. First the yes.

Resembling is always time-bound. Resembling works only during the time of resembling. It always functions in a context of culture, history, language, experience, etc. This is the inescapably relational character of meaning, and it is incurable. If relativity is a different way of spelling insistent relationality, then there is no escape.

If there is an entitativeness about resemblances, there can also be a dialogue among them and a dialectic between them. Then, perhaps, the dialogic/dialectic structure can have a normativeness that no resemblance can claim. Perhaps participation in that dialogue could even be a criterion for inclusion in a community. You belong as long as you are in the conversation. Perhaps the Christological question "Who do you say that I am?" can play a constitutive role that time-bound answers to the question have played in the ages that preceded historical consciousness. Having the momentous question gives one entry.

Watching Metaphors Act

U.S. pragmatists would have found kindred spirits among the Hebrews of the early scriptures. You know what "God" means by watching what "God" does. Jesus had the same sense: By their fruits you will know what they are. Charles Sanders Peirce[6] and William James [7] insisted that words and sentences mean what they *do.* So too Jabes says that "we have to meet words half way, watch them act, listen to them. . . . We cannot tell one truth from another except by their different fates."[8] In our long western history, Christianity has watched *Logos* act, has been engaged by its truth, and fascinated by its splendor. However, the retrieval of the Jewish origins of Christianity engenders a hermeneutic of suspicion about *Logos* and *Sophia.* It broaches the is-not-like limits of these resemblances. "Resemblance cannot but be its own limit. Defining the limit means honing in on resemblance."[9] In other areas, the feminist hermeneutical critique does the same, especially with the language of male resemblance. By the same token, of course, *Ruach* and *Dabhar* yield meaning but also run out of meaning when arriving at their own limits, at the is-not-like.

It is my intention in the final volume to assemble an unbook that I hope resembles a book of constructive theology, giving *Ruach/Dabhar* a Christological centrality and watching it act. It will not necessarily speak more or speak less than other Christologies. It will speak differently and with inevitable insufficiency. A negative criterion is that it must not violate the original voice of the Jesus event, as best as that can be retrieved. A positive criterion is that it must accost human history anew and help it resemble the resemblances of God's reign that the life and words of Jesus resemble.

If I have worn out the word "resemble," it's a risk I take. The word "resemble" conjures up a sense that something is only "sort of like" something else, and that what resembles also dissembles. But oh the power of the tenuous resemblance and the trembling metaphor!

Notes

1. Edmond Jabes, *The Book of Resemblances,* tr. Rosmarie Waldrop (Hanover: Wesleyan/Univ. Press of New England, 1990), p. 44.

2. Jabes, 1990, p. 48.

3. Edmond Jabes, *The Book of Dialogue,* tr. Rosmarie Waldrop (Middletown: Wesleyan, 1987), p. 27.

4. Jabes, 1990, p. 74.

5. Jabes, 1990, p. 70.

6. Charles Sanders Peirce, *Charles Sanders Peirce: Selected Writings,* ed. Philip Wiener (New York: Dover, 1958), Ch. 6 "How to Make Our Ideas Clear." "Consider what effects, which might conceivably have practical bearing, we conceive the object of our conception to have. Then, our conception of these effects is the whole of our conception of the object" (p. 124).

7. William James, *Pragmatism* (Cleveland: World Book Meridian, 1955), "What Pragmatism Means." "You must bring out of each word its practical cash value, set it at work within the stream of your experience. . . . There can *be* no difference anywhere that doesn't *make* a difference elsewhere" (pp. 46, 45).

8. Jabes, 1990, p. 63; Jabes, 1987, p. 79.

9. Jabes, 1990, p. 92.

WORKS CONSULTED
FOR VOLUME TWO

Anderson, Bernhard, *Understanding the Old Testament* (Englewood Cliffs: Prentice-Hall, 1986).

Arendt, Hannah, *The Human Condition* (Chicago: Univ. of Chicago, 1971).

Berger, Peter L., *The Sacred Canopy* (Garden City: Doubleday, 1967).

Blass, F., and Debrunner, A., *A Greek Grammar of the New Testament and Other Christian Literature* (Chicago: Univ. of Chicago, 1961).

Boman, Thorlief, *Hebrew Thought Compared with Greek* (Philadelphia: Westminster, 1960).

Botterweck, G. Johannes and Ringgren, Hilmer, eds., *Theological Dictionary of the Old Testament,* Vol. III (Grand Rapids: Wm. B. Eerdmans, 1978).

Brown, Raymond E., *The Community of the Beloved Disciple* (New York: Paulist, 1979).

Brueggemann, Walter, *Israel's Praise* (Philadelphia: Fortress, 1988).

Bynum, Carolyn Walker, *Jesus as Mother: Studies in the Spirituality of the High Middle Ages* (Berkeley: Univ. of California, 1984).

Cady, Susan, Ronan, Marian, and Taussig, Hal, *Sophia The Future of Feminist Spirituality* (San Francisco: Harper & Row, 1986).

Cooke, Bernard J., *The Distancing of God* (Minneapolis: Fortress, 1990).

Crites, Stephen, "The Narrative Quality of Experience," *Journal of the American Academy of Religion,* 39 (1971).

Davies, W.D., *Paul and Rabbinic Judaism* (Philadelphia: Fortress, 1980).

Dunn, James D.G., *Christology in the Making* (Philadelphia: Westminster, 1980).

Dunn, James D.G., *The Evidence for Jesus* (Philadelphia: Westminster, 1985).

Eliot, T.S., "East Coker," *The Four Quartets* (New York: Harcourt, Brace and World, 1971).

Fiorenza, Elisabeth Schüssler, *In Memory of Her* (New York: Crossroad, 1983).

Geertz, Clifford, *The Interpretation of Culture* (New York: Harper & Row, 1973).

Gerhart, Mary and Russell, Alan, *Metaphoric Process: The Creation of Scientific and Religious Understanding* (Fort Worth: Texas Christian Univ., 1984).

Gertz, Clifford, "On the Native's Point of View," *Meaning and Anthropology,* Keith Basso and Henry Selby, eds. (Albuquerque: Univ. of New Mexico, 1976).

Goldberg, Michael, *Jews and Christians: Getting Our Stories Straight* (Nashville: Abingdon, 1985).

Gregg, Robert C. and Groh, Dennis E., *Early Arianism: A View of Salvation* (Philadelphia: Fortress, 1981).

Grillmeier, Aloys, *Christ in Christian Tradition,* Vol. 1 (Atlanta: John Knox Press, 1975).

Habermas, Jurgen, *Knowledge and Human Interests* (Boston: Beacon, 1979).

Havener, Ivan, *Q: The Sayings of Jesus* (Wilmington: Glazier, 1987).

Heidegger, Martin, *Introduction to Metaphysics* (Garden City: Anchor Doubleday, 1961).

Heschel, Abraham Joshua, *The Prophets,* Vol. I (New York: Harper, 1962).

Hillers, Delbert R., *Covenant: The History of a Biblical Idea* (Baltimore: Johns Hopkins, 1969).

Jabes, Edmond, with Cohen, Marcel, *From the Desert to the Book,* tr. Pierre Joris (Barrytown: Station Hill, 1990).

Jabes, Edmond, *The Book of Dialogue,* tr. Rosemarie Waldrop (Middletown: Wesleyan Univ. Press, 1987).

Jabes, Edmond, *The Book of Resemblances,* tr. Rosemarie Waldrop (Hanover:: Wesleyan Univ. Press, 1990).

James, William, *Pragmatism* (Cleveland: World Book Meridian, 1955).

James, William, *Varieties of Religious Experience* (New York: Mentor 1958).

Jeremias, Joachim, *The Prayers of Jesus* (Philadelphia: Fortress, 1978).

Johnson, Elizabeth, "Jesus the Wisdom of God: A Biblical Basis for Non-Androcentric Christology," *Ephemerides Theologicae Lovaniensis,* LXI (4), December 1985.

Kelly, J.N.D., *Early Christian Doctrines* (San Francisco: Harper & Row, 1978).

Kittel, Gerhard, ed., Bromley, G.W., tr., *Theological Dictionary of the New Testament,* Vol. III (Grand Rapids: Wm. B. Eerdmans, 1965).

Lee, Bernard J., *The Galilean Jewishness of Jesus: Retrieving the Jewish Origins of Christianity* (New York: Paulist, 1988).

Lee, Bernard J., "Christians and Jews in Dialogue Community," *Journal of Ecumenical Studies,* Winter 1991.

Lodahl, Michael E., *Shekhinah/Spirit Divine Presence in Jewish Christian Religion* (New York/Mahwah: Paulist, 1992).

Lohfink, Gerhard, *Jesus and Community* (Philadelphia: Fortress, 1984).

McCarthy, D.J., *Treaty and Covenant* (Rome: Pontifical Biblical Institute, 1963).

McFague, Sally, *Metaphorical Theology* (Philadelphia: Fortress, 1982).

McIntyre, John, *The Shape of Christology* (Philadelphia: Westminster, 1966).

Mendenhall, George, *Law and Covenant in Israel and the Ancient Near East* (Pittsburgh: The Biblical Colloquium, 1955).

Miller, David, *Christs* (New York: Seabury, 1981).

Montague, George T., *The Holy Spirit: Growth of a Biblical Tradition* (New York: Paulist, 1976).

Murphy, Roland E., *Wisdom Literature* (Grand Rapids: Eerdmans, 1981).

Neve, Lloyd, *The Spirit of God in the Old Testament* (Tokyo: Seibunsha, 1972).

O'Leary, Joseph S., *Questioning Back: The Overcoming of Metaphysics in the Christian Tradition* (Minneapolis: Winston, 1985).

Peirce, Charles Sanders, *Charles S. Peirce: Selected Writings,* ed. Philip Wiener (New York: Dover, 1958).

Pritchard, J.B., ed., *Ancient Near Eastern Texts Relating to the Old Testament* (Princeton: Princeton Univ., 1954).

Ricoeur, Paul, *The Rule of Metaphor* (Toronto: Univ. of Toronto, 1979).

Ricoeur, Paul, *The Symbolism of Evil* (Boston: Beacon, 1967).

Robinson, H. Wheeler, *The Christian Doctrine of Man* (Edinburgh: T.&T. Clarke, 1958).

Robinson, H. Wheeler, *Corporate Personality in Ancient Israel* (Philadelphia: Fortress, 1964).

Robinson, H. Wheeler, *The Religious Ideas of the Old Testament* (London: Duckworth, 1964).

Ross, Sir David, *Aristotle* (London: Methuen, 1960).

Schillebeeckx, Edward, *The Eucharist* (London: Sheed & Ward, 1968).

Schmidt, W.H., "Dabhar," *Theological Dictionary of the Old Testament,* Vol. III, Johannes Botterweck & Hilmer Ringgren, eds., (Grand Rapids: Wm. B. Eerdmans, 1978).

Schoonenberg, Piet, *The Christ* (New York: Herder and Herder, 1970).

Spencer, John, "Meland's Alternative in Ethics," *Process Studies,* 6/3 (1976).

Theissen, Gerd, *The Social Setting of Pauline Christianity: Essays on Corinth* (Philadelphia: Westminster, 1982).

Whitehead, Alfred North, *Adventures of Ideas* (New York: Mentor, n.d.).

Whitehead, Alfred North, *Process and Reality,* corrected edition (New York: Macmillan Free Press, 1978).

Whitehead, Alfred North, *Symbolism* (New York: Capricorn, 1959).

Wolff, Hans Walter, *Anthropology of the Old Testament* (Philadelphia: Westminster, 1981).

Wolfson, Harry Austryn, *The Philosophy of the Church Fathers* (Cambridge: Harvard Univ. Press, 1970).

INDEX

Clemens Thoma and Michael Wyschogrod, editors, *Parable and Story in Judaism and Christianity* (A Stimulus Book, 1989).

Eugene J. Fisher and Leon Klenicki, editors, *In Our Time: The Flowering of Jewish-Catholic Dialogue* (A Stimulus Book, 1990).

Leon Klenicki, editor, *Toward a Theological Encounter* (A Stimulus Book, 1991).

David Burrell and Yehezkel Landau, editors, *Voices from Jerusalem* (A Stimulus Book, 1991).

John Rousmaniere, *A Bridge to Dialogue: The Story of Jewish-Christian Relations;* edited by James A. Carpenter and Leon Klenicki (A Stimulus Book, 1991).

Michael E. Lodahl, *Shekhinah/Spirit* (A Stimulus Book, 1992).

George M. Smiga, *Pain and Polemic: Anti-Judaism in the Gospels* (A Stimulus Book, 1992).

Eugene J. Fisher, editor, *Interwoven Destinies: Jews and Christians Through the Ages* (A Stimulus Book, 1993).

Anthony J. Kenny, *Catholics, Jews and the State of Israel* (A Stimulus Book, 1993).

STIMULUS BOOKS are developed by Stimulus Foundation, a not-for-profit organization, and are published by Paulist Press. The Foundation wishes to further the publication of scholarly books on Jewish and Christian topics that are of importance to Judaism and Christianity.

Stimulus Foundation was established by an erstwhile refugee from Nazi Germany who intends to contribute with these publications to the improvement of communication between Jews and Christians.

Books for publication in this Series will be selected by a committee of the Foundation, and offers of manuscripts and works in progress should be addressed to:

Stimulus Foundation
785 West End Ave.
New York, N.Y. 10025